W9-DGV-785

NUMBER TWO
Eastern European Studies

Stjepan G. Meštrović, Series Editor

serbia's
secret war

*Serbian president Milan Nedić on a state visit to Adolf Hitler,
September 18, 1943. This photo first appeared in the November, 1943,
Spanish edition of* Signal.

serbia's secret war

Propaganda and the Deceit of History

by Philip J. Cohen
foreword by David Riesman

TEXAS A&M UNIVERSITY PRESS
College Station

The paper used in this book meets the minimum requirements
of the American National Standard for Permanence
of Paper for Printed Library Materials, Z39.48–1984.
Binding materials have been chosen for durability.

Library of Congress Cataloging-in-Publication Data

Cohen, Philip J., 1953–
    Serbia's secret war : propaganda and the deceit of history / by
Philip J. Cohen ; foreword by David Riesman.
        p.   cm. — (Eastern European studies ; no. 2)
    Includes bibliographical references and index.
    ISBN 0-89096-688-5 (alk. paper); 0-89096-760-1 (pbk.)
        1. World War, 1939–1945—Yugoslavia—Serbia. 2. World War,
    1939–1945—Yugoslavia—Serbia—Historiography. 3. World War,
    1939–1945—Collaborationists—Yugoslavia—Serbia. 4. National-
    ism—Yugoslavia—Serbia. 5. Serbia—History—1918–1945.
    I. Riesman, David. II. Title. III. Series: Eastern European studies
    (College Station, Tex.) ; no. 2.
    D802.Y82S434593   1996
    940.54'864971—dc20
                                                        95-46662
                                                        CIP

To
ROCHELLE, CHARLES,
and DOROTHEA CAMILLA
for their unfailing support

Table of Contents

Maps and Tables

Series Editor's Statement

This book by Philip J. Cohen is the second in the series on Eastern European Studies and follows Norman Cigar's *Genocide in Bosnia-Herzegovina: The Policy of Ethnic Cleansing*. It will be up to historians, Balkanologists, and political scientists to sort out the impact of Cohen's study upon their disciplines. In the following pages, I intend to discuss briefly the larger, contextual significance of this study. The most important context, of course, is that the current Balkan War raged (and continues still) even as Cohen was writing this book.

The now standard responses to the current Balkan War can be summarized as follows: All sides are equally guilty; the fighting is horrible, but we can't do anything to stop it; the bloodshed is contained in the territory of the former Yugoslavia, so it has no larger meaning for those who do not live there. These rationalizations have eased Western consciences in the short-run, but will not stand up to honest scrutiny in the long run. In the first place, respected Western fact-gathering organizations have concluded that the overwhelming majority of the atrocities and one hundred percent of the genocide in the current Balkan War were committed by Serbs. Genocide is the most serious of international war crimes, and the West failed to put a stop to it. Second, and in contrast to other instances of genocide, this one in the Balkans was televised. Thus, the rationalization given for genocide in World War II, that "we didn't know," does not hold for the genocide in the Balkans. Thanks to the information revolution, nearly everyone in Western countries knows about this genocide. But this fact raises serious moral issues, ranging from the question, Would genocide in World War II have been stopped had people known about it? to, Why did knowledge of genocide in 1990 not lead to the appropriate moral action to put a stop to it? Third, the current Balkan War became internationalized early because of the involvement of NATO, the United Nations, Russia, much of the Islamic world, and many European Nations. It is already a "world war," not in the sense of many countries going to war with each other but in terms of the focus, money, alliances formed (Russia, Serbia, and Greece against the West) and alliances discredited (such as NATO, the CSCE, the European Community, and the UN).

The evil of mostly secret genocide in World War II led to numerous scholarly efforts to understand the minds of the Nazi criminals who were responsible for it. The evil of the highly visible genocide in the Balkans in the 1990s must eventually lead to scholarly efforts to understand not only the minds of the criminals who perpetrated it, but also the minds of those who stood by, watched it, and failed to stop it.

Cohen's study is significant primarily because it is on the cutting edge of such coming anatomies. I use the word anatomy deliberately, harking back to Erich Fromm's *The Anatomy of Human Destruction,* in which he examined the criminal minds of Hitler, Himmler, and Stalin. But for reasons stated above, the circumstances surrounding genocide in the Balkans have changed because of massive media coverage. In this contemporary context, Cohen's study is a double-edged sword: In line with Hannah Arendt, Erich Fromm, and others who analyzed the "minds of the criminals" in the Nazi era, he examines outpourings from the mind of the indicted Serb war criminal. But in addition, and in contrast to previous studies in genocide, Cohen's study probes into the reasons why Western intellectuals were generally taken in by the rationalizations for genocide offered by indicted Serbian war criminals.

The rationalizations I am referring to include the following by Radovan Karadžić: The Serbs were forced to commit preemptive genocide against Croats and Muslims due to fears that stem from atrocities committed by the World War II Croatian Nazi collaborationist regime, the Ustasha, and to fears of Bosnian Muslims harking back to the Turkish victory over the Serbs in 1389. Karadžić's right-hand man, Gen. Ratko Mladić, adds that the Serbs have been the West's consistent allies. For example, Roger Cohen writes in the *New York Times:*

> General Ratko Mladic, the commander of the Bosnian Serbs, accused NATO of attacking the Serbs in a more brutal way than Hitler. . . . The reference to Hitler by General Mladic underscores the way in which the Serbs' war-ravaged history, marked at times by stoical heroism, and their contribution to allied victories in two world wars, has been repeatedly

invoked by political and military leaders. . . . They ask why the Serbs are thus persecuted and conclude that it is all an American-led plot against them. . . . They have suffered unduly. (September 8, 1995, p. A1)

As David Riesman suggests in his foreword, Philip Cohen shows that real history in the former Yugoslavia is much more complex: The crimes of the Croatian Ustashas were terrible, but the Serbian Chetniks also collaborated with the Nazis in addition to opposing them at times during World War II. Serbia was not just *occupied* by the Nazis, but it actively *collaborated* with them.

But any respectable historian and journalist should know that puppet regimes in World War II Yugoslavia, including that of Serbia, collaborated with the fascists. This should not be surprising given the larger context of fascist collaboration even by America's allies, France and Italy. The rationalizations and distortions offered by Serbian war criminals in the 1990s should have been challenged and debunked on scholarly grounds prior to the publication of Cohen's book, but clearly were not. Most commentators who denounced Serbian atrocities in the 1990s nevertheless reserved sympathy for Serbian fears of Croats and Muslims that led them to commit evil—as if others would not have good grounds to fear the Serbs based upon their history. This widespread acquiescence by Western intellectuals and journalists really raises the haunting question of how post–World War II genocide is possible. Even with regard to the Holocaust, one ought never to forget that the standard cliché, "we didn't know," was more a rationalization than a truism. Too many Germans and non-Germans had more than ample reason to suspect that the fate of the Jews as they were carted away from their residences would be none other than the fate of the mentally retarded in 1935, the burning of whose corpses, as Lucy Dawidowicz points out in her *War Against the Jews,* could be smelled in major population centers in Germany from the mid-thirties onward. Similarly, one had ample reason to suspect the fate of Bosnian Muslims, whose bodies continue to be found in massive graves, given past Serbian rhetoric and Serbian actions taken against Muslims earlier in this century.

Having raised the question of why historians and other intellectuals failed in making the connections and analyses mentioned above, I leave it up to the reader to decide upon an answer. I will close with the observation that path-breaking works in all disciplines are frequently made by outsiders who are marginal to mainstream disciplines. The Nobel-Prize winner, Rene Dubos, demonstrates this convincingly in his *Mirage of Health,* wherein he shows that major medical and public health achievements were not made by the medical profession. The celebrated American sociologist, David Riesman—who came to sociology from law—has argued that the stranger to an established discipline necessarily introjects an appreciable dose of objectivity into discussions because he or she remains free of the prejudices and paradigms that eventually stifle objectivity in any profession. Cohen's pathbreaking study follows in the distinguished tradition established by two other physicians who made major contributions to the social scientific understanding of human evil, Erich Fromm and Robert J. Lifton. The result of Philip Cohen's meticulous and excruciatingly well-documented study is bound to be the realization that this time, we cannot deny that we know.

Stjepan G. Meštrović
Series Editor

Foreword

Philip Cohen has shown a remarkable ingenuity in finding source material not only in arcane sources in the former Yugoslavia but also by pursuing leads that take him into nineteenth-century British parliamentary proceedings and a Jewish Encyclopedia in the United States from before the First World War. The Nazis were meticulous in keeping records; so too, according to this volume, were many officials in what was once Serbia and the other arenas that then made up the former Yugoslavia after the Second World War. And if there is a statistic to be found as to the number of Jews living in a certain region of Serbia—or the number of Ustashas who were trained in Italy—those figures will be found in proper setting in this volume.

It will be astonishing to contemporary readers to find that the term *ethnic cleansing* was used by militant Serb nationalists well before the current assaults in Croatia or Bosnia and Herzegovina. Indeed, there is not much new but much that is tragic in Serbian actions going back to the last century.

This reader had already, through diligent but amateur scrutiny, concluded that the Serbs now engaged in warfare and ethnic cleansing are primarily Serbs from peasant backgrounds—Hill or Mountain Serbs, not the cosmopolitans of Belgrade, or indeed the cosmopolitans of cosmopolitan Sarajevo.[1] An understanding of this limited sensibility has been intensified and strengthened in these chapters, which further serve as a reminder that the pan-Yugoslav fascist movements had Serbian and, to a lesser extent, Slovenian roots. A minor puzzle in the book is the news that not only the Nazi Party and the German intelligence services supported the anti-Semitic and anti-capitalist movements in Serbia, but also the German industrial firms. One must ask why these companies supported National *Socialism*. Perhaps they realized that this movement would eliminate competitors and not be the threat indicated by the label National Socialism.

What this reader finds remarkable is the expedition with which Serbian intellectuals and propagandists change their tune: first, to support the Nazis while the latter held power; then, in some cases, to turn to the Partisans and become influential under the regime of Tito; and now, to claim that the Serbs were the greatest friends of the Jews in the former Yugoslavia. What is startling about this facility is also the fact that, as this volume makes fully explicit and documents, Serbian nationalism was subordinate to German National Socialism and, in much smaller measure, to Italian Fascism. One must ask: what kind of nationalism is that? It is a nationalism with a remarkable degree of subordination. But it also becomes clear to the reader who has even the slightest background in the area that intellectuals—it is astonishing how many officials of the Serbian and Yugoslav ministries held doctoral degrees—were able to swing the peasant population easily through maniacal anti-Semitism, in which the small number of Jews in Belgrade and in a few towns were given majestic power in capitalism and in communism alike, as in other familiar anti-Semitisms in the Western World. Often it was only European intervention, British in many cases, that led to the lessening of anti-Semitic regulations during the periods of Serbian independence.

The author's scrupulousness makes clear that he is not "anti-Serb" out of zealotry. He recognizes instances of Serbian public and private decency and also examples of Croatian anti-Semitism and treachery. But, as his account makes clear, there is an important cultural difference between Serbia and Croatia: it is in Serbia that illiterates could rise to leadership and even to the monarchy—something inconceivable in better-educated Croatia and Slovenia. Moreover, the Serbian Orthodox Church authorities are in many cases the leaders of the pan-Serbian movements and, despite their education, or perhaps in some respects with the aid of their education, are fiercely and actively anti-Semitic. Again and again, Orthodox Church leaders take principal part in the political culture.[2]

There are also, not surprisingly, Serbian crimes against Muslims on behalf of what the Chetnik directive of December 20, 1941, specified as an "ethnically pure" Greater Serbia cleansed ". . . of all national minorities and non-national elements" (see chapter 2).

One of the contributions of the volume is to show that the Chetniks are mistakenly portrayed as anti-fascist and even protective of the Jews. Philip Cohen describes a much more complicated set of constellations.

There are ever so many vignettes in this volume which will haunt the reader. One that particularly struck me was the attack on October 23, 1940, by the White Eagles of the Zbor Youth Movement at Belgrade University. Revolvers were put to the necks of professors, and unarmed students were stabbed with knives—according to this volume, a favorite Serbian weapon—as the attackers hailed Hitler and Mussolini and screamed "Down with the Jews!" (See chapter 1).

The author goes back generations in Serbian history and, indeed, in the history of the region, to trace the routes of Serbian nationalism, the epochs of anti-Semitism in the last century, and the rise to power of illiterates. In so doing, these chapters show again the hegemony of the non-cosmopolitan Serbs, whose very lack of education could seem to be an asset, but also makes them vulnerable to the ideologies created by Serbian intellectuals leaning a century later toward Hitler and, to a lesser degree, toward Mussolini.

At this point I need hardly say that the volume will be useful to scholars specializing in the history and current politics and policies in the Balkans and in Serbia in particular. But the book will be useful to a far wider audience, for whom it will bring scrupulously gathered material—not previously available—which required a felicity with language and an ingenuity in what might be regarded as detective work to find. This semi-amateur reader had no difficulty whatever in following the text, but only a difficulty in putting it down, because it is so absorbing!

I cannot emphasize enough the importance of this book in that it might affect contemporary judgments in the United States and elsewhere. The fact that the author is Jewish should not matter. But in this case it does because, for example, the government of Israel has refused to recognize Croatia, blaming it for persecuting and killing Jews, but has exempted the Serbs from blame. The author cites Jewish scholars who have been convinced by the exceptional propaganda talents of the Serbs that Serbian forces defended the Jews against the Nazis. Such beliefs are in contrast to the reality made clear in this volume: the Serbians were anti-Semitic long before there were Nazis, and the Serbs in part made use of the Nazis and in part were captivated by them because of the shared ideologies of German National Socialism and Greater Serbian expansionism.

David Riesman
Henry Ford II Professor
of Social Sciences Emeritus
Harvard University
Cambridge, Massachusetts

Preface

As the twentieth century draws to a close and Serbia finds itself at war for the fifth time in this century, historians have drawn attention to the haunting parallels between Serbia's role in the Balkan Wars of 1912–13 and the events of the 1990s. To be sure, the primary strategic goals of the Serbian leadership regarding territorial expansion and the extermination of "alien populations" were present in the two Balkan Wars. The same determination among the Serbian leadership to create an ethnically homogeneous Greater Serbia was also found during the two world wars. The similarities between Serbia's record in World War II and developments in the 1990s are striking—and critical to an understanding of present-day Serbian nationalism. This study examines Serbia's World War II record, a neglected historical issue, and delineates the historical continuity of state-orchestrated genocide and expansionist nationalism in Serbian political culture from the pre-twentieth century to the present day.

To date, the internal history of Serbia in the Second World War has received only superficial treatment in English-language studies. Serbia's role in World War II, a complex period of history, is often clouded by a mythology that casts the Serbs as synonymous with anti-Nazi resistance and the Croats and Bosnian Muslims as synonymous with pro-Nazi collaboration. Such a conventional wisdom, however, is not borne out by the historical record.

A central thesis of this book is that the mainstream of Serbia's political, intellectual, and religious leadership collaborated extensively with the Axis powers, contrary to the mythology of resistance as promoted by subsequent official accounts. The Serbian establishment participated actively in the Holocaust against Serbia's Jewish community. Key societal institutions involved in the extermination of Serbia's Jews included the Nazi-backed regime of Gen. Milan Nedić, the Serbian fascist movement Zbor, and various Serbian state security forces, including the Serbian State Guard, the Serbian Volunteer Corps, the Belgrade Special Police, the Serbian Gestapo, as well as the Chetnik guerrilla bands of Kosta Pećanac, and the Chetniks of Draža Mihailović.

It is well known that the nominally "Yugoslav" Chetniks, committed to the formation of Greater Serbia, operated in Slovenia, Croatia, Bosnia-Herzegovina, Montenegro, and Macedonia, as well as Nedić's Serbia. It is not so well known, however, that Serbia's collaborationist institutions—including the Serbian Gestapo, Serbian State Guard, and Ljotić's Serbian Volunteer Corps—also operated beyond the borders of Nedić's state with the knowledge and approval of the Axis occupying powers.

At the urging of prominent Serbian intellectuals and leaders, Serbs in Serbia and Montenegro collaborated extensively with the Nazis and Italian fascists in suppressing the resistance or in conducting a mode of resistance that was passive in comparison to that in Croatia and Bosnia-Herzegovina. Outside of Serbia and Montenegro, ethnic Serbs were divided between the largely Axis-collaborating Chetniks and the far more vigorous Partisan resistance. In the Croatian puppet state, there was widespread rejection of the Nazi-installed Ustasha regime among the Croats and Muslims as well as Serbs, who progressively consolidated a Partisan resistance. It was only after the withdrawal of the Germans and the overthrow of the Nedić regime by advancing Soviet forces and their Partisan allies in October, 1944, that the Serbs in Serbia began to join the Partisans in large numbers. These new Partisans included tens of thousands of former Nazi collaborators responding to Tito's promises of amnesty, as well as to the call of the Serbian king-in-exile—reluctantly and under British pressure—for Serbian Chetniks to join Tito's forces. With the German withdrawal in October, 1944, the war in Serbia ended six months before it would end in Croatia, Bosnia-Herzegovina, and Slovenia.

After the war, the British forcibly repatriated tens of thousands of "Yugoslavs" from Bleiburg, Austria. This led to massacres, carried out by the Communists, of many of the repatriated Croats and Slovenes, and even a number of Chetniks. The "Bleiburg" massacres of May and June, 1945, had less to do with the punishment of collaboration (most of the victims were innocent peasants) than with the institution of state terror to ensure the Communists' postwar monopoly of power. The massacres also served another purpose for Tito's Communist Party; for Serbian Chetniks had risen in the Partisan ranks near the war's end, and the massacres—primarily a Serb-driven blood-letting—helped cement Serbia's adherence to the Communist movement, which Serbia had mostly opposed. Without Serbian adherence to the party, the reconstitution of the Yugoslav federation under Communist auspices would have been impossible. Tito made further concessions to Serbia by reestablishing Belgrade as the administrative center of Communist Yugoslavia.

These events led to Serb numerical domination of Yugoslavia's Communist Party and provided the window of opportunity for a substantial core of former Serbian Nazi collaborators to attain influential positions in the postwar Yugoslav government. Although some of the most prominent Serbian pro-Axis collaborators were condemned and punished after the war, Tito nevertheless allowed a significant degree of historical revisionism by Serbian apologists rather than risk antagonizing this much-needed constituency. The portrayal of wartime Serbia as primarily anti-Axis, as innocent of complicity in the Holocaust, and as a victimized nation would shape significantly its postwar affairs. Particularly in the years following Tito's death in 1980, the reinvention of Serbia's role in World War II became a crucial factor in its efforts to win foreign sympathy and support for a revived nationalist agenda.

As a consequence of having reinvented its past ethnic policies, the way was cleared for Serbia once again to commit genocide. Since 1991, Serbia, first covertly and later openly, has conducted a systematic campaign to destroy non-Serbian culture in the region. Ethnic- and religious-based expulsions and the mass murder of civilians throughout the territories coveted by Serbia have taken place—most notably in Croatia and Bosnia-Herzegovina but also in the Albanian-populated province of Kosovo, in the predominantly Muslim-inhabited region of Sandžak along the Serbian-Montenegro border, and to a lesser extent in the Vojvodina province, home to a substantial population of Hungarians, Croats, and other minorities. At the same time, the Belgrade regime has mounted an intensive propaganda campaign through media and diplomatic channels to justify Serbia's aggression against neighboring countries and non-Serbian populations, to gain political support from the international community, to undermine sympathy for Serbia's victims, and to portray the victims as responsible for the war.

A key aspect of this propaganda campaign has been the representation of Serbs as an oppressed and endangered people rising to their own defense—and sharing a moral position with the Jews of the post-Holocaust era. Thus, while Serbian opinion makers have portrayed the Serbs as the purest of victims in the Second World War—indeed, Serbs constituted approximately half of all Yugoslav war losses—they simultaneously have concealed the genocide carried out by various Serbian parties against various ethnic communities. And they have failed by design to give an honest accounting of Serbia's own responsibility for the Holocaust.

Most Serbian historians have neglected the extensive documentation recording Serbia's collaboration with the Nazi regime, perhaps for fear of shattering conventional views which have become ingrained in official and popular Serbian historiography. This work examines an important part of the historical record and challenges more than half a century of Serbian historical revisionism.

I am indebted to those individuals who assisted in collecting documentation, reviewing the manuscript, providing helpful discussion and criticism, and offering professional skills in translation and research. I am also grateful for the library skills of Ivan Miletić, the translations of Anto Knezevich and Branimir Anzulović, and the editorial skills of Katherine J. Rosich and Alan F. D. Potter. Henry L. de Zeng IV conducted critical research on military history, and Ljubica Štefan provided me with essential documentation on the Holocaust period in Serbia. The Cartographic Service Unit of the Department of Geography at Texas A&M University provided the maps. I have greatly benefitted from the insights and suggestions of the following people (in alphabetical order): Barry Brkić, Norman Cigar, Thomas Cushman, Mitchel W. Fidel, Michael J. Harpke, Alan F. D. Potter, András Riedlmayer, Chandler Rosenberger, Nedzib Sacirbey, and Susan Woolfson. I am also grateful for the contributions of many other individuals, including Serbs of conscience, who assisted in this work.

Guide to Croatian and Serbian Pronunciation

Croatian and Serbian are phonetic languages, pronounced as they are written. Standard Croatian is written in the Latin alphabet with special diacritical marks. Standard Serbian is written in Cyrillic (somewhat different from the Russian Cyrillic alphabet) but transliterates easily into Latin letters. Those consonants for which the pronunciation differs from English usage are shown in the table.

For Croatian and Serbian words, proper spellings, rather than English transliterations, are used. Exceptions are "Ustasha" and "Chetnik," for which the common English spellings are used, rather than *Ustaša* and *Četnik*. Accordingly, the plurals of Ustasha and Chetnik are obtained by the English convention of adding a final "s," rather than the grammatically correct *Ustaše* and *Četnici*.

For geographical names, familiar English designations are used whenever possible. Thus, Croatia is preferred to *Hrvatska,* and Belgrade to *Beograd.* Where familiar English designations do not exist, place names follow local usage, so that the Macedonian capital is called *Skopje,* rather than its Croatian or Serbian version, *Skoplje.*

In direct quotations, the original spellings are preserved. For example, *Servia,* rather than *Serbia,* appeared in English-language texts until the early twentieth century.

c	=	*ts,* as in "tsar"
ć	=	*ch* (soft), as the "t" in "future"
č	=	*ch* (hard), as the "tch" in "watch"
dj	=	*j* (soft), as the "g" in "fungicide"

đ = *j* (soft), as the "g" in "fungicide"

dž = *j* (hard), as the "j" in "jar"

h = more guttural than English
and always pronounced

j = *y,* as in "yes"

lj = as the "li" in "medallion"

nj = as the "ny" in "canyon"

r = lightly rolled

š = *sh,* as in "she"

ž = *zh,* as in "Zhivago"

serbia's
secret war

Chapter One
The Roots of Serbian Fascism

The Plan for Greater Serbia

The idea of an ethnically homogeneous Greater Serbia, deeply rooted in Serbian political culture, was first codified in 1844 by Ilija Garašanin, then an influential minister in the Principality of Serbia under the crown of Prince Aleksandar Karađorđević.[1] Garašanin's internal memorandum titled "Načertanije" (The Outline)—a blueprint for the creation of Greater Serbia through the conquest of lands inhabited by Bulgarians, Macedonians, Albanians, Montenegrins, Bosnians, Hungarians, and Croats —was kept secret until 1906.[2] In the introduction, Garašanin asserts that "a plan must be constructed which does not limit Serbia to her present borders, but endeavors to absorb all the Serbian peoples around her."[3] Elsewhere in the document, Garašanin, in regarding Croats and Slavic Muslims as Serbs of the Catholic and Islamic faiths, describes various strategies for the bloodless conquest of neighboring populations:

> Special attention must be paid to the problem of diverting the peoples of the Roman Catholic faith [Croats] from Austrian influence, and evoking a sympathy for Serbia. Through the Franciscans there, this goal would be best achieved. The Franciscans must be won over to the idea of the union of Bosnia and Serbia. To this end, several prayer books and hymnals should be printed in Belgrade, as well as prayer books for Orthodox Christians [Serbs] and anthologies of national songs which would be in the Latin alphabet on one side and Cyrillic on the other. As a third step, it would be advisable to print a short and general history of Bosnia, in which the names of some Bosnians who converted to the

Mohammedan faith [Slavic Muslims] and their renowned deeds would be included. . . . Through the printing of these and similar patriotic works. . . . Bosnia will be liberated from the influence of Austria and incline more to Serbia. Croatia and Dalmatia, in this way, would procure books which would be impossible to print in Austria. The natural result would be a merger of these lands in a closer relationship with Bosnia and Serbia.[4]

Notably, Garašanin's program for the expansion of Serbia called for the extension of Serbian domination to regions in which Serbs, if present at all, constituted a minority of the population.

Although "The Outline" implied merely the political assimilation of the various non-Serbian peoples living within the envisioned Greater Serbia, by regarding these non-Serbian populations as really Serbian, it set the stage for treating them as traitors to the nation in the event that their political allegiance and cultural conformation were not voluntarily forthcoming. In 1902, Nikola Stojanović (1880–1965), a lawyer, politician, and newspaper publisher, also commented on Croatian assimilation in a piece titled "Do istrage vaše ili naše" (Until Your or Our Extermination):

The Croats . . . are not and cannot be a separate nation, but they are on their way to becoming—Serbs. By taking Serbian as their literary language, they have taken the most important step towards unification. Also, the process of merging continues apart from the language. By reading every single Serbian book, any folk song, by singing any Serbian song, an atom of fresh Serbian democratic culture is passing into their organism. . . . This struggle must be fought until extermination, yours or ours. One party must succumb.[5]

After first appearing in Belgrade, the same piece was published in the Croatian capital of Zagreb, causing violent demonstrations.[6] Hardly an aberration, however, Stojanović's refusal to recognize a Croatian identity independent of the Serbs was echoed in Serbian elementary and secondary school textbooks of the period, which rarely mentioned the existence of Croats at all. When mentioned, Croats were designated as Serbs of the Catholic faith.[7]

In 1937, an official memorandum titled "Iseljavanje Arnauta" (The Expulsion of the Albanians) emerged from the mainstream Serbian political establishment. It was written by Vasa Čubrilović, a political adviser to the royal Yugoslav government and conspirator in the 1914 assassination of Austrian Archduke Franz Ferdinand in Sarajevo, the event which helped spark the First World War. "The Expulsion of the Albanians" argued that Hitler's and Stalin's success in expelling Jews and others presaged the success of a plan to render the lives of Albanians so intolerable and terror-filled that they would leave for Albania and Turkey:

If Germany can evict hundreds of thousands of Jews, if Russia can transport millions of people from one part of the continent to another, a few hundred thousand evicted Albanians will not provoke a world war. The deciding bodies must know what they want in order to carry through with their plan and not worry about world opinion. . . .

The only effective way is evicting Albanians from their triangle [Debar-Rogožna-Niš] *en masse*. To cause the massive emigration the first prerequisite is to generate fear. It can be created in many ways. It is well known that Muslim masses are generally easily susceptible to influences, especially religious, that they are gullible and even fanatical. Therefore, for the Albanians to emigrate, it is necessary, first of all, to win over their clergy and men of influence, either by money or by threats. Agitators should be found as soon as possible to promote eviction, especially if Turkey is willing to give us some of these agitators. . . .

The second condition is the pressure by the state apparatus. It should make the utmost use of all legal means in order to make the Albanian existence here as bitter as possible: fines; arrests; the ruthless application of all the police sanctions; punishments for smuggling, cutting trees and letting dogs loose; forced labor; . . . Old deeds should be rejected, land registry should be stopped, but all the taxes as well as all public and private debts should be ruthlessly collected. The use of state and community pasture lands should be banned; all concessions . . . should be abolished; they should not be granted monopoly licenses and should be fired from state, private and self-employment. . . . Sanitary measures, such as the forceful implementations of regulations even inside their homes, knocking down the walls and high fences around their dwellings, the rigid implementation of veterinary laws which would continually prevent the selling of cattle at the market and so forth can all be done effectively and practically. Albanians are most sensitive in religious matters. That is where we should hit hardest. It can be done by molesting their clergy, plowing their graveyards. . . .

Even private initiative can have great effect. Our colonists should be given arms, if necessary. The traditional Chetnik method should be used in those areas. Chetnik actions there would need secret support. A horde of Montenegrins from the mountains should be sent down to provoke massive clashes with the Albanians. . . . With the help of our secret forces the conflict should be prepared in advance. It should even be encouraged, which will not be difficult if the Albanian resistance is fierce. The whole case should be calmly presented as a conflict between clans and tribes and if necessary, it should be characterized in economic terms. In extreme cases, some local uprisings can be provoked which would later be put down by blood—the most effective means. This should not be done directly by the army, but rather by our colonizers, that is, Chetniks and Montenegrin tribes.

There is one more method which Serbia very effectively used after 1878, the secret burning of Albanian villages and town quarters.[8]

An insight into the racist mindset that Čubrilović represents is offered by his proposed Serbian eugenics program to improve Montenegrin genetic stock by cross-breeding with Serbs:

The very first question is, who should colonize there?. . . As a means of pushing out Albanians, the Montenegrins are the most convenient because they are most similar to the [Albanians] in mentality and temperament. They [the Montenegrins] should be accompanied by Serbs from Lika [the Croatian hinterland north of Dalmatia], the *krajina* [the Croatian border], [and the Serbian towns of] Čačak, Užice, and Toplica. This should be done because the Montenegrins lack the necessary work habits and organization and in order to break their mountain community by intermixing and cross-breeding Montenegrins with the Serbian people from various parts of the Dinaric Mountains to create a new breed, less Montenegrin and more Serbian.[9]

Čubrilović's suggestion in the 1937 memorandum that the Chetniks could be organized and secretly assisted by the government to shed Albanian blood while the official army maintained its distance was not without precedent. During the Balkan Wars of 1912 (against Turkey) and 1913 (against Bulgaria), when Serbia annexed Kosovo, the Sandžak, and Macedonia, the Chetniks were responsible for the worst atrocities, primarily against civilians, following in the path of the Serbian Army's military campaigns.[10]

Ethnic Cleansing for Greater Serbia

The concept of ridding Serbia of "Turks" (among Serbians, a pejorative term for Muslims) had been a recurrent theme in Serbian political culture since the nineteenth century. Even before the independence of

Serbia in 1878, Serbs had driven Muslims from their homes and expropriated their properties.[11] After 1878, so many of the Muslims who had populated many towns and fortresses in Serbia vanished in a series of expulsions and massacres that, by the eve of the Balkan Wars, Serbia was virtually Muslim-free. After Serbian statehood, nearly all of the hundreds of mosques that stood in this former Ottoman principality were systematically destroyed.[12] During the Balkan Wars of 1912–13, the term *cleansing* was used explicitly to describe Serbia's method of acquiring territory.[13] In northern Albania Serbian and Montenegrin fighters turned whole villages into crematoriums, where women, children, and the disabled were burned alive.[14] Their brutality was vividly portrayed in the eyewitness accounts of M. Edith Durham, a British war correspondent and nurse, who administered care to Montenegrin soldiers. Durham reported that Montenegrins and Serbs routinely mutilated the Albanian, Turkish, and Bosnian Muslim civilians, and she particularly noted their practice of cutting off the noses and upper lips of their still-living victims:

> [The Montenegrins] all gloried in their bestiality, and related in detail their nose-cutting exploits, imitated the impaling of a Turk upon a bayonet, and the slicing off of his nose and upper lip, and they shouted advice to the still living man: "Go home and show your wives how pretty you are!" All, with very few exceptions, had taken noses. An old man of seventy had only taken two, but excused himself on the grounds of having fallen ill at the beginning. . . .
>
> A Russian surgeon, the only foreign doctor who had been allowed in the Kosovo district, came to work with us for a few days, and corroborated the [Montenegrins'] statement that they had scarcely left a nose on a corpse between Berani [Montenegro] and Ipek [Kosovo].
>
> Some warm partisans of Montenegro have declared that they do not see anything horrible in the mutilation of dead bodies . . . but the men's own account was that they mutilated the wounded before giving them a final bayonet prod. . . .
>
> A report came to me that . . . in Kosovo [region] the ground in many places was simply strewn with the bodies of women and children. . . . I did not . . . attach much belief to the report till a Servian officer turned up at the dinner table, and related, with glee, the valorous deeds of the Serbs. "We have," he boasted, "annihilated the Ljuma tribe."[15]

Durham further described how Serbian troops had tortured civilians with slow death, simply for their own entertainment. The following episode occurred in the village of Arzi from 1912 to 1913:

When passing through the village in November, the Serbs had merely disarmed the people who had not resisted. But when the troops returned in April, they amused themselves by bleeding some of their defenceless victims to death. [The villagers attested:] "Not quickly, as you do sheep, but slowly. They made little cuts on the wrists and elbows and on the necks so that they should be a long time dying." Some women, with hideous and vivid pantomime, described the manner of the cuts and how the Serbs had danced round the dying victims and imitated their last shudders. . . . Nor were the Serbs themselves ashamed of their exploits, for a Serb officer told a doctor I know, that he had helped to bury people alive in Kosovo.[16]

Repression and Persecution in the First Yugoslavia

The pattern of Serbian persecution of Muslims continued after the creation of Yugoslavia in 1918, when the acquisition of Bosnia-Herzegovina brought a sizable Slavic Muslim population under Serbian rule. During the first years of Yugoslavia, Serbian Chetniks, encouraged by the government, terrorized and murdered the Slavic Muslims in eastern Herzegovina. In 1924, Serbs massacred several hundred Slavic Muslims in the Sandžak (which had been seized by Serbia in 1913), also with the encouragement of Serbian authorities.[17]

From the first days of the Kingdom of Serbs, Croats, and Slovenes in 1918, virtually the entire state apparatus was in the hands of the same Serbian ruling class that had run the small pre–1918 Serbian kingdom. For example, in the first twenty-four Yugoslav governments (1918–29), Serbs held the post of prime minister 97 percent of the time; defense minister, 100 percent; interior minister, 92 percent; foreign minister, 83 percent; finance minister, 98 percent; education minister, 83 percent; and justice minister, 87 percent.[18] Croats had comprised over 15 percent of the generals and admirals in the Austro-Hungarian armed forces, and Croatian regiments had a centuries-long reputation for military prowess. Nevertheless, in Royal Yugoslavia only Serbian military traditions, governing everything from uniform and rank to regulations, were maintained.[19] Serbian officers were retained automatically in the new Yugoslav army, while those of Croatian or Montenegrin background (or even Serbs from Croatia) needed to apply to join. If accepted, often these former Austrian-Hungarian officers or soldiers were given reduced pay and sent to distant posts.[20] Former Austro-Hungarian officers with at least twelve years of education occupied ranks inferior to those of younger Serbian officers, often unschooled peasants. Although the Latin script of the Croatian language was recognized along with the Cyrillic script under the constitution, the use of the Latin alphabet by the Croatian officers was taken as evidence of antipatriotism and even punished. Montenegrins, however, were soon accepted as brother Serbs, while Croats, who had served as former Austro-Hungarian officers, resigned. By the eve of World War II, 161 of 165 generals in the Royal Yugoslav Army were Serbs or Montenegrins.[21]

Immediately after the declaration of the Yugoslav state in December, 1918, the Serbian army and police were installed throughout the former Austro-Hungarian lands—including Croatia, Bosnia-Herzegovina, Slovenia, and Vojvodina—as had been done in Macedonia and Kosovo upon their annexation by Serbia several years earlier. Serbian forces imposed a brutal martial law on the civilian non-Serbian populations, who were treated as enemies, and whose lands were treated as Serbian conquests. For example, an edict of April 28, 1919, plainly stated: "The inhabitants of enemy districts, occupied by the army, are subject to the jurisdiction of military courts."[22] Such justice was administered under Serbian military codes, which were never publicized. Daily beatings with clubs became commonplace in Croat- and Muslim-populated areas.[23] Not uncommonly, innkeepers and waitresses were taken to military barracks and beaten for refusing to use "Greater Serbia" as a designation for Yugoslavia.[24] The military routinely pillaged private property, confiscated boats without explanation or compensation, and confiscated guns from respected burghers. Some local Serbian military commanders even devised their own rules for corporal punishment. One Lt. Col. Petar Teslić, commander of the Zagreb Infantry Regiment, prescribed his own penal code: affronts to the king were punishable by twenty-five blows, plunder would be punished "immediately on the spot" by firing squad, and "He who beats mildly will have the same number of sharp blows measured to himself."[25]

Serbian authorities routinely imprisoned and murdered Croatian political leaders and prominent intellectuals.[26] The most significant of these political murders took place on the floor of the Parliament in Belgrade on June 20, 1928, when Puniša Račić—a deputy of the Serbian Radical Party and the former president of an extremist Chetnik organization—pulled out his revolver and shot five members of the Croatian Peasant Party for denouncing government corruption.[27] Two victims died immediately, and the popular leader of the Croatian Peasant Party, Stjepan Radić, died six weeks later. As punishment, Račić spent a period confined to his home. Radić was then succeeded by Vladko Maček, who demanded Croatian autonomy, called for a new federal constitution, and conducted a rump parliamentary session in Zagreb. In response, on January 6, 1929, King Aleksandar Karađorđević jailed Maček, abolished the Constitution of 1921, dissolved the Parliament, and outlawed all political parties. He also proclaimed a royal dictatorship and changed the name of the country from the Kingdom of Serbs, Croats, and Slovenes to Yugoslavia, in an apparent move to annihilate the identity of the constituent nations of the Serbian-ruled kingdom.[28]

Under Aleksandar's dictatorship, the Serbian ruling circles consolidated their control over the military, police, and legal apparatus. The press was rigidly censored, and the campaign of repression—especially against the Croats and Macedonians—intensified. Typically, taxation in Croatia and Slovenia was often ten times greater than in Serbia, but the revenue was devoted almost only to Serbian agriculture, commerce, industry, railroads, and government employees.[29]

A dissident Serbian lawyer in Belgrade, Rajko Jovanović, decried Yugoslavia's systematic, state-sponsored violence in a pamphlet titled *Glavnjača kao sistem* (The Glavnjača Prison as a System). According to Jovanović's documentation, the first ten years of the Kingdom of Serbs, Croats, and Slovenes were marked by twenty-four political death sentences, about six hundred political assassinations, thirty thousand political arrests, three thousand political emigrants, and numerous political expulsions. The overwhelming majority of political victims were Croats, Macedonians, and Albanians.[30] Jovanović was the first in the country to collect systematically the evidence of Yugoslav terror.

The political murder of the Croatian historian Milan Šufflay in early 1931 prompted international protest. His murder, carried out by two police agents, followed years of threats against his life for advancing the opinion that the Albanians, descended from Illyrian ancestors, were earlier inhabitants of the Balkan peninsula than the Serbs and Croats—a belief which ran counter to official Serbian history. Šufflay's murder was carried out by two police agents on the orders of Nikola Jukić, a member of the pro-Serbian organization *Mlada Jugoslavija* (Young Yugoslavia), and arrangements for the murder had been worked out one week earlier in the home of Gen. Beli Marković, the Serbian military commander of Zagreb.[31] On February 18, 1931, the official Yugoslav newspaper *Naša sloga* (Our Unity), published in the coastal town of Sušak (today, part of the city of Rijeka), announced that "skulls will be split." That very evening in Zagreb, Šufflay's skull was smashed open by an iron rod.

Prompted by the murder of Šufflay, Albert Einstein publicly condemned King Aleksandar's campaign of "horrible brutality" and "terrorism" against the Croats. This condemnation made the front page of the *New York Times* in May, 1931, when Einstein and Heinrich Mann, the brother of novelist Thomas Mann, issued a joint appeal to the Paris-based

League for the Rights of Man to intervene on behalf of the Croats and to "muster all possible aid to protect this small, peaceful and highly civilized people."[32]

In the portion of Macedonia that Serbia occupied in the Balkan War of 1913 and conveniently renamed "Southern Serbia," Serbian authorities undertook a program to "Serbianize" the Macedonian population through the destruction of Macedonia's centuries-old cultural and religious heritage. In *Black Hand over Europe,* Henri Pozzi describes the cultural state of Macedonia upon its becoming a Serbian province in 1918:

> Macedonia had more than 700 churches; she also possessed 86 colleges or secondary schools, with 2,800 students and 460 professors; 556 primary schools with 33,000 scholars and 850 teachers. The convents and churches contained inestimable treasures—the fruits of a thousand years of Macedonian culture and thought.
>
> The churches, monasteries and schools have been confiscated, all the priests, all the teachers have been expelled, imprisoned, or deported into Old Serbia. The churches and monasteries, which even the Turks themselves had respected, have been pillaged from top to bottom.[33]

As part of the program to extend Serbian control to Macedonia, the Serbian language was forcibly imposed on the population, and Macedonian surnames were changed to Serbian forms.[34] Brutal police measures were applied systematically. Common methods of interrogation included crushing toes with a hammer, drilling teeth, and mutilating men's and women's genitals. Prisons were filled with men, women, and children crowded in cells too small to permit movement. Macedonian women were typically whipped, beaten, and raped, but also subjected to gruesome tortures, such as pouring fuel on their armpits and loins and setting them on fire.[35] Such atrocities were instituted as policy by Žika Lazić, the chief of the state police (and later the Yugoslav minister of the interior), of whom the following description was offered by a French author:

> I was at Belgrade, in July 1932, dining at the Excelsior Restaurant behind the royal palace. . . . Lasitch [Lazić] came to sit down next to us. . . . He had just returned from Macedonia where he had been organising the State Police. I noticed one thing particularly, all the while he was animatedly telling us risqué stories about women, he did not stop picking little flies from the table cloth which he would hold for a moment struggling between his fingers. Then, without stopping his flow of talk, gently one by one, he tore off their wings, and with the end of his cigarette, tapping lightly, unhurriedly, he forced them to crawl by

burning their abdomens. "With the Macedonian women also," he said to us, "in order to render them amorous, when they are insensible, we place hot irons on a good spot."[36]

The Serbian Fascist Movement of the 1930s

As elsewhere in pre–World War II Europe, fascist movements emerged in Serbia during the early 1930s. Relatively little, however, has been written in English about that stage of Serbian history. This was a turbulent period, marked by political strife within Yugoslavia, economic crisis throughout Europe, and the rise of fascism in several nearby countries, such as Italy, Germany, Hungary, and Romania. In Yugoslavia, the major fascist groups—distinctly pro-Serbian in character and primarily Serbian in composition—arose in response to and in support of Aleksandar Karađorđević's royal Yugoslav dictatorship, declared on January 6, 1929.[37] Supporters of a Serbian monarchy, these groups—most notably, *Združenje borcev Jugoslavije* (Association of Fighters of Yugoslavia), originally formed in Slovenia; *Jugoslovenska akcija* (Yugoslav Action); and the *Jugoslovenski narodni pokret Zbor* (Yugoslav National Movement Zbor)—would reach the zenith of their influence during the Nazi occupation of Serbia (1941–44).[38]

The Yugoslav Action movement was formed in Belgrade in 1930 and, within three years, was calling for a totalitarian state. Soon, the Yugoslav Action adopted symbols imitative of the Nazis. Appropriating a blue swastika as their symbol and the raising of the right hand as their salute, they attracted considerable interest in Berlin. In 1934, Viktor von Heeren, the German envoy in Belgrade, reported to his Ministry of Foreign Affairs that the Yugoslav Action "shows a kinship with National Socialism, even in its external characteristics."[39] Velibor Jonić, who would later play a prominent role in the Zbor and was a minister in the Serbian collaborationist governments of Aćimović and Nedić, was elected secretary-general of the Yugoslav Action.[40]

Older than the Yugoslav Action but similar in outlook was the *Zveza slovenskih vojakov* (Union of Slovene Soldiers), which was formed in 1929 to support King Aleksandar's newly declared dictatorship and, by the end of 1930, was renamed *Zveza bojevnikov* (Union of Fighters). By July, 1931, the Union of Fighters had the official approval of the administration of *Banovina dravska* (Slovenia). This paramilitary organization included World War I volunteers, Serbian Chetniks, and Yugoslav reserve officers (primarily Slovenes and Serbs). As the organization grew, it increasingly attracted individuals from political parties that had been banned by Aleksandar for their alleged anti-state activities, and for this reason, in 1933, the Union of Slovene Soldiers was itself disbanded by official decree.[41]

Nevertheless, in December, 1933, the organization was revitalized and united with several other soldiers' organizations—the Union of Volunteers, the Association of Reserve Officers and Warriors, the Association of War Military Invalids, and another banned organization, the Union of Fighters—to form *Združenje borcev Jugoslavije–Boj* (Association of Fighters of Yugoslavia). Like the earlier Union of Slovene Soldiers, it was formed with the intent of supporting the royal Serbian dictatorship. On October 13, 1934, in Belgrade, representatives of various pro-fascist organizations met, including the Yugoslavia Action, the Ljotić-led *Otadžbina* (Fatherland), the Serbian Herzegovinian movement *Zbor* (Rally), the *Buđenje* (Awakening) movement from Vojvodina, the Slovenian movement *Borci* (Fighters), and *Zveza bojevnikov* (Association of Fighters).[42] Each participating group agreed to dissolve itself and create a unified movement. The thirteen signatories to this agreement included Ratko Parežanin, Velibor Jonić, and Đorđe Perić, all of whom would later hold official positions in the Nazi-collaborationist Serbian governments of 1941–44. Three days after the signing of this agreement, King Aleksandar was assassinated, which further destabilized the political situation in Serbian-dominated Yugoslavia. On December 4, 1934, in the interest of forming a stronger, unified pan-Yugoslav movement, the leadership of the Association of Fighters of Yugoslavia met in Zagreb with other like-minded groups, including the one led by Dimitrije Ljotić, a critical figure in the history of the Serbian fascist movements.[43]

Dimitrije Ljotić, the son of the Serbian consul to Salonika (Greece), had been religious in his youth and was strongly influenced by the Christian doctrine of nonviolence as advocated by Russian author Leo Tolstoy. After completing his law studies in Belgrade in 1913, Ljotić was sent to Paris to study, financed by King Petar I Karađorđević.[44] After 1913, while studying at the Institute of Agriculture in Paris, Ljotić came under the influence of Charles Maurras, whose social and political philosophies were a rejection of the French Revolution, democracy, and individualism and would support Hitler and inform the ideology of the Vichy French government of Henri Philippe Pétain.[45] During the years of World War I, Ljotić rejected Tolstoy's doctrine of nonviolent Christianity, as he reflected on "how people can be led." He began to believe that Providence had destined the Serbian people for "a certain grand role," a recurrent theme in his writings.[46]

Ljotić served in the military until 1920, also working concurrently for the Yugoslav intelligence service of the Fourth Army District in Croatia.[47] In 1919, the commander of the Fourth Army District was Gen. Boža Janković, the founder and first president of *Srpska narodna odbrana* (Serbian National Defense), a pan-Serbian organization closely connected with the 1914 assassination of Archduke Franz Ferdinand. However, since Janković was old and infirm, the real power was in the hands of his chief of staff, Col. Milan Nedić. Intimately connected with this web was Ljotić's and Nedić's common friend, Stanislav Krakov, the Fourth Army District code officer responsible for sending secret-coded reports from Croatia to the Supreme Command in Belgrade.[48]

In 1920, Ljotić joined the Radical Party of Nikola Pašić, stating that it was "God's will."[49] A staunch believer in the Karađorđević dynasty and supporter of King Aleksandar's dictatorship, Ljotić in 1929 received his first of several audiences with the king. His loyalty was ultimately rewarded when he was appointed minister of justice on February 16, 1931. Four months later, Ljotić submitted to Aleksandar a written proposal of a new Yugoslav constitution established on the model of Germany and Italy. The King rejected this.[50] On August 17, 1931, the government decided to create one government-backed political party. Ljotić, who opposed the creation of any party, resigned from his post. According to Ljotić's memoirs, he kept the king informed of his future political plans at the king's request.[51]

Ljotić established contacts with three pro-fascist groups organized respectively around three newspapers which began in 1934: the weekly *Otadžbina,* published in Belgrade; the monthly *Zbor,* published in Herzegovina; and the weekly *Buđenje,* published in Petrovgrad (modern Zrenjanin, Vojvodina).[52] Ljotić himself was a contributor to all three publications, and he became particularly influential among the *Otadžbina* group.

At the December, 1934, meeting in Zagreb, attended by the Association of Fighters of Yugoslavia and others, Ljotić and his group prevailed in assuming leadership, in part because of his connections with the Royal Court. The name *Zbor* was adopted for the entire movement.[53] The following month, in an act of intended symbolism, the Yugoslav National Movement Zbor—which merged the Yugoslav Action from Zagreb, the Fighters from Ljubljana, and the Awakening from Petrovgrad—was officially established in Belgrade on January 6, 1935, the sixth anniversary of the imposition of King Aleksandar's dictatorship.[54]

Soon, the members of the new, unified Zbor movement elected their leadership: Dimitrije Ljotić as president, Juraj Korenić as first vice president, Fran Kandare as second vice president, and Velibor Jonić as secretary-general. The Belgrade-based *Otadžbina* became Zbor's official newspaper in February, 1934. The stated program of Zbor was the imposition of a planned economy and "the racial and biological defense of the national life-force and the family"—a formulation which corresponded closely to Hitler's own ideology.[55] Concerning the question of nationalities and their rights within Yugoslavia, Ljotić firmly opposed any dialogue with the Croats or any other nationals within Yugoslavia.

Not all constituent groups were enthusiastic about their membership in the new, unified Zbor movement. Although members of the paramilitary Association of Fighters of Yugoslavia were divided on whether to join the unified Zbor, their leadership unanimously decided in favor. The leadership of the Yugoslav Action, on the other hand, decided not to join.[56]

Although the Yugoslav Action and Zbor movements operated independently, both were openly supportive of Hitler's National Socialism and advocated warm relations with Germany, which was noted with interest by German envoy Viktor von Heeren.[57] Von Heeren's enthusiasm was echoed in the communiqué of still another German observer: "The movement Zbor represents a kind of national-socialist party. . . . Its principles are the struggle against Freemasons, against Jews, against communists, against Western capitalism."[58] Ljotić's Zbor movement began to receive financial support from German industrial firms and the German intelligence services as early as 1935.[59]

When founded, the new Zbor movement was illegal, since political parties, with few exceptions, had been banned in Yugoslavia since 1929. On September 2, 1935, Velibor Jonić and attorney Milan Aćimović petitioned the Ministry of the Interior to officially approve Zbor. On November 8, 1935, the Ministry of the Interior communicated official government approval of the Rules and Program of the Zbor and recognized it as an official political party.[60]

Ljotić enjoyed close relations with the Serbian Orthodox Church, in which he held an official position. As a member of the Patriarchal Council of the Serbian Orthodox Church in Belgrade, Ljotić established a close and long-lasting association with the highly influential Bishop Nikolaj Velimirović. Under Ljotić's influence, Bishop Velimirović's clerical organization *Bogomoljci* (Devotionalists) officially joined Zbor, and some of Velimirović's followers became Zbor functionaries.[61]

As the Zbor movement continued to grow, it attracted the offspring of orthodox priests, police, government officials, and wealthy farmers. Ljotić also drew into the organization more than a dozen high officers from the

Royal Yugoslav Army, including Col. Kosta Mušicki, who would later command the Serbian Volunteer Corps.[62]

In 1937, Ljotić promoted his loyal collaborator Stanislav Krakov to the chief of the Propaganda Section of the Zbor. Krakov, who would later become editor in chief of the collaborationist Belgrade newspaper *Obnova*, was a student of Adolf Hitler's *Mein Kampf*, to which he referred admiringly.[63] The Zbor participated in the 1935 and 1938 Yugoslav elections. In the National Assembly elections in May, 1935, Zbor offered 8,190 candidates throughout Yugoslavia. This list of candidates was officially approved by the Yugoslav government, as were three other lists: that of the Yugoslav government, led by Bogoljub Jevtić, premier and minister of foreign affairs; that of the United Opposition, led by Vladko Maček, leader of the Croatian Peasant Party; and that of Božidar Ž. Maksimović, the recently resigned justice minister and a Radical Party dissident. In the elections of 1935, Ljotić's candidates received less than 1 percent of the 2,778,172 votes cast. The candidates led by Bogoljub Jevtić won the elections with 62.6 percent of the vote.[64] Only a month later, however, Prince Pavle replaced Jevtić with Milan Stojadinović, who formed his own political party, the Yugoslav Radical Union. Stojadinović headed the royal Yugoslav government as premier from June, 1935, until February, 1939.

Stojadinović initially led with political flexibility and pro-democratic rhetoric. He relaxed police oppression, abandoned censorship of the newspapers, and granted amnesty to political prisoners.[65] By 1937, however, his government increasingly emulated the fascist models of Italy, Hungary, Romania, and Germany. Stojadinović established pro-regime trade unions, as was the practice in Germany and Italy. He organized the "green shirts," a paramilitary youth group in imitation of Germany's brown shirts and Italy's black shirts. Special salutes were introduced, and Stojadinović's intelligence service intensified its surveillance of the citizenry, while ignoring Germany's growing espionage of Yugoslavia.[66] Stojadinović advocated closer relations with Hitler and, like Ljotić, he proved unsympathetic and uncompromising in handling Croatian complaints of government corruption and demands for increased autonomy.[67] Indeed, with time, Stojadinović's ideology became less distinguishable from that of Ljotić, and, perhaps because their political agendas converged, Stojadinović and Ljotić became political adversaries.[68]

Ljotić repeatedly attacked Stojadinović though Zbor publications, accusing him of various acts of treason against Yugoslavia—and even charging him with involvement in the 1934 assassination of King Aleksandar. Stojadinović, in turn, attempted to discredit Ljotić by disclosing that Ljotić was funded by Germany.[69] Some of the compromising materials used against Ljotić came from Marshal Hermann Göring, the head of the German air force and a Stojadinović supporter.[70] A number of Zbor functionaries were already questioning Ljotić's effectiveness as a leader, and, since 1935, some of the Union of Fighters and some Zbor members already had left Ljotić's movement.[71] To further weaken Zbor, Stojadinović offered money and power to a number of its most prominent members. Indeed, at the end of 1937, Ljotić purged a number of high-ranking Zbor leaders, who soon reemerged in official or semi-official positions in the Stojadinović government.

Danilo Vulović was appointed to a ministerial post in the Stojadinović government. Đorđe Perić, the Zbor press section chief, soon headed the semi-official Yugoslav news agency, Avala. Danilo Gregorić, the Zbor propaganda section chief and supreme youth leader, was installed as the editor in chief of the government journal *Vreme* (Time) and was furnished with a home, a luxury automobile, and money. Velibor Jonić, the secretary-general of the Zbor movement, became a teacher in the royal court.[72] The defections of Perić, Jonić, and Gregorić, all of whom would play prominent roles during the German occupation, advanced the careers of still other Zbor members, who would later assume influential positions in wartime Serbia. For example, Gregorić was replaced by Ratko Parežanin, later the editor in chief of the collaborationist *Naša borba,* and Jonić was replaced by Milorad Mojić.[73] (The reconciliation between Ljotić and the defectors from Zbor would occur during the German occupation, when they would once again unite on the same political platform.)

Ljotić repeatedly used the Zbor organ *Otadžbina* to attack Stojadinović, who, in turn, frequently banned issues of *Otadžbina*. By the end of 1939, almost all Zbor publications, including *Otadžbina, Naš put, Vihor, Zbor,* and *Buđenje,* would be banned. In 1938, during the months preceding the elections, Stojadinović prohibited Zbor rallies and newspapers, seized Zbor propaganda materials, and arrested Zbor leaders. In September, 1938, Royal Yugoslav Gendarmes opened fire on a crowd of Zbor supporters, killing at least one person, and Ljotić was arrested.[74]

On October 10, 1938, Stojadinović's government dissolved the National Assembly, proclaimed new elections, and arrested some members of Zbor. Ljotić asserted that the authorities were "arresting us not because we have deserved arrests but because they want in this way to prevent our participation in the elections."[75] Indeed, speaking with one high-ranking Zbor member, Stojadinović indicated that he would not tolerate the existence of Zbor because "what the Zbor wants is what I want; therefore, there is no place for Zbor. In the autumn, I will have militarily trained youth in uniforms. And then I will go to the elections."[76] In response, Ljotić published a brochure. Titled "A Message to the Fascist Apprentice," it criticized Stojadinović for, above all, lacking originality of thought and purpose; Stojadinović was merely an imitator of Mussolini and the "hero and martyr," Adolf Hitler, while Ljotić claimed for himself an equal status with both Mussolini and Hitler as an innovator of native fascism.[77]

The elections of December, 1938, offered three candidate lists: that of the Stojadinović government, that of the Croatian leader Vladko Maček, and that of Dimitrije Ljotić. Of the 3,039,041 votes cast, these lists won fifty-four, forty-five, and one percent of the vote, respectively.[78] Zbor's poor showing among the Serbian voters in 1938 cannot be interpreted as a popular rejection of fascism, since the majority of Serbian voters, in fact, elected the pro-fascist candidates running under Milan Stojadinović. In the election battle between the two pro-fascists, Stojadinović's victory over Ljotić was due to several factors: Stojadinović's advantage of incumbency; his pre-election public attacks on Zbor; the arrests of its leaders and the suppression of its publications; and Stojadinović's courtship of key Zbor leaders. Notably, in the Croatian regions, including areas with a Serbian population, Maček's list won nearly seventy percent of the 1,373,296 votes cast.[79]

In February, 1939, however, due to the heightened internal crisis resulting from Stojadinović's failure to resolve the Croatian national question, Prince Pavle removed him as premier. Stojadinović's dismissal dismayed the Reich authorities in Berlin, for, on Hitler's orders, the *Volksdeutsche* (ethnic German) minority of Vojvodina, roughly five hundred thousand, had voted en bloc for Stojadinović.[80] The Italian authorities also were upset by Stojadinović's removal, since Stojadinović had made a secret agreement with Mussolini acknowledging Italy's territorial aspirations in Albania in exchange for Mussolini's restraining of Ustasha activities.

Stojadinović was replaced by the undistinguished but more malleable Dragiša Cvetković. The Germans' disappointment was partially assuaged when Aleksandar Cincar-Marković, Stojadinović's ambassador to the Third Reich, was appointed foreign minister in the new government. Cincar-Marković was unabashedly pro-Hitler, and he would collaborate with the Germans throughout the Nazi occupation of Serbia.[81]

In August, 1939, Gen. Milan Nedić was appointed minister of the army and the navy in the Cvetković-Maček government. Ljotić frequently contacted Nedić, who happened to be a relative of his, through Col. Miloš Masalović, who was Nedić's chief of cabinet and a Zbor member.[82] With the assistance of Masalović, the Zbor organ *Bilten* (Bulletin) was published illegally in the military printing house and was distributed throughout Yugoslavia by Serbian military couriers. Ljotić was its editor in chief and main contributor, and from March, 1939, to October, 1940, fifty-eight issues of *Bilten* appeared.[83] The later issues were printed in nearly twenty thousand copies each. *Bilten* proved especially influential in the Royal Yugoslav Army, and Ljotić particularly was satisfied to exert influence among young trainees in the military academy as well as among certain high-ranking officers.

Ljotić's other writings from these same months revealed an unbridled admiration for Adolf Hitler as the savior of Europe. For example, soon after Germany's occupation of Czechoslovakia in March, 1939, Ljotić wrote an article, "Behind the Dark Clouds God's Golden Sun Shines," in which he proposed that this seemingly gloomy day for Slavdom actually represented salvation:

> That day, March 15, I was returning home by a train. I was completely alone in the whole car. It was getting dark. I was wondering why did I not feel depressed. Just the opposite. I was wondering why I felt some crazy confidence during a day so difficult for Slavdom . . . and then I understood why was I not depressed. Hitler is an instrument of God's Providence.[84]

In 1939, Vladko Maček, the president of the Croatian Peasant Party, engaged in five months of negotiations, under the instructions of Prince Pavle, with Serbian counterpart Dragiša Cvetković. These negotiations were intended to address the growing list of Croatian grievances. The result was the Cvetković-Maček *Sporazum* (Agreement) of August 26, 1939, which created a semi-autonomous Croatian political unit, *Banovina Hrvatska,* within Yugoslavia that would remain closely tied to Yugoslavia through finance and banking, the military, foreign policy, and joint legislation. Prince Pavle then replaced the Stojadinović government with the Cvetković-Maček government.

The terms of the 1939 agreement, however, were never fully implemented, and many Serbian members of the Yugoslav government remained vehemently opposed to any concession to the Croats. Indeed, the agreement stimulated activity among various political groups advocating Greater Serbia. One such group, the Serbian Cultural Club, included such notables as Vasa Čubrilović (author of "The Expulsion of Albanians") and Nikola Stojanović (author of "Until Your or Our Extermination"). During one of his frequent speeches at the Serbian Culture Club, Ljotić blamed the Croats for the internal problems of Yugoslavia and suggested that the Serbian military should crush any movements which threatened the hegemony of Serbs. Speaking for the Zbor movement, Ljotić repeatedly attacked

Cvetković for making concessions to the Croats.[85] On foreign policy, Ljotić maintained that Yugoslavia should support the Axis powers and make a sincere gesture of friendship toward the Third Reich by removing the influence of Jews and Freemasons on Yugoslav policy.[86]

The Zbor movement, long funded by the German industry and intelligence services, was infiltrated by the Gestapo (*Geheime Staatspolizei,* or the Secret State Police), the *Abwehr* (German military intelligence), and the SS (*Schutzstaffel,* or Protective Formation). Ljotić's contacts with the SS were specifically through the SD (*Sicherheitsdienst*), the branch of the SS that would engineer the Holocaust.

The German spy network had also infiltrated the Stojadinović government. For example, ministers Ante Mastrović, Đuro Čejović, and Dušan Pantić were all clandestinely connected with the SS *Reichssicherheitshauptamt* (RSHA, the Reich Security Central Office) in Berlin, where the Yugoslav section was headed by Karl Kraus and his assistant Hans Helm. Their agents also included Dušan Pantić, Stevan Klujić, and Lazar Prokić (future publishers of the Nazi propaganda magazine *Signal*), as well as Milan Aćimović, Dragomir (Dragi) Jovanović, and Milan Banić, all of whom would play prominent roles in the collaborationist Serbian governments.[87] Ljotić himself played a central role in this German spy network and would later assist Kraus in establishing contacts with Milan Nedić.[88]

On October 23, 1940, at Belgrade University, the Zbor youth movement, known as *Beli orlovi* (White Eagles), violently clashed with pro-Communist students of the Department of Technology. Members of *Slovenski jug* (Slavic South), another Serbian nationalist group, also participated in the two days of bloody attacks on students and professors, punctuated by slogans such as "Long live Ljotić!" "Heil Hitler!" "Viva il Duce!" "Down with the Jews!" "Down with the Freemasons!"[89] The police, who had foreknowledge of the attack, were withdrawn from the area.[90] The university president, Petar Micić, sympathized with Zbor. The riots were orchestrated by Ljotić, who hoped that the crisis would provoke the imposition of the equivalent of martial law at the university, thereby bringing Belgrade University under more centralized control.[91] However, the plan backfired, generating public outrage, and the royal government in response further curtailed Zbor activities.

On October 24, 1940, the royal government quietly revoked Zbor's legal status, leaving even the Zbor unaware of its decision. On November 2, 1940, the Ministry of the Interior sent a list of Zbor members to all district administrators. The next day, the administration of the City of Belgrade entered the headquarters of the secretariat of the Zbor movement and informed Zbor members that their organization had been disbanded. Yugo-slav police were ordered by the government to search for and compile lists of Zbor functionaries.[92] The police often instructed Zbor members to deny their affiliation with Zbor, however. Many did so, with the result that rela-tively few Zbor members were confirmed to exist in Yugoslavia. During October and November of 1940, only about 160 members of Zbor were arrested.[93]

Maček's Croatian constituency regarded Ljotić as an enemy of Croats. In-deed, Ljotić repeatedly wrote letters to Prince Pavle, urging him to annul the semi-autonomous Croatian *Banovina* that was created as the result of the 1939 Agreement. In a characteristically shrill tone, Ljotić wrote to Prince Pavle: "*Stop the Croatian experiment immediately.*"[94]

Pavle—who had labored to achieve internal stability—ordered the prosecution of Ljotić, largely because of Ljotić's militantly anti-Croatian stand. Actions against Zbor, particularly against Ljotić, however, were un-dertaken with some trepidation, lest the Germans be provoked. Although the government investigation concluded that Zbor was guilty of high trea-son and accepting funds from another country (Germany), Ljotić was never arrested but instead was placed under surveillance from which he soon escaped. Ljotić hid with friends in Belgrade and maintained frequent com-munications with Milan Nedić and Bishop Nikolaj Velimirović.[95]

On November 6, 1940, the same day that police actions were initiated against the Zbor, Pavle had obtained the resignation of the minister of the army and navy, Gen. Milan Nedić, because of his advocacy of a strong alliance with the Axis powers.[96] Following Nedić's resignation, and despite police surveillance, there appeared additional issues of Ljotić's *Bilten* sup-porting a pro-Axis foreign policy and criticizing the government's contin-ued tolerance of Jews and Freemasons. Ljotić also attacked the pro-British elements of the government who would oppose the signing of the Tripar-tite Pact.[97]

The Tripartite Pact and the 1941 Coup

The Tripartite Pact, which formalized the Axis alliance between Germany, Italy, and Japan, was signed in September, 1940. Soon after, Ber-lin began to urge the Yugoslav government to join the Axis, and, once Bul-garia's King Boris signed the pact, this pressure intensified. From the beginning, Hitler's preferred course of action was the preservation of Yugo-slavia rather than the creation of an independent Croatian entity. Most German leaders were pro-Serbian, inspired, in part, by the warm welcome given to Hermann Göring in Belgrade, when he represented Germany at the 1934 funeral of King Aleksandar.[98] Pro-Serbian views were also held by Franz Neubacher (the German consul-general highly respected by Göring), Viktor von Heeren (the Belgrade ambassador), and Paul Schmidt (the chief of the Press Section of the German Foreign Ministry). Schmidt had been particularly influenced by Danilo Gregorić, who, as a member of the Zbor and the editor in chief of the government journal *Vreme*, had become his principal source of information on Yugoslavia. According to the postwar writings of a German intelligence officer, Gregorić had led Schmidt to publish "a number of pro-Yugoslav articles in the German press,"

> his primary object being to awaken a sympathetic interest in Hitler and the other leaders for Yugoslavia and, in particular, for the Serbs. He lauded the centuries-old and heroic struggle of the valiant Serbian people against the Turkish oppressor, the military virtues of the warlike Serbs, their chivalrous characteristics and so on, and succeeded in making quite a plausible case for a moral relationship which he professed to see between Germans and Serbs. By this means he greatly strengthened the pro-Serb feeling which already existed among the German leaders. Hitler himself repeatedly declared that he regarded an alliance with the brave and warlike Serbs as an object particularly worth striving for.
>
> The Croats, on the other hand, had no really influential man in Berlin to plead their cause.[99]

On March, 4, 1941, Adolf Hitler and Prince Pavle met at Berchtesgaden, Germany. In return for Yugoslavia's joining the Tripartite Pact, Hitler agreed to a number of Prince Pavle's demands: that Salonika would be ceded to Yugoslavia, albeit after the war; that Yugoslavia's territorial integrity would be protected against invaders, particularly Italy; that Yugoslavia would have no obligation to enter the war on behalf of the Axis; that no Axis arms or troops, not even the wounded, would cross Yugoslavia's territory; and that the terms of the agreement would be published. Hitler consented to all terms except the last.[100]

Two days later, on March 6, Prince Pavle convened a meeting of the Crown Council (the executive committee of the cabinet) in Belgrade to consider Hitler's offer.[101] After hearing the minister of the army and navy, Gen. Petar Pešić, state that he favored collaboration because Yugoslavia was in no position to defend itself militarily, Maček asked whether German promises could be trusted, and Foreign Minister Aleksandar Cincar-Marković replied that they could. On March 10, a second Crown Council meeting was called to consider the pact. At this meeting, Milan Antić, minister of the Royal Court, proposed that Yugoslavia insist on not only the annexation of the Greek port city of Salonika, but additional Greek territory as well. Maček and Kulovec both strongly refused to be party to plans for territorial aggrandisement.[102]

On March 20, the Crown Council met for the last time to vote on the Tripartite Pact. Attending the meeting were six Serbian high officials, one Slovene, and one Croat.[103] The Slovene, Fran Kulovec, was concerned over Slovenia's borders with Austria and Italy and was the first to suggest signing the pact. The Croat, Vladko Maček, asked if refusal to sign would mean war with the Axis, and Foreign Minister Aleksandar Cincar-Marković replied that it would. The willingness of the Croatian and Slovenian representatives to sign the pact was contingent on the understanding that they were prepared to renounce it once Yugoslavia's forces were built up to the point that the country could defend itself.[104] The Crown Council then voted unanimously in favor of signing the Tripartite Pact. On the same day, the cabinet voted to accept the pact, sixteen to three.[105]

By March 23, rumors of a planned coup d'état had reached Prince Pavle and Cvetković; one of the coup plotters, General Simović, warned Pavle that he would not be able to restrain his officers from bombing the Royal Court if the Tripartite Pact were signed. On March 25, 1941, Cvetković and Cincar-Marković, representing Yugoslavia, signed the Tripartite Pact in Vienna. Not present at the signing was Maček, the leader of the Croatian majority party, who refused to attend the ceremony, stating beforehand that "even four oxen couldn't drag me to go."[106]

The next morning, Yugoslav newspapers reported the signing of the Tripartite Pact. As foreign radio stations broadcast the news, demonstrations broke out in the streets and schools throughout Yugoslavia.[107] Then, during the early hours of March 27, a group of Serbian officers carried out a coup against Prince Pavle and installed seventeen-year-old Petar II Karađorđević as the ruling king. The same day, Simović appointed Momčilo Ninčić, the president of *Nemačko-Jugoslovensko društvo* (German-Yugoslav Society) of Belgrade, who had excellent connections with official Italian circles, to be the Yugoslav foreign minister. Although Ninčić's appointment met strong opposition from the Croatian leadership and the Independent Democrats—a Serbian party with a history of cooperation with the Croatian Peasant Party—Ninčić had the almost unanimous support of the Serbian ministers.[108]

Following his appointment on March 27, Ninčić's first order of business was to assure the German ambassador, Viktor von Heeren, that Yugoslavia would *uphold* the terms of the Tripartite Pact.[109] Unaware of this double game, British prime minister Winston Churchill proclaimed that "early this morning the Yugoslav nation found its soul" and officially recognized the Simović government on the very day of the coup.[110]

In Serbian nationalist historiography, the March 27 coup has been interpreted as a popular Serbian revolt against the Tripartite Pact. The coup, however, was the work of the British intelligence service and a handful of British-funded high-ranking Serbian officers.[111] The motivations of the British and the Serbs were quite different. While the British sought to undermine Yugoslavia's cooperation with the Axis, the Serbian officers wanted to remove Pavle largely because of his accommodations to the Croats. Moreover, there was a rival coup faction, which was entirely pro-German and supported by Ljotić's Zbor. Whatever their differences in foreign policy, the internal policy of both coup factions was the same: the installation of a Serbian military dictatorship. Toward the end of 1940, the Zbor counterconspiracy revealed their plans to the German intelligence service, but Hitler refused to support the plot. Since Hitler was already working toward establishing closer cooperation with Yugoslavia's Prince Pavle, to support a *putsch* not only would have been superfluous, but potentially harmful as well.[112]

The British involvement in the preparations for the coup had begun several months earlier, in the summer of 1940, when the British government tried openly to influence the ruling group, which included Prince Pavle, Cvetković, and Maček, while covertly supporting the Serbian nationalist-oriented opposition that wanted to overthrow Pavle. The British cultivated contacts in Yugoslav military and political circles through business contacts, diplomacy, and the British intelligence service—the Special Operations Executive (SOE). For example, T. G. Mapplebeck was a member of the British embassy and a businessman whose joint British-Serbian aviation firm supplied military equipment to the Yugoslav Air Force. Mapplebeck forged close links with a number of high-ranking officers, including the three generals who plotted the coup and to whom he channeled funds from the British government.[113]

The SOE also provided funds to and bribed key leaders of the Serbian Agrarian Party and the Democratic Party. Months before the coup, the SOE had delivered a railroad car full of weapons and radio communication equipment to the Serbian Agrarian Party. The SOE had also infiltrated a number of Serbian nationalist organizations such as the Chetniks, the veterans associations, the Order of the White Eagles with Swords, and *Narodna Odbrana* (the National Defense), headed by Ilija Trifunović-Birčanin, the influential president of all Chetnik organizations (and later war criminal). The SOE established especially close ties to Trifunović-Birčanin and funded his organization whose origins were in the conspiracy to assassinate Archduke Franz Ferdinand.[114]

Three air force generals on the British payroll—Borivoje Mirković, Dušan Simović, and Bogoljub Ilić—would play a critical role in the March 27 coup. Simović had first considered a coup against Prince Pavle in 1938, when the Yugoslav government was negotiating a concordat with the Vatican, an initiative bitterly opposed and ultimately prevented by the Serbs. Again in 1940, in planning the March 27 coup, Simović had also received guarantees of support from the Russians and intended to foster closer ties between Yugoslavia and the Soviet Union. Mirković, who would become the principal commander of the coup, was a strong supporter of Greater Serbia and had resolved years earlier to oust Pavle in favor of Serbian military rule. Mirković saw Pavle as too liberal and too conciliatory to the Croats' demands for more independence from Belgrade. It is doubtful that Mirković's sentiments were particularly anti-German, since in his own quarters he prominently displayed a signed photograph of his fellow airman, Marshal Hermann Göring. Mirković, in turn, recruited his friends, the Knežević brothers, each of whom provided useful contacts with the British. Maj. Živan Knežević commanded a Royal Guard infantry battalion, and Professor Radoje Knežević was prominent among intellectuals in the influential Serbian Cultural Club.[115]

The plotters considered two plans for the coup. In one plan, the coup would be executed before the signing of the Tripartite Pact. Prince Pavle would remain in power but would be forced to replace the Cvetković government with an entirely Serbian government, which would exclude the participation of Croats or Slovenes. The new government would be led by Gen. Dušan Simović. According to the second plan, the coup would be executed after the signing of the Tripartite Pact. Pavle would be expelled, young King Petar II would be proclaimed the ruler, and the government led by Simović, including Croats and Slovenes, would declare a general mobilization. This plan was adopted on March 11.[116]

By March 24, while the Yugoslav delegation was en route to Vienna for the signing of the pact, the British intensified pressure on the plotters to go forward with the coup. The SOE was reassured by Chetnik leader Trifunović-Birčanin that plans for the coup were well advanced. As late as March 26, T. G. Mapplebeck persuaded General Mirković to proceed with the coup within forty-eight hours.[117]

The almost bloodless coup d'état (one gendarme was killed) began late on March 26 and was completed by the early hours of the next morning. At the time of the coup, Prince Pavle was in Zagreb, where Maček offered to lead Croatian troops in a march on Belgrade to crush the rebellion. Pavle, however, rejected Maček's offer, which he saw as carrying the risk of civil war and as jeopardizing the unity of Serbs and Croats. Following Simović's demand, Prince Pavle returned to Belgrade and tendered his resignation. Simović, as the new premier, announced the formation of his government, which included Vladko Maček as a vice-premier—a move intended to prevent Croatian opposition to the coup. In fact, Simović's announcement of Maček's inclusion in the coup government was undertaken before the Croatian leader had been contacted at all. On April 1, Maček convened a meeting of the leadership of the Croatian Peasant Party and insisted that Croatia must defend Serbia in the event of war, and this was affirmed in a unanimous resolution. Summoned by Simović, Maček proceeded several days later to Belgrade, where, seeing no alternative, he reluctantly joined the coup government.[118]

The other vice-premier of the newly formed Simović government was Slobodan Jovanović of the British-funded Serbian Agrarian Party. The events that followed, however, bore little resemblance to British expectations. The new government not only continued the policy of accommodation to Hitler but began to recruit Serbian pro-Axis supporters. In one of its first acts, the coup government released all of Ljotić's followers from prison and halted judicial proceedings against them. Moreover, the newly appointed minister of the army and navy, Gen. Bogoljub Ilić—one of the British-funded coup leaders and known as notoriously hostile to the Croats—promptly invited Ljotić, the vocal Nazi supporter, to join the new government. Ljotić had previously been encouraged to join the new government by Bishop Nikolaj Velimirović, who had foreknowledge of the impending coup d'état. However, Ljotić was excluded from the new government, largely due to the objections of Branko Čubrilović, a Freemason undoubtedly offended by Ljotić's anti-Masonic demagoguery and a friend of Simović. Although Ljotić himself did not join, a number of his followers were accepted into government service. For example, during the first hours of the coup, Col. Miloš Masalović, a member of the Zbor movement, presented himself for duty. Previously dismissed in 1940 from military service—along with Milan Nedić—by Prince Pavle's government for his strong pro-Axis views, Masalović was reactivated and appointed the commander of the Infantry Regiment of the Royal Guard.[119]

Thus, the March 27 coup d'état, carried out by a relatively small number of conspirators, was more a testimony to the efficacy of the British intelligence service and the opportunism of its plotters than to any widespread popular Serbian sympathy for the Allied cause. In reality, the coup was never so clearly anti-Axis as it was anti-Pavle and anti-Croatian, and from the beginning it was in part driven by pro-Axis Serbs. Despite revisionist attempts to portray pre–World War II Serbia as staunchly antifascist, Serbia indeed bred its own fascist movement.

Chapter Two
The Serbian State, 1941-1944

Conquest by the Axis Powers

The effect of the March 27 coup was felt in Berlin. Hitler, who was at this time preoccupied with his plans to invade Russia and considered German-Yugoslav issues settled, became furious, having worked to reach an agreement with Prince Pavle.[1] Hitler had little confidence in coup leaders supported by Great Britain, despite their immediate overtures to the Third Reich. Publicly attributing the coup to "Communists," Hitler resolved to impose his own brand of stability in the Balkans.[2] On April 6, 1941, Axis forces invaded Yugoslavia. The Italians immediately implemented long-standing designs and annexed most of the Croatian coast. To encourage the cooperation of Hungary and Bulgaria, Hitler had offered them parts of Yugoslav territory to which they had claims or aspirations. Hungary annexed Bačka (Vojvodina), Međimurje and Baranja (Croatia), and Prekomurje (Slovenia). Bulgaria received most of Macedonia, part of eastern Serbia, and a small part of Kosovo.

The Royal Yugoslav Army had been poorly equipped and poorly trained. Most of the weapons and uniforms were World War I–era, and the air force consisted of World War I–vintage biplanes with open cockpits. Furthermore, almost all of the Yugoslav commanding generals—virtually all Serbs—were opposed to fighting the Nazis and sought an armistice.[3] The Axis forces easily prevailed—and were surprised by the lack of resistance.

By April 12, the first German units had reached Belgrade. On April 14, the supreme command of the Royal Yugoslav Army ordered its units to stop fighting and sought a truce with the Germans, who demanded instead

an unconditional surrender.[4] The same day, the king and his family were
evacuated from the air base in Nikšić, Montenegro, to Greece. Before de-
parting, King Petar named Gen. Danilo Kalafatović the military chief of
staff. On April 15, Prime Minister Simović and his cabinet decided that
the government should not capitulate and that only the military should
surrender. Simović and his cabinet then joined King Petar II in Greece, from
where the royal government-in-exile would ultimately relocate to London.
Two days later, when German troops captured the military command headquarters in the town of Pale, near Sarajevo, Kalafatović designated Gen.
Radivoje Janković and Foreign Minister Aleksandar Cincar-Marković to
sign the unconditional surrender in Belgrade. During the twelve days of
onslaught, the Germans took 345,000 Yugoslav soldiers as prisoners of
war, while German losses were light: 151 killed, 392 wounded, and 15
missing in action.[5] Most of the several dozen captured officers from Ljotić's
Zbor movement were soon released.[6] Ljotić received written notice from
the German authorities assuring his freedom.[7]

Serbian nationalists—including coup leader General Simović and even
King Petar himself—blamed Yugoslavia's failure to resist the Axis invasion
on "fifth columnist" Croats; the primary failure of the Yugoslav Army and
its virtually all-Serbian leadership was ignored.[8]

Serbian State

The Emergence of the Collaborationist Government

The German division commanders prior to the invasion did not have instructions on how to administer the conquered territories. Rather, the plans were developed during the course of the twelve-day April war. The Germans had considered creating a collaborationist government utilizing Dragiša Cvetković, who sought a return to power. On April 17, 1941, the day of the Yugoslav military's capitulation, the Germans brought Cvetković at his request from Niška Banja to Belgrade, where he met with the two regents, Radenko Stanković and Ivan Perović, to discuss the creation of a collaborationist pan-Yugoslav government.[9] This plan, however, was frustrated by Hitler's decision to divide Yugoslavia. Moreover, in his own bid for power, Cvetković had no shortage of competitors.

The same day that Cvetković offered his services to the Nazis, a number of individuals who would become prominent collaborators also converged on Belgrade: retired army general Đura Dokić from Sarajevo; Boško Kostić from Goražde; Božidar (Boško) Bećarević from Montenegro; Velibor Jonić from Foča; and Col. Tanasije Dinić and journalist Danilo Gregorić, who were transported from Niš to Belgrade by a German military vehicle.[10] Treated with particular deference by the Germans was the former foreign minister Aleksandar Cincar-Marković. By the personal order of von Ribbentrop, Cincar-Marković was offered a cottage in Germany.[11]

From April 17 until the establishment of the first Serbian collaborationist administration on April 30, pro-Nazi politicians—including Dimitrije Ljotić, Milan Aćimović, Dragi Jovanović, Đorđe Perić, Stevan Klujić, and Col. Tanasije Dinić—were holding meetings almost daily to determine the composition of the new government. They kept the Germans informed of their meetings.[12] The German authorities at first thought that Ljotić should organize the collaborationist administration, but they ultimately concluded—and Ljotić concurred—that a Ljotić-led government would be a political failure.[13] Ljotić's bitter political struggle with Stojadinović years earlier had compromised him as a public figure. As he explained it to Gestapo officer Karl Kraus, an "uncompromised man with generally recognized authority and force of personality" was needed to convince the people that "the Germans are their friends, that they want the best for the people, and that they are the saviors of humankind from communism."[14]

On April 22, Gen. Helmut Förster was appointed the military commander of Serbia (the first in a long line of commanders). After reviewing the reports prepared by Gestapo agents Kraus and Helm, Förster decided to form a Serbian government in accordance with their suggestions: under the leadership of Milan Aćimović, the administration would include Tana-

sije Dinić, Đorđe Perić, Momčilo Janković, Dušan Pantić, Stanislav Josifović, Dimitrije Ljotić, and Milosav Vasiljević.[15] After Berlin gave its
consent, Harald Turner convened a meeting on April 29 with the collaborationist candidates. Ljotić, however, retracted his offer to join the government and instead promised as a lawyer to support and defend it, assuming
"the role of attorney before the domestic and foreign public." Ljotić recommended in his place the inclusion of Zbor members Stevan Ivanić and Milosav Vasiljević, both of whom received appointments.[16] Col. Tanasije
Dinić was appointed assistant commissar for interior affairs and assumed
responsibility for organizing the Serbian Gendarmes.[17]

On April 30, 1941, the Government of Commissars was formed under
Milan Aćimović, an attorney, former Belgrade chief of police, and minister
of interior affairs (1938–39) in the pro-Nazi government of Milan Stojadinović. These commissars, who had been closely associated with the prewar
Yugoslav governments, represented a spectrum of Serbian political parties
and constituencies, excluding Communists and the British-supported Serbian Agrarian Party. The Royal Yugoslav Gendarmes continued to function
as the Serbian Gendarmes, which along with the Serbian police maintained
order for the first three months of the German occupation.[18]

Prior to Hitler's invasion of Russia, the Yugoslav Communists had not attacked German forces out of obedience to Moscow and the Molotov-
Ribbentrop Pact. Two weeks after Hitler's invasion of Russia, on July 7,
1941, the anti-German uprising led by Josip Broz Tito commenced in Serbia. At this time, due to the transfer of German troops to the Russian Front,
occupation forces in Serbia were reduced to three German divisions, containing only two instead of the usual three regiments. The German soldiers
who remained in Serbia were mainly older men, poorly equipped, inade-
quately trained, and thinly dispersed throughout the towns, and even more
thinly dispersed in the countryside. Thus, the Germans' ability to respond
to Partisan sabotage was limited. Individual battalions were separated by
as much as twenty-five to thirty miles and had no armored vehicles, while
their trucks were in bad repair.[19] The German authorities had anticipated
some degree of guerrilla resistance, but their strategy primarily was to rely
on the Serbian police to suppress the insurgency. The scale of the
Communist-led uprising exceeded German expectations, however. German
reprisals were swift. By July 22, a total of 111 people, Jews included, had
been executed by the Germans, and by the end of August the total had
reached approximately 1,000.[20]

The National Call to Suppress the Resistance

At the outbreak of the war, the Yugoslav Communist Party had only about two thousand members in Serbia proper.[21] The German reprisals drove many Serbs to the Communist-led insurgency as well as to the Chetnik movement, which generally avoided confrontation with the Germans. Over the next few months, while the Partisan uprising continued to gain momentum, mainstream Serbian intellectuals and leaders urged collaboration with the Nazis.

On August 13, 1941, under the leadership of Velibor Jonić, 545 Serbs, including some of the country's most prominent and influential figures, issued an "Appeal to the Serbian Nation," which called for loyalty to the Nazis and condemned the Partisan resistance as unpatriotic.[22] The following text appeared in the major Belgrade newspapers:

The Serbian nation is experiencing trying days. In these fateful hours, it is the duty of each Serb, each true patriot, to help the country preserve peace and order with all his might. Only thus can the great work of the national renewal of the fatherland be carried out and a better future for our tormented nation be secured. At a moment when the overwhelming majority of our people clearly perceives that this is the only path toward our national salvation, a handful of alien mercenaries and saboteurs under the command of criminal Bolsheviks senselessly jeopardizes all efforts to settle our situation. They are intentionally attempting to provoke a conflagration of ruin and extermination in the country, in the treacherous hope that they will thereby aid their masters. Criminal bands, comprised of communists and runaway slaves who have escaped the authorities, are destroying national property, killing and robbing our fellow citizens, while endangering the lives of innocent women and children. By their misdeeds and crimes, they jeopardize the existence of our entire population, the whole Serbian nation. Every sober and intelligent Serb, every well-meaning son of this land who thinks for himself, realizes the danger threatening us. This fear is justified when one remembers the dangers confronting a conquered country when peace is disturbed. His revulsion is especially evident when the appeal from the victor for loyal collaboration is answered with shots from a position of ambush. Such perfidious and unworthy fighting does not correspond to the chivalrous spirit of our people, and inflicts a serious blemish upon the honor of the entire Serbian nation. Our nation is not communist nor does it have any connection with the international destroyers of the most sacred currents of European culture. Therefore, we can no longer fold our hands as we watch them push our nation into an abyss. We must not permit this part of our country, this island of salvation for the entire Serbian nation, to be endangered and our nation to be decimated and exiled from its homeland because of their crimes. The final moment has come for us to rise up in the defense of our existence. The duty of each true Serbian patriot is to thwart the infernal intentions of the communist criminals with all his might. Therefore, we call upon the entire Serbian nation to assist our authorities in the struggle against these enemies of the Serbian nation and its future by acting decisively in every situation, using all available means.[23]

The list of the signatories was published over two days. The first three to sign were bishops of the Serbian Orthodox Church. Four Serbian Orthodox archpriests also signed, as well as at least eighty-one professors (including the university president) at Belgrade University. The list reflected a vast range of occupations, including school directors and teachers, Yugoslav army generals, former government ministers and legislators, bank directors, industrialists, merchants, attorneys, physicians, pharmacists, engineers, architects, journalists, writers, painters, sculptors, opera singers, musicians, and actors. The signatories' titles included trade group and business association presidents, as well as leaders of various professional organizations and of the arts (see appendix A). On the day the Appeal was issued, the Bar Association, meeting in Belgrade, unanimously passed a resolution supporting it.[24]

Two weeks after the publication of the "Appeal to the Serbian Nation," with the Partisan insurgency continuing to gain momentum and with German displeasure increasing, approximately seventy-five prominent Serbs convened an emergency meeting in Belgrade, where it formally was resolved that Gen. Milan Nedić should form a "Government of National Salvation" to replace the existing Government of Commissars. In attendance were former and then-current government ministers, military officers, university professors, industrialists, and representatives from all political parties (except the Serbian Agrarian Party and the Communist Party). Many at the emergency meeting urged close cooperation with the Nazi occupiers (a partial listing appears in table 1). At least half of the commissars of the Aćimović government, including Aćimović, were present at this meeting.[25]

Prior to the Nazi invasion of Yugoslavia, Gen. Milan Nedić, a World War I hero, in 1940 had been relieved as Yugoslav minister of the army and navy for urging that Yugoslavia join the Axis and for suggesting the ceding of Yugoslav territory to appease Germany.[26] On August 29, 1941, two days after the Belgrade emergency meeting, the German authorities

Table 1. Prominent Serbs urging Nazi collaboration at Belgrade meeting of August 27, 1941

	Societal position held	Aćimović regime	Nedić regime	Signed appeal
Aćimović, Milan	Yugoslav minister	yes	yes	yes
Cincar-Marković, A.	Yugoslav minister			yes
Dinić, Tanasije	colonel, Royal Yugoslav Army	yes	yes	yes
Draškić, Panta	general, Royal Yugoslav Army		yes	
Ilić, Vlada	president, Chamber of Industry			yes
Ivanić, Stevan	physician; Zbor member	yes		yes
Janković, Momčilo	lawyer; National Assembly	yes	yes	yes
Jojić, Risto	Yugoslav minister	yes		yes
Jonić, Velibor	university professor	yes	yes	yes
Kostić, Josif	general, Royal Yugoslav Army		yes	yes
Kostić, Lazar	university professor	yes		
Kostić, Mirko	university professor			
Kotur, Đuro	senator	yes		yes
Kumanudi, Kosta	president, National Assembly			yes
Ljotić, Dimitrije	Yugoslav minister; Zbor founder			yes
Marković, Lazar	Yugoslav minister			yes
Mihajlović, Ilija	industrialist			
Nedić, Milan	general; Yugoslav minister		yes	
Olćan, Mihailo	Zbor member		yes	
Pešić, Dušan	general, Royal Yugoslav Army			
Pržić, Ilija	university professor			yes
Radosavljević, Miloš	politician		yes	
Radovanović, Stevan	general, Royal Yugoslav Army			
Spalajković, Miroslav	National Assembly			yes
Trivunac, Miloš	university professor and dean		yes	yes
Vasiljević, Milosav	politician	yes		yes

SOURCES: Borković (1979), pp. 95–97; Kostić (1949), pp. 44–46; Karapandžić (1958), p. 84.

installed General Nedić and his *Vlada narodnog spasa* (Government of National Salvation) in power. Seven of Nedić's eleven ministers had been present at the August 27 meeting in Belgrade; three were generals in the Royal Yugoslav Army; and four were held over from the Aćimović Government of Commissars.

The German authorities relied on Nedić to build up larger Serbian armed forces to subdue the Partisan uprising, nearly two months in progress.[27] Nedić assumed command over the Serbian Gendarmes, the Serbian Volunteer Command (the military arm of Zbor), and those Chetniks under Kosta Pećanac who had vowed loyalty to the Nedić government. The shortage of German police and military forces in Serbia was a significant factor in the German decision to rely upon armed Serbian formations to maintain order.[28] Indeed, according to Nedić's own postwar testimony, he began to introduce order with the help of these troops, since there were not enough German troops in Serbia.[29] On September 1, 1941, three days after the

SERBIA'S SECRET WAR

Nedić government came to power, the following communiqué was sent from Col. Jovan Trišić, then commander of the Serbian Gendarmes, defining their new responsibilities and autonomy:

> Beginning with the day of activation of this [Nedić's] government, German military forces do not interfere in any interior affair of Serbia, and therefore not in the work of the Gendarmes either. Since the German military forces had undertaken—before the creation of the Serbian government—certain action on the ground in order to prevent communist brigand bands, which action has not been completed, it has been ordered that the German military forces stop their action against these bands as of September 3, 1941. The Gendarmes shall act entirely autonomously, exclusively in the interests of the Serbian people . . . according to orders from the Serbian government.[30]

On September 5, 1941, two days after this order went into effect, the minister of interior affairs ordered the creation of nine new armed detachments under the direct command of Nedić. These detachments consisted of just under one thousand Serbs, armed by the Germans to fight against the resistance along with the Serbian Gendarmes, Kosta Pećanac's Chetniks, and Ljotić's 120-man 1st Detachment of Serbian Volunteers.[31] These relatively small forces proved inadequate to suppress the sabotage and ambush tactics of the Communist-led insurgency in Serbia, and Nedić soon requested the help of German troops to crush the Partisan uprising.

Because of the deteriorating German military position in Serbia, Gen. Franz Böhme was appointed the military commander for Serbia. The 342nd German Division was sent from France to Serbia, joining the 125th Regiment, which had been sent from Greece.[32] By mid-September, a portion of Mihailović's Chetniks had begun to participate in the uprising in Serbia, driven, in part, by concerns that the Communists were eclipsing the Chetniks as a resistance force.[33]

On September 18, General Böhme arrived in Belgrade, intending to replace Serbian police actions with German operations. Soon after his arrival, however, Böhme learned that Chetnik leader Kosta Pećanac had broken with Mihailović, openly allying himself with Nedić. Böhme was persuaded that Nedić had a significant following, that he was working for the German cause, and that Nedić's government and police could still be useful. After a personal meeting with Nedić, Böhme left impressed that he was a "thoroughly honorable man."[34] On September 29, Böhme ordered the German authorities to resume arming the Serbian police. By the end of October, 1941, armed Serbian forces under German supervision were performing with increasing effectiveness.[35]

By the eighth month of German occupation, Minister of the Economy Mihailo Olćan boasted that Serbia "has been allowed what no other occupied country has been allowed [and that is] to establish law and order . . . by means of our own armed forces."[36] On November 21, 1941, Nedić issued an order for the creation of a unified Serbian command structure, specifying that the commander of the Serbian Gendarmes would also coordinate the activities of the Serbian Volunteer Command of Ljotić and the Chetniks of Kosta Pećanac.[37] According to German estimates of December 1, 1941, Nedić was in command of forces numbering nearly eighteen thousand. On December 13, 1941, the Nazi military command ordered the arming of all Serbian formations.[38]

The Belgrade Special Police

On the day of the Yugoslav military's surrender to invading Axis forces, Dragomir (Dragi) Jovanović arrived in Belgrade from Gornji Milanovac. The following day he was warmly received by Gestapo officers Karl Kraus and Hans Helm, who suggested that he reorganize the Belgrade police and head the local Belgrade government.[39] On April 21, Col. Ernst Moritz von Kaisenberg, the field commandant in Belgrade, appointed Jovanović extraordinary commissar for the City of Belgrade. The Gestapo accepted Jovanović's recommendations to divide Belgrade into sixteen boroughs and two commissariats and to reestablish the Belgrade police as an apparatus of political repression in Belgrade.[40] Jovanović and Božidar (Boško) Bećarević revitalized the former political police, continuing its previous organizational charter.[41]

The Belgrade Special Police was organized in mid-May, 1941, under the guidance of the Gestapo. As Jovanović stated in his postwar testimony: "I changed only the name of the Department of General Police into the Department of the Special Police, according to instructions."[42] Initially consisting of 55 agents, it grew to 878 police guards and 240 agents by late June, 1941.[43] The chief of this unit was Ilija Paranos, a signatory of the "Appeal to the Serbian Nation." Paranos reported to Jovanović.[44] The 4th Anti-Communist Section of the Special Police was headed by Boško Bećarević, who was responsible for hundreds of arrests, tortures, executions, and deportations.[45] Salaries for the Special Police—as well as rewards for captured or killed Communists and Jews—were subsidized by the Fund for the Prevention of Jewish-Communist Action, which was paid for by the Jews of Belgrade.[46]

The Serbian Volunteers of Dimitrije Ljotić

Srpska dobrovoljačka komanda (Serbian Volunteer Command) was a relatively small but highly effective military formation in occupied Serbia. Later renamed *Srpski dobrovoljački korpus* (Serbian Volunteer Corps), this formation was organized by Dimitrije Ljotić, who had established a relationship with the SS as early as 1935, the year his Zbor movement was expanded into *Jugoslovenski narodni pokret Zbor* (Yugoslav National Movement Zbor), the pan-Serbian fascist party modeled on the Nazi party.[47] For years, the funding for Ljotić's political activities had come from German industrial firms and intelligence services.[48] In the early days of the German occupation, Ljotić founded the Serbian Volunteer Command as the military branch of Zbor.

The Volunteers remained unarmed until mid-September, 1941. At a September 14 government meeting, Mihailo Olćan, the minister of finance and a Zbor member, suggested arming Ljotić's Volunteers to suppress the Partisan uprising, which was continuing to gain momentum.[49] Olćan's office was established as the temporary recruitment headquarters for the Serbian Volunteer Command, and on the following day 234 Zbor members reported for duty. Within the next few days, over 600 had enlisted.[50]

The Volunteers were sent immediately into combat missions—jointly with Nedić's newly formed detachments and the Chetniks of Kosta Pećanac—against the Partisans.[51] In the same month, Harald Turner, the chief Nazi civil administrator for Serbia, reported to his superiors that Ljotić's Serbian Volunteers had demonstrated "extraordinary results" in their "cleansing actions" and could be fully trusted.[52]

On October 6, 1941, at the suggestion of Ljotić, Col. Kosta Mušicki was appointed by Nedić to head the Serbian Volunteer Command. A member of Zbor and a former aide to King Aleksandar and Queen Marija, Mušicki had demonstrated his support for the Nazis by helping them to enter Yugoslavia during the Axis invasion of April, 1941. Mušicki at the time was stationed in Slavonski Brod (Croatia) as the Royal Yugoslav Army commander of the railroad between Belgrade and Zagreb.[53] For several months after the Axis conquest, Mušicki remained in Slavonski Brod, where he attempted to join the Ustasha Militia. Failing that, in mid-August Mušicki went to Belgrade, where he was warmly received by Ljotić.[54] Mušicki served as commander of the Volunteers until the end of 1941, when he was removed from this post amid accusations concerning his loyalty.

In October, 1941, the Serbian Volunteer Command participated in the notorious massacre of civilians at Kragujevac. After ten German soldiers were killed and twenty-six wounded around Kragujevac in an ambush by

Partisans and Chetniks, German forces retaliated by shooting civilians in Kragujevac. German wartime records indicate that 2,300 civilians were executed; Yugoslav postwar publications have claimed as many as 7,000 victims.[55] German soldiers, however, were not alone in their responsibility for the massacre—nor were the victims only Serbs.

The first persons arrested on October 18, 1941, were all of the Jewish males in Kragujevac and a number of Communists, altogether about seventy persons. The total fell short of the designated number of 2,300 to be shot, as required by the German retaliation formula. Therefore, all males from the town between the ages of sixteen and sixty were assembled and the victims—including high school students—were selected from among them.[56] What is usually omitted from most accounts of the Kragujevac massacre, however, is that the 5th Detachment of the Serbian Volunteer Corps, commanded by Marisav Petrović, was responsible for rounding up the victims and surrendering them to the Germans for execution. The Serbian Volunteers, armed with German arms and wearing German helmets, brought the arrested civilians to barracks, which they guarded until the execution. On the day after the execution, the Volunteers recruited new members in Kragujevac.[57]

The involvement of Ljotić's forces in the murder of Serbian citizens was not unusual. On December 7, 1941, in the town of Čačak, in an attempt to identify suspected Communists, the Germans ordered that all Serbian males between the ages of fifteen and sixty must report to receive identity cards. It was also announced that the town was encircled and that anyone who tried to escape would be killed. By one o'clock that afternoon, five thousand were arrested. A commission composed of Germans, Nedićites, Ljotićites, and Chetniks selected out the suspected Communists, and a court under the leadership of the local Serbian Orthodox priest and prominent Zbor member, Father Dragutin Bulić, was established the next day. Because Bulić taught at the high school, he was familiar with the political persuasions of both students and teachers. He rendered his judgment, drawing a cross next to the names of those who would be executed, and the sentence, death by machine gun, was carried out immediately. Col. Kosta Mušicki, the leader of Ljotić's Volunteers, participated in these proceedings. Between December, 1941, and January, 1942, about six hundred people were condemned to death, and a larger number were sent to concentration camps.[58] Joint Serbian-German courts martial were established in other towns as well.[59]

On May 16, 1942, the Nedić government decreed that the officers of the Serbian Volunteer Command would begin to "receive a salary according to the law."[60] Between April and December, 1942, the number of Ljotić's Volunteers increased from 3,500 to 5,000. At the beginning of 1943, the Serbian Volunteer Command was renamed the Serbian Volunteer Corps, and Kosta Mušicki, who had in the meanwhile been promoted to general, resumed command. In the first half of 1943, the armed forces of the Serbian State Guard, the Serbian Border Guard (administered by the Ministry of Finance), and the Serbian Volunteer Corps numbered about 25,000.[61]

The Serbian State Guard

Srpska državna straža (Serbian State Guard) was established by Milan Nedić in March, 1942, with the support of SS general August Meyszner. On February 4, 1942, Meyszner and Nedić met to discuss the creation of a new Serbian police force with 15,000 to 16,000 members.[62] The nucleus of the Serbian State Guard was the Serbian Gendarmes, a direct continuation of the Royal Yugoslav Gendarmes. Within less than three months of existence, the State Guard (which was divided into the City Guard, the Field Guard, and the Border Guard) totaled 18,622 personnel, an approximate level maintained throughout the period of the German occupation.[63]

In the summer of 1942, Meyszner appointed Jovanović as chief of *Srpska državna bezbednost* (Serbian State Security), which assumed the administration of the State Guard, and in October, 1942, the administration of the Serbian Border Guard was transferred to the Ministry of Finance.[64] In October, 1943, both the State Guard and the Border Guard were placed under the operational control of *Höhere SS und Polizeiführer Serbien* (Higher SS and Police Leader for Serbia).[65]

The State Guard routinely executed captured Partisans, often with the assistance of legalized Chetniks. For example, when six Partisans were hanged publicly in the Serbian towns of Valjevo, Ub, and Obrenovac, on March 27, 1942, the Serbian chief of the Valjevo district issued the following report to Nedić's Ministry of Interior: "Several thousand people as well as representatives of the German army attended the carrying out of the death sentence in all three places. The execution was carried out by our authorities, the Serbian State Guard, and Chetnik detachments."[66]

As former Gendarmes accustomed to wielding power in Yugoslavia, members of the State Guard were unenthusiastic about having to play a subservient role relative to the Germans. What preserved their morale, however, was the dream of restoring a royalist Greater Serbia. Most members of the State Guard sympathized with Mihailović's Chetnik movement and its goals and provided Mihailović with intelligence and even logistical support. Jovanović himself provided financial support to Draža Mihailović from his discretionary funds.[67]

The Chetniks

Unlike the Serbian State Guard and the Serbian Volunteer Corps, both of which operated with Nazi support from the start, the ultra-nationalist Chetniks began as irregular guerrilla formations from the remnants of the Royal Yugoslav Army. Chetnik leader Kosta Pećanac was an early and open collaborator with the Nazis, and his followers were legalized in Nedić's Serbia. The most prominent Chetnik leader, however, was Dragoljub (Draža) Mihailović, a Yugoslav Royal Army colonel who would emerge as the leader—or at least the figurehead—for the Chetnik movement throughout Yugoslavia. Appointed minister of the army, navy, and air force by the Yugoslav government-in-exile in London in January, 1942, Mihailović was a devoted royalist, whose relationship to the Axis powers evolved into a pattern of complexity and compromise.

DRAŽA MIHAILOVIĆ

The Chetniks under the command of Mihailović initially had planned to resist the German occupation but soon fell into a pattern of military passivity compared to Communist resistance groups. The reasons for this transformation were complex. They were in part due to fear of German reprisals, especially after the Serbian losses suffered in the Independent State of Croatia during the first four months of the war. Adding to the complexity of their wartime actions was the Chetnik—and Communist—realization that in carefully choosing their battles and forging alliances, the means of postwar succession to power would be secured.

By late 1941, Mihailović's Chetniks effectively had abandoned resistance to the Axis in favor of the struggle against Tito's Partisans, and thereafter maintained a pattern of collaboration with both Germans and Italians against the Partisans, notwithstanding sporadic acts of anti-Axis sabotage. Indeed, during late 1943 and 1944, and especially after Allied support had shifted to Tito, the Chetniks made a point to openly fight the Axis in the presence of American and British military observers.[68]

Even at the beginning of the German occupation of Serbia, Mihailović had not only avoided clashes with the Axis, but initiated and maintained contact with the occupation forces and their collaborators. In August, 1941, German analyses noted that Communists formed most of the insurgency, while Serbian nationalist Chetniks were deliberately avoiding military confrontation with the Germans. In a report sent to Berlin on September 11, more than five months after the Nazi occupation, the plenipotentiary of the German Ministry of Foreign Affairs in Serbia, Felix Benzler, wrote that there had been to date no battles between German forces and Chetniks.[69] In fact, Mihailović's efforts to establish cooperation with the Germans had so favorably impressed Capt. Josef Matl of *Abwehr* (German military intelligence) that, in October of 1941, Matl reported that the Chetnik detachments of the Yugoslav army under the command of Col. Draža Mihailović had placed themselves at the disposal of the German Wehrmacht.[70]

At Mihailović's request, the German military command met with him in mid-November.[71] The German delegation was led by Colonel Kogard, assistant to the chief of staff of the Military Command of Serbia. Accompanying Mihailović were Col. Branislav J. Pantić, Maj. Aleksandar Mišić, and Capt. Nenad Mitrović. Mihailović promised to continue fighting against the Partisans and emphasized that his forces would not attack the Germans. Mihailović requested from the Germans 20,000 rifles, 200 heavy machine guns, 2,000 machine guns, 100 mortars, 100,000 hand grenades, and 20,000 Yugoslav military uniforms and boots. He also proposed that the Germans withdraw to Niš and Belgrade, while his Chetniks would secure all communications and roads in Serbia's interior. Typewritten copies of these requests were prepared for both the Germans and Milan Nedić.[72]

During the meeting, Kogard and Mihailović agreed that their common enemy was the Partisans. Kogard, however, stated that he could not trust the Chetniks because, unlike "Nedić, Ljotić, Pećanac, and many others, who had openly sided with us from the beginning," Mihailović's Chetniks "were waging an open struggle against the German Wehrmacht."[73] According to Pantić's eyewitness account, Mihailović protested that "he had never issued any order to attack the German forces. Just the opposite. All of his orders were directed to avoid that struggle, except when his forces are attacked by the Germans. Thus had it been until that moment, thus would it be in the future."[74]

Kogard then produced several photographs of the mutilated bodies of German soldiers killed near Kragujevac in October, 1941. Their penises had been cut off and inserted into their mouths—a form of mutilation typically practiced by the Chetniks. He maintained that Mihailović must be held responsible for crimes committed by his Chetniks. Mihailović stated that the crime had been committed by the Partisans, not by his men. Kogard, however, insisted that he had information to the contrary. Mihailović then conceded that it was possible his men were responsible, but that he was aware of neither the attack nor the mutilations. Kogard responded,

"That does not diminish your responsibility as the commander. You are responsible for the crimes committed by your subordinates." [75] Largely because of Nazi suspicions regarding the Chetniks' role in the mutilations, the mid-November meeting ended without any agreement between the two sides. The meeting, however, would not be Mihailović's final overture to the Germans.

Prior to the November meeting, Mihailović also had attempted to forge cooperative relationships with committed Axis collaborators. As early as May, 1941, a little more than one month after the German's had invaded Yugoslavia, Mihailović sent his second lieutenant, Vladimir Lenac, to Belgrade to meet with Ljotić. Lenac, who had headed the Zbor youth movement at Zagreb University, informed Ljotić of Mihailović's interest in collaboration and asked for the names of Belgrade civilians who could provide financial assistance to the Chetniks. [76]

On August 29, the day Nedić formed his government, Nedić sent a message to Mihailović offering to collaborate in opposing the Partisans. [77] During early September, in response to Nedić's request, Mihailović sent a delegation to meet with Nedić in Belgrade. In Nedić's testimony at his war crimes trial on January 9, 1946, he explained Mihailović's goals of and conditions for collaboration:

> (1) To establish order and peace in Serbia. (2) To begin a joint fight against the communist-led Partisan detachments, precisely against units of the Communist Party. (3) That I should establish a connection with [the Germans] and legitimize Draža to the Germans. (4) To remit him [Draža] a certain sum of money for paying the wages of his officers and non-commissioned officers. (5) Having pacified Serbia, to take military action in Bosnia for pacification. (6) To assist the government of [General Blažo] Đukanović in Montenegro for its pacification. All these proposals and conditions were accepted by my side. Draža got money, and the Germans approved this. [78]

Accordingly, on September 7, 1941, the commander of the Serbian Gendarmes issued an order to the commander of Nedić's 5th Detachment stating that Nedić's detachments "will make contact with the Chetnik detachments which are under the command of General-Staff Colonel Draža Mihailović," and that "in each detachment there must be one person who speaks German very well, because of the possibility of maintaining connection with the German military authorities." [79] Nevertheless, it is widely believed that Mihailović was engaged in resistance as late as October, 1941, when he and Tito supposedly were still attempting to link forces in resisting the Germans. Indeed, Tito and Mihailović did meet on September 19, 1941, at which time Mihailović voiced his opposition to large-scale attacks on German positions, citing fear of German reprisals. Four days later, when Tito's Partisans and Mihailović's Chetniks entered the western Serbian town of Užička Požega, the two forces clashed. Over the next six weeks, Partisans and Chetniks fought for control of the town. Amid this open conflict, Tito and Mihailović met for a second time on October 26, but could establish no new common ground. Throughout most of this period, Mihailović maintained a liaison officer at Tito's headquarters in Užice.[80]

At the end of September, Gen. Heinrich Danckelmann, the German military commander for Serbia, informed Nedić that Mihailović had deceived both Nedić and the Germans, having reached an agreement with the Partisan leadership.[81] Nevertheless, even as Mihailović offered to cooperate with Tito against the Germans, he promised to join the Nazis in fighting the Partisans. It appears that Mihailović kept his word only to the Nazis. During November, 1941, Partisan-held territory near the Serbian town of Požarevac was attacked jointly by one German battalion, the Hungarian Danube Flotilla, and four Serbian formations: Ljotić's 6th Volunteer Detachment, two of Nedić's detachments, six Chetnik detachments led by Pećanac, and Mihailović's Chetniks.[82] It was during this time that Mihailović had requested the meeting with the Germans that would end in failure.

On November 18 and 20, one week after Mihailović's meeting with the Germans, Tito's and Mihailović's delegates met to negotiate a prisoner exchange, a cessation of hostilities, and a supposed continuation of joint action against the Germans. On November 25, however, Mihailović's Chetniks joined German troops and other Serbian collaborationist forces in an intensive attack on the Partisan stronghold in the western Serbian town of Užice, where Tito's headquarters and armaments factory were located. By December 5, 1941, with Serbian help, the anti-Nazi uprising in Serbia effectively was crushed.[83] A German military assessment, titled "Serbia at the end of 1941," stated: "The creation of the Serbian government under President General Milan Nedić has fulfilled expectations. The Serbian people have entered the struggle against Bolshevism, and in that way a seed has been planted that could—as a fruit—bring friendship toward Germany and active collaboration with both the Axis and the New Europe."[84]

The same report proposed to increase the number of the Serbian Gendarmes from 10,000 to 20,000; to release 500 Serbian officers and 10,000 soldiers loyal to Nedić from prisoner-of-war camps; and to create a transitional Serbian state, as a prelude to an autonomous, independent Serbia in the New Europe.[85]

Throughout the Second World War, the Chetniks functioned as the instruments of a policy of genocide, which was accepted broadly by the intellectual and political leadership in Serbia and which extended beyond Serbia's borders. Chetnik ideology was elaborated in the memorandum "Homogeneous Serbia" by Stevan Moljević (dated June 30, 1941, two months before its author joined the executive council of the Chetnik National Committee and became a key adviser to Mihailović).[86] An excerpt follows:

> The primary and essential duty of Serbs today is: to create and organize a homogeneous Serbia which must encompass the entire ethnic territory where Serbs live, and to secure for Serbia all necessary strategic and communication lines and centers as well as economic regions that would forever enable its free economic, political and cultural development.
>
> These strategic and communication lines and centers are necessary for the security, life, and survival of Serbia, and if in some regions today we do not have a Serbian majority, those regions must serve Serbia and the Serbian people.[87]

Although written following two-and-one-half months of German occupation, the document's primary concern is not the question of resistance but the creation of Greater Serbia. The territories to be incorporated were essentially those identified in "The Outline," Ilija Garašanin's 1844 blueprint of Serbian expansionism.[88]

In December, 1941, Moljević drafted a letter that was sent to Dragiša Vasić, a Belgrade intellectual who had joined Mihailović's staff in the summer. Reiterating the themes of "Homogeneous Serbia," Moljević proposed taking possession of a substantial portion of Croatian territory and "cleansing the land of all non-Serb elements." Moljević continued: "With regard to the Muslims, our government in London should immediately resolve the issue [of emigration] with Turkey, with which the English will help us." Significantly, this document was endorsed with Mihailović's handwritten instruction, "forward to Dr. Vasić."[89]

In their pursuit of Greater Serbia during the Second World War, the Chetniks regarded non-Serbian populations with a contempt that paralleled the Nazis' attitude toward non-Aryan populations.[90] As early as the summer of 1941, the Belgrade Chetnik Committee proposed that, in order to make Greater Serbia purely Serbian in composition, 2,675,000 people would have to be expelled (including 1,000,000 Croats and 500,000 Germans), and 1,310,000 Serbs would be brought into the newly annexed areas. Although no figures were suggested for population shifts of Muslims, the committee identified Muslims as "a grave problem."[91]

A Chetnik directive of December 20, 1941, specified their goal to create an "ethnically pure" Greater Serbia, consisting of Serbia, Macedonia, Montenegro, Bosnia-Herzegovina, and Vojvodina, "cleansed . . . of all national minorities and non-national elements." This directive further specified the necessity of "cleansing the Muslim population from the Sandžak and the Muslim and Croatian populations from Bosnia and Herzegovina."[92] Between 86,000 and 103,000 Muslims died during the Second World War.[93] The majority of these perished at the hands of the Chetniks.

PAVLE ĐURIŠIĆ

Most responsible for Chetnik operations against Muslims, especially in Montenegro and the Sandžak (both within the Italian zone of occupation), was Pavle Đurišić, commander of the Montenegrin Chetniks.[94] Supported and armed by the Italians, Đurišić's Chetniks operated primarily in the Italian occupation zone but at times crossed into the German zone.[95] For example, in one campaign in early 1943, Đurišić's forces killed ten thousand Muslims, ninety percent of whom were civilians, in the vicinity of Foča in southeastern Bosnia (the German zone of occupation). Chetnik losses were reported to be thirty-six dead and fifty-eight wounded.[96]

After the capitulation of Italy in 1943, Đurišić established closer ties with Dimitrije Ljotić, whose Serbian Volunteer Corps provided weapons, food, typewriters, and other supplies. Nedić promoted Đurišić to the rank of lieutenant-colonel and appointed him assistant commander of the Serbian Volunteer Corps, and, on October 11, 1944, Adolf Hitler awarded Đurišić the Iron Cross.[97]

FATHER MOMČILO ĐUJIĆ

Although the Chetniks killed a number of Serbian Orthodox priests who opposed them, it is noteworthy that roughly three-quarters of Yugoslavia's Serbian Orthodox priests supported the Chetniks throughout the war.[98] One prominent Orthodox clergyman and Chetnik leader was Father Momčilo Đujić. Born in Knin, Croatia, in 1907, and a self-proclaimed *vojvoda* (warlord), he operated in northern Dalmatia and western Bosnia, where, as early as April, 1941, his Chetniks began murdering and mutilating Croatian civilians.[99]

Father Đujić negotiated an official pact of nonaggression with the Italians, who approved his command of three thousand Chetniks. He established a consistent record of cooperation with the Italian authorities in anti-Partisan raids, although one Italian assessment of April, 1943, concluded that Đujić's Chetniks were good for little more than plunder.[100] Following the surrender of Italy in September, 1943, some of Đujić's Chetniks fled to the hills or defected to the rapidly growing Partisan movement, but a few thousand almost immediately began to collaborate with the Germans.[101] This new Chetnik-Nazi relationship was reinforced when, in a short-wave transmission on November 19, 1943, Mihailović instructed Đujić to cooperate with the Germans, adding that Mihailović himself could not openly do so "because of public opinion."[102]

Unlike the Italians, who strongly supported him, the Germans were wary of Đujić and limited his activities to protecting the rail lines between Knin and Split from Partisan sabotage. Recognizing his own weakening position, Đujić began to cultivate direct ties to Ljotić's Zbor movement.[103] By the end of 1944, with Partisan victories and the demoralization of his own troops on the increase, Đujić urgently appealed to the Germans to permit him and his Chetniks to take refuge in German-controlled Slovenia. When the German authorities in Zagreb refused, Ljotić, now headquartered in Slovenia, traveled to Vienna and obtained Hermann Neubacher's approval.[104] Đujić's escape to safety along with six thousand Chetniks was assisted by the Nazis and Ustashas, at the request of Ljotić.[105]

Some details of Đujić's activities in late 1944 provide insight into the nature of Chetnik collaboration with the Germans. On November 25, 1944, Partisan forces began to attack the town of Knin, which was defended by fourteen thousand German troops, forty-five hundred Chetniks under Đujić, and about fifteen hundred Ustashas. After six days of fighting, Đujić was wounded, and, on December 1, he sent an emissary to Gen. Gustav Fehn of the German 264th Division in Knin with the following message:

> The Chetnik Command with all of its armed forces has collaborated sincerely and loyally with the German Army in these areas from September last year. Our common interests demanded this. This collaboration has continued to the present day. . . . The Chetnik Command wishes to share the destiny of the German Army in the future, too. . . . The Command requests that [the village of] Pađene be the base for supplying our units, until a further common agreement is reached.[106]

The Chetniks received some ammunition and food from the Germans and, on December 3, 1943, waged a joint German-Chetnik offensive against the Partisans, before Đujić's forces of about six to seven thousand withdrew to Bihać, with the assistance of the German 373rd Division. General Fehn organized the transport of Đujić's wounded Chetniks through Zagreb to the Third Reich.[107] Đujić then requested a written guarantee from Pavelić that the rest of his Chetniks may withdraw to Slovenia. In addition, Ljotić and Nedić appealed to Hermann Neubacher in Vienna to secure Pavelić's cooperation, and the Slovene collaborationist Gen. Lev Rupnik also requested safe passage for Đujić's troops.[108]

On December 21, 1944, Pavelić issued an order to the Croatian military forces to give unconditionally free passage to Đujić's Chetniks.[109] However, the routes offered by Pavelić were unsecured because of constant Partisan attacks, and so Đujić took an alternate route toward the Istrian peninsula, terrorizing and murdering the local Croatian population along the way.[110] Once in Slovenia, Đujić's forces joined Jevđević's Chetniks, Ljotić's Volunteers, and Nedić's Serbian Shock Corps to form a single unit under the command of Odilo Globočnik of the *Höhere SS und Polizeiführer im Adriatischen Küstenland* (Higher SS and Police Leader in the Adriatic Littoral).[111] In 1947, Đujić was tried in Yugoslavia in absentia as a war criminal and found guilty but has never been extradited, despite a 1988 request by Yugoslavia.[112] Đujić lives in the United States, where he has resided for decades.

THE COMPLEX ALLIANCES OF THE CHETNIKS

A number of scholarly works have argued that the Chetniks were first and foremost a resistance force allied with the anti-Axis powers, but they offer an incomplete picture of the Chetnik movement.[113] Like the Nazis, who believed that all Germans must live within one large, ethnically-pure German state, the Chetniks believed that all Serbs must live in one large, ethnically pure Serbian state.[114] In the Chetnik vision, Greater Serbia would consist only of Serbs, under a Serbian king, encompassing Serbia, Vojvodina, Bosnia-Herzegovina, Macedonia, Kosovo, Montenegro, and portions of Croatia, including the Dalmatian coast as far north as Šibenik and the inland provinces of Lika and Slavonia. The Chetnik plan specified that the non-Serbian populations of the coveted lands would be eliminated and that these lands would finally be legally incorporated into a Greater Serbia.[115]

Regarding the realization of a Greater Serbia, the Chetniks and the Nedić government worked in a parallel fashion toward a common goal. The Chetniks contributed to the cause of Greater Serbia by executing a policy of genocide against non-Serbs in the territories they coveted, while Nedić maneuvered politically with Berlin to secure the creation of Greater Serbia under German patronage. The final step of the Chetnik plan was to seize power after the Germans were ousted in an anticipated invasion by the Allies. Thus, Serbia would be restored to full autonomy under the Serbian monarchy, and the Chetniks would establish their military authority over the ethnically homogenous Greater Serbia. It is this part of the Chetniks' endgame—their anticipation that the Allies would eventually oust the Germans—that has provided the basis for the claim that the Chetniks were really a resistance force all along. In the final analysis, however, the Chetniks' legacy was principally one in which opportunism overshadowed resistance in a near-total eclipse. Thus, the Chetniks variously collaborated with the Partisans against the Nazis, the Nazis against the Partisans, the Italians against the Ustashas, and the Ustashas against the Partisans. As late as February, 1943, Mihailović was so indiscreet as to state to a British colonel that the Chetniks' principal enemies were, in order, Tito, the Ustashas, the Muslims, the Croats, and last the Germans and Italians.[116]

For example, the safe evacuation of 417 Allied pilots, including 343 Americans, from Chetnik-held territories in Serbia during the latter half of 1944 has often been cited as evidence of the Chetniks' strong pro-Allied sympathies.[117] Indeed, with Allied support shifted from Mihailović to Tito, Mihailović's Chetniks were courting renewed Allied support and made great efforts to demonstrate their willingness to assist the Allies.[118] However, none of these sources mentions that the Chetniks rescued German aviators as well, as indicated in a Nedić government report of February, 1944, and, on still other occasions, Mihailović's men hunted down Allied aviators on behalf of the Germans.[119]

Despite claims that the Chetniks were devoted to a common cause with the Allies, the Chetniks were neither genuinely anti-Axis nor pro-Allied in orientation, but primarily opportunists for Greater Serbia, for which cause they solicited both Axis and Allied support.

The Serbian Role in the Concentration Camps

The fate of the Jews in concentration camps in Serbia will be discussed in the next chapter. Here we consider the internment and murder of Serbs. Although much of the evidence related to Serbian concentration camps was destroyed under orders of the retreating Nazis, the memoirs of survivors of the Banjica concentration camp in Belgrade offer insight into the role played by the Serbs in exterminating members of the resistance.[120] After the German military command gave orders for the creation of the concentration camp, Belgrade mayor Jovanović took steps to convert the former 18th Infantry army barracks into a camp, which operated from July 5, 1941, until October 3 or 4, 1944.[121] One-half of the inmates were dispatched to Banjica by the SS, and another one-third were sent by the Serbian State Guard, Ljotić's Volunteers, Pećanac's Chetniks, various urban police units, and the Special Police of Belgrade.[122]

The Banjica camp, which mainly held members of the resistance, was run by the Belgrade police commissioner, Svetozar Vujković, remembered by concentration camp survivors for his enthusiastic collaboration with the

Gestapo, his role in ordering murders, and his penchant for devising tortures.[123] In the early days of Banjica, the camp was guarded jointly by the Gestapo and the Serbian State Guard, but later this function devolved to the Serbian State Guard alone.[124] Execution lists in Banjica were drawn up by Vujković, who often selected victims at random.[125] Executions of inmates were a daily event. There were no execution lists at first, but, from 1942, the lists, written entirely in Cyrillic, were prepared by the Gestapo and Special Police.[126] According to the memoirs of Banjica survivors, these executions were performed by the Belgrade Special Police and the Serbian State Guard, and the victims included children. According to preserved records, 23,697 inmates passed through Banjica, of whom 3,849 were slain at various killing sites, primarily by the Germans but also by members of the Serbian State Guard. The actual number of victims may have been higher.[127]

The Russian Corps

Another collaborationist formation in Serbia wholly loyal to the Nazi cause was the Russian Protection Corps, known throughout its existence by a variety of official Russian designations.[128] The Russian Corps was founded in Belgrade by Russian émigrés on September 12, 1941, under the guidance of the German Command and in cooperation with the Nedić government.[129] Although their aim was to assist the Germans in destroying the Bolshevik regime in the Soviet Union, the Russian Corps never fought in Russia, but rather in Serbia (1941–44), Bosnia (1944–45), and Slovenia (1945) and almost exclusively against Tito's Partisans.

The Russian Corps was composed mainly of émigré Russians and officers of the Russian Imperial Army defeated in the civil war that followed the Russian Revolution of October, 1917.[130] In September, 1944, the Russian Corps would reach their numerical peak of 11,197; the total number of Corps members serving during the war was 17,090.[131] They were armed by the Germans with the captured weaponry of the Yugoslav army.

Between the fall of 1941 and the spring of 1944, the Russian Corps primarily protected weapons factories, mines, roads, and railroads throughout Serbia in accordance with the priorities established by the German High Command.[132] To Berlin, Serbia represented an important source of raw materials. Its railroads and roads provided vital links to the eastern Mediterranean. Beginning in the spring of 1944, the Russian Corps increasingly focused on fighting against the Partisans, who were penetrating Serbia from the Sandžak and Bosnia. Partisan ranks grew by tens of thousands when Chetniks responded to Tito's offer of amnesty in August, 1944, and grew further when in September, 1944, at the urging of the British, Petar II told his followers to join the Partisans.[133] After October, 1944, with the German withdrawal from Serbia and the arrival of the Red Army, the Russian Corps withdrew to Bosnia-Herzegovina and later to Slovenia.

Throughout the war, in their operations against the Partisans, the Russian Corps acted in close cooperation with the Serbian State Guard, Ljotić's Serbian Volunteer Corps (with whom they were most closely allied), Mihailović's Chetniks, and the Ustashas.[134] On December 1, 1942, the Corps was incorporated into the Wehrmacht, and all members of the Russian Protection Corps were required to take an oath of allegiance to the Führer.[135] Members of the Russian Corps believed that their only hope to return to a Russia free of Bolshevism depended upon a German victory.

As early as November, 1941, the Russian Corps had established a pattern of collaboration with the Chetniks against Partisans, and it was not until 1944 that clashes occurred between the Chetniks and the Russian Corps.[136] Nevertheless, in the summer of 1944 the Corps mediated an agreement between the Chetniks under Petrović and the Germans to fight against the Partisans, and the Chetniks were joined by a Russian company.[137] The Russian Corps maintained loyal and friendly relations with the Serbian government of Nedić, and the Russian Corps commander, Gen. Boris Aleksandrovich Shteifon, had warm personal relations with Nedić.[138]

The Serbian Gestapo

In mid–1942, the German Gestapo formed a secret Serbian Gestapo in Belgrade without the knowledge of Milan Nedić or his government.[139] SS lieutenant colonel Emanuel Schäfer, the newly appointed chief of the German Security Police in Serbia, wanted to create an indigenous Serbian entity through which the Gestapo could exert more control over the Nedić regime. Schäfer selected Janjić to head this new organization. According to German intelligence, Janjić was a promising candidate. Appointed secretary of the presidency by Dragiša Cvetković during Royal Yugoslavia, Janjić, a member of Zbor, had used his position to disseminate pro-Nazi propaganda. During the Belgrade coup of March 27, 1941, Janjić fled from Belgrade, but he was soon reinstated as a temporary official in the collaborationist government of Milan Aćimović. When Janjić volunteered his services to the Belgrade Special Police in the summer of 1941, his offer was rejected. He then assembled his own detachment of one hundred soldiers to fight against the Partisans near Kragujevac.[140]

It was in Kragujevac—where the Germans, assisted by the 5th Detachment of the Serbian Volunteer Command under Marisav Petrović, brutally massacred civilians in October, 1941—that Janjić captured the interest of the Gestapo. He had joined Petrović's detachment only shortly before the massacre, and afterward, Petrović appointed Janjić president of the munici-pality.[141] In this capacity, Janjić subjected the local population to punish-ments that included beatings, earning him praise from the German secret police, local German officers, and even Nedić for maintaining order.[142] Jan-jić also engaged extensively in looting, blackmail, and rape. When the Ser-bian police attempted twice to arrest Janjić over the next few months, he was released each time following the intervention of the German Gestapo. In March, 1942, Nedić promoted Janjić to chief of the newly formed Spe-cial Detachment at the Presidency of the Government, which served as Nedić's bodyguard.[143]

After receiving his secret commission from Emanuel Schäfer, Janjić be-gan to recruit members from his own Special Detachment, the Serbian State Guard, the Serbian Volunteer Corps, and from among Nedić adminis-tration officials, high school students, and merchants. The members them-selves would soon call it *Srpski gestapo* (Serbian Gestapo).[144] Janjić saw himself as replacing Nedić to become the führer of a nationalist-socialist Serbia. In July, 1942, he called his first twelve members "apostles" and intended to promote them to the highest state positions in Serbia when he assumed power. He proposed to Felix Benzler of the Reich Ministry of Foreign Affairs and August Meyszner of the SS in Belgrade that he should be entrusted to form two Serbian SS divisions, one for the Eastern Front and one for the front in northern Africa.[145]

When Nedić learned of Janjić's political ambitions, he disbanded the Special Detachment and ordered Janjić's arrest.[146] Janjić was taken to the Banjica concentration camp. The German Gestapo, however, secured Jan-jić's release within days. Serbian State Guards again tried to arrest Janjić in August, 1942, but abandoned the attempt when Janjić produced his iden-tity card bearing the imprimatur of the Gestapo.[147]

By the end of 1942, Janjić's organization had grown to 145 members. The first Belgrade Headquarters was a converted primary school, where tortures and murders were carried out in the basement.[148]

The Germans had envisioned the Serbian Gestapo as an elite formation operating against the Partisans, but Janjić's main preoccupation was Nedić, whom he continued to denounce as insufficiently loyal to the Germans. On occasion, the Serbian Gestapo wore the uniform of Mihailović's Chetniks, while at other times they dressed in German uniforms and pretended not to know the Serbian language. On February 22, 1943, Nedić sent a memo-randum to the German military administrative commander of Serbia, pro-testing the activities of the Serbian Gestapo:

What is this organization doing? What purpose is it serving? How and what are its goals? All of this is not clear to me, since I have not been officially informed about this from any source. According to all reports, without exception, from all regional authorities, this impossible organization is severely harming the authority of both the Serbian administration and the German uniform. I personally, and my ministers, high state functionaries, loyal and sincere collaborators with the occupation authorities, are the constant object of wicked, ruthless, and most insulting attacks by these people, without regard for place or occasion. It is easy to suppose what feeling is provoked among the Serbian government and its organs, as well as the public, by such acts.[149]

In fact, there was constant friction between the Serbian Gestapo and both the Belgrade Special Police and the Serbian Volunteers. After receiving Nedić's memorandum, Emanuel Schäfer split the Serbian Gestapo into two parts.

In late April, 1943, Janjić and twenty-six members of his Serbian Gestapo left Belgrade for Berlin, where they continued to work for the German Gestapo.[150] Thirty-three Serbian Gestapo members remained in Belgrade under the leadership of Janjić's deputy, Svetozar Nećak, one of Janjić's apostles.[151] However, their operations were restricted: they were given specific tasks to fulfill; they were not permitted to wear German uniforms; and they were redirected to undermine the Partisan movement rather than Nedić's government. Members posed as captured Partisans in prison camps in order to learn the location of Partisan units. But they generally met with only limited success. Nećak's group was disbanded in February, 1944, yet its former members individually chose to continue working for the Gestapo in Belgrade.[152]

In Berlin, Janjić's apartment became his command headquarters. His followers infiltrated the Yugoslav (mainly Serbian) forced labor ranks there, using such methods as blackmail, robbery, and entrapment to ferret out Partisan sympathizers. A Gestapo report of January, 1944, observed that "among the Serbian laborers on the Reich territory, Janjić is applying Serbian methods and is harming German interests." Defending Janjić, SS major Bruno Sattler wrote in the margin of this report: "This evaluation is unjust toward this absolutely Germanophile man." Nevertheless, in May, 1944, Janjić was replaced in Berlin by two of his apostles.[153]

Nedić and Fascist Greater Serbia

Clashes among Serbian collaborationist organs—such as those between the Serbian Gestapo and both Nedić's government and Ljotić's

Volunteers—were hardly unusual. For example, during 1942, infighting among Nedić's ministers aligned to either of two strong pro-Nazi factions, Zbor and the Yugoslav Radical Union of Milan Stojadinović, became so great that it threatened to paralyze the government. In October, Harald Turner asked Nedić to propose which ministers should be kept or dismissed. Nedić recommended the removal of four ministers and their replacements, which the Germans approved. On November 7, Nedić announced the restructuring of his government (see appendix B).[154]

Nedić's greatest priority, however, was the creation of Greater Serbia, which had also preoccupied the preceding Aćimović administration. Indeed, during June, 1941, the Government of Commissars had sent a memorandum to Gen. Ludwig von Schröder, the military commander in Serbia, stating the need "to give the Serbian people its centuries-old ethnographic borders."[155]

From December, 1941, Nedić repeatedly advocated the creation of Greater Serbia in his public speeches and in private discussions with the German occupation officials. Nedić's plans for expansion included the entire Dalmatian coast of Croatia, all of Bosnia-Herzegovina (except the predominantly Muslim-populated northwest province of Bihać), Croatia's eastern Slavonia, all of Vojvodina (except the German-populated province of Banat), all of Macedonia, all of Montenegro, and part of Albania.[156]

Nedić began seeking an audience with Hitler as early as the end of 1941. During secret meetings with Felix Benzler, Nedić insisted upon being received by the highest functionaries of the Third Reich in Berlin. By 1942, Nedić was advancing proposals for the creation of a nationalist-socialist Serbian state, which would draw its strength from the Serbian peasantry and traditional village life. Typically, in an address on May 10, 1942, Nedić praised the Serbian peasants as the "untouched Serbian race" that has no "mixed foreign blood."[157]

On January 1, 1943, the presidency of the Ministerial Council sent a long memorandum, titled "Explanation of the Necessity of Organizing the Serbian People as a National Community," to Gen. Paul Bader, whose authority matched that of the military commander of Serbia. The memorandum asserted that the Serbian peasants had had the greatest role in the history of the Serbian state but that this class was not represented adequately in the creation of Nedić's state. Therefore, the memorandum suggested that a Serbian peasant state should be organized as had been done in Germany and Italy:

An individual in Serbia, the householder and members of his family, especially among village populations . . . should no longer feel alone

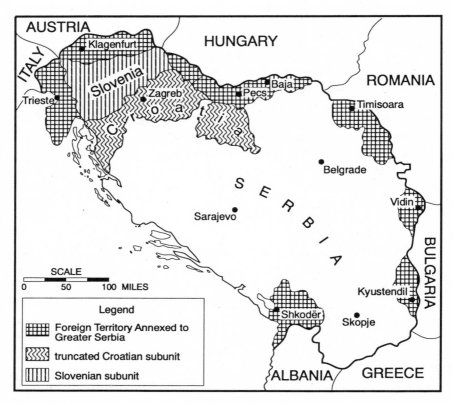

Greater Serbia

and left to fend for himself. Therefore, it seems necessary to encompass and unite all of them into organic communities as has been achieved in Italy on the fascist basis and in Germany on the National Socialist basis. . . . As opposed to the Jewish anarcho-materialist mentality, the Serbs, as well as all other Aryan peoples, are characterized by a natural racial instinct to consider the family, nation, and the state as the highest spiritual and material values. . . . The constructiveness of Serbian National Socialism is based on the blood connections of the family, the peasant cooperative, and the clan.[158]

Nedić's memorandum was carefully examined by Bader, who consulted with Franz Neuhausen at the Ministry of Foreign Affairs, SS general Meyszner, and Gen. Alexander Löhr, military commander in Southeast Europe, as well as with colleagues in the intelligence service. A number of German high officers were at least partially supportive of Nedić's proposal. Meys-

SERBIA'S SECRET WAR

Yugoslavia after 1945

zner, however, rejected it because Nedić had requested extraordinary powers for himself in the memorandum. According to Meyszner, the proposed
"organization shows a dictatorial character at the hands of the President
Minister." At the end of the month, Bader informed Nedić that his proposal
was rejected because of the difficulties of implementing changes during
wartime, but it could be favorably considered after the war.[159]

Finally, on September 18, 1943, Nedić was received by Adolf Hitler
during an official state visit to Berlin, long awaited by the Serbian leader-
.ship, to discuss plans for creating Greater Serbia under Hitler's protection.
Nedić also wanted to reestablish his command over the Serbian State
Guard and Serbian Volunteer Corps and to increase the latter's numbers
from five thousand to fifty thousand.[160]

In a three-hour meeting with Foreign Minister Joachim von Ribbentrop, Nedić demanded an increase in his own authority and the expansion
of Serbia's borders. According to the minutes of this meeting, Nedić spe-

cifically asked for more *Lebensraum* (living space) for the Serbian people. He proposed the annexation of Montenegro, the Sandžak, eastern Bosnia, Srijem, and, most especially, Kosovo.[161] Von Ribbentrop refused to discuss the issue of expanding the border of Serbia—or of any other occupied country, for that matter—while the war was in progress, but suggested that Serbia would be independent after the war. By the end of the meeting, Nedić was so agitated that Hermann Neubacher, the recently appointed German Foreign Office plenipotentiary for Southeast Europe, intervened to calm him. Neubacher was himself an advocate for a Serbian federation encompassing Serbia, the Sandžak, and Montenegro. He suggested to von Ribbentrop that, rather than permit Nedić's meeting to end unsuccessfully, Nedić should meet with Hitler.[162]

In the fifteen- to twenty-minute meeting that followed at Hitler's bunker, Hitler calmed Nedić by promising that he could resume the command of the Serbian State Guard and Serbian Volunteer Corps, double the number of battalions in the Serbian Volunteer Corps, and reopen Belgrade University. Hitler, however, made no concession on Greater Serbia.[163] Goebbels wrote a brief note in his journal about Nedić's meeting with Hitler: "The Serbian Prime Minister, Nedić, has paid a visit to the Führer. He acted very obediently and loyally during this visit. The Führer believes he can make good use of him in re-establishing order in Serbia."[164]

Neubacher continued to lobby the German command for a larger Serbia as serving Germany's military and political interests. Furthermore, a group of German high officers around Neubacher—including Gen. Hans-Gustav Felber and Field Marshal Maximilian von Weichs, the military commander of Southeast Europe from August, 1943—supported the creation of a Serbian unit which would include Serbia, Montenegro, and the Sandžak.[165] Later, the German supporters of Greater Serbia envisioned it to encompass Srijem, eastern Bosnia to the Bosna River, and Kosovo.[166]

In a meeting of December 14, 1943, Hitler expressed his willingness to consider Neubacher's proposal for a Greater Serbian Federation.[167] Nevertheless, in August, 1944, when Germany's military situation was worsening on all fronts, when Tito's Partisans were beginning to build up strength in Serbia, and when Hitler's military staff was proposing a plan for the unification of all of the Serbian nationalist forces under Nedić, Mihailović, and Ljotić against the Communist-led Partisans, Hitler railed against the "danger of a Greater Serbia," even suggesting that Communism was more acceptable.[168]

Just weeks before Nedić's long-awaited visit to Hitler, Milosav Vasiljević, a prominent follower of Ljotić, independently submitted to the German authorities his own proposal for Greater Serbia, a memorandum titled "Deutsch-serbische Verständigung" (The German-Serbian Understanding). Describing the Independent State of Croatia as unstable and powerless to effect order and peace over its territory, the memorandum called for the creation of an "Independent State of Serbia" to be a committed ally of the Third Reich. The memorandum further proposed "a solemn declaration of gratitude and respect of the Serbian people toward the Führer for the liberation of the Serbian Independent State from Yugoslavia and its other enemies." The Greater Serbian state was envisioned to extend as far as the Dalmatian coast of Croatia, the northern Albanian city of Shkodër, and the Greek port city of Salonika.[169]

Critical to understanding the collaborative role played by the Serbian state during the Nazi occupation is an examination of the activities of various Serbian forces—including the Serbian Gestapo, Serbian State Guard, and Ljotić's Serbian Volunteer Corps—*beyond* the borders of Nedić's state. From 1942 to 1944, the Serbian Gestapo was active not only in Serbia but also in Srijem, a region of the Independent State of Croatia.[170] On April 14, 1943, the German Military Command of Serbia praised units of the Serbian State Guard for their "successful action" against Partisans near Bijeljina in eastern Bosnia (within the borders of the Independent State of Croatia).[171] In February, 1944, Nedić sent the 2nd Battalion of the 5th Regiment of the Serbian Volunteer Corps to assist Pavle Đurišić's Chetniks in Montenegro, where 543 of 893 Volunteers were lost in battles against the Partisans.[172] Such military actions beyond the borders of Serbia were consistent with Serbian expansionist aims.

The Collapse of Nedić's Serbia

In mid-August, 1944, Dragi Jovanović, Milan Nedić, and Draža Mihailović secretly met in the village of Ražani. Nedić agreed to provide one hundred million dinars for wages and to request that the Germans supply Mihailović with arms and ammunition.[173] All the money and a portion of the requested arms were soon delivered. On September 6, under German authority and formalized by Nedić, Mihailović took command of the Serbian State Guard, the Serbian Volunteer Corps, the Serbian Border Guard, and all Chetniks. On the same day, the first group of Germans, as well as some two hundred Serbian officials, left Belgrade.[174] At the end of September, Jovanović revealed to Mihailović that the Germans were evacuating from the Balkans and proposed that Mihailović's Chetniks should occupy the towns throughout Serbia before the Communists do. But Mihailović had already made the decision to shift his forces to Bosnia.[175]

With the withdrawal of German forces from Serbia, Serbian collaborators were left with only a few options: to withdraw with the Nazis, to accept Tito's offer of amnesty and join the Partisans, or to pretend they had not collaborated at all. Many collaborators sought German protection from the Allies, and, indeed, the Nazis assisted many in reaching German-controlled territory.[176]

On August 28, 1944, Nedić appointed Minister of Education and Religion Velibor Jonić as state secretary of the government's Presidium, replacing Cvetan Ceka Đorđević, who had been assassinated. Among Jonić's primary responsibilities was preparing for an eventual evacuation of the Nedić government. On September 15, all of Nedić's ministers, except Minister of Agriculture Veselinović and Finance Minister Đorđević, voted to leave Belgrade for the Third Reich.[177] During the same month, Education Minister Velibor Jonić devised a plan to shield some five thousand Serbian intellectuals who had publicly supported the Nazis: some of the older intellectuals would be given refuge in Serbian monasteries, while the rest would be immediately transported to Germany.[178] The Nedić government continued to operate in Belgrade until October, when Soviet forces drove the Germans from Serbia, allowing Tito's Partisans to assume control.

In preparation for their departure from Belgrade, Nedić's ministers and leading officials began to amass large sums of money. On September 29, Nedić himself received 3.5 million Serbian dinars from the safe of the Ministry of Finance.[179] Nedić's government convened its last cabinet meeting in Belgrade on October 3. That night Milorad Nedeljković, Nedić's minister of economy, wrote in a letter to his ministry's office:

> From this moment (midnight) martial law is imposed in Belgrade. The German authorities take over the function of the Serbian government. The Serbian government removes to Germany in order to take over its political and national duty there, bringing together all Serbs who have already been over there (more than 300,000), as well as those who will be evacuated one of these days, and these are all of our intellectual circles, clerks, and Serbian armed detachments (the Serbian State Guard, the Serbian Volunteer Corps, the Border Guard, and the Serbian Guard). All members of the Ravna Gora [Chetnik] movement and many politicians of democratic factions get their passports in the German legation today. . . . I inform you and all of the officials that everyone who wants to be evacuated should report at the Presidency of the Government. Train after train will go non-stop. The Cabinet of the Presidency will do all formalities. Belgrade has been encircled and in a few days

fighting will start from all directions. When [Belgrade] is occupied by communists and Tito's Partisans-Croats, all educated people and the economic elite of the Serbian nation will surely be butchered. They must be saved and this is our task now. . . .[180]

On September 6, 1944, a group of Germans departed from Belgrade, and with them came a group of about two hundred Serbs. On October 4 and 5, more Serbs left Belgrade for Vienna. Among them were Belgrade mayor Dragi Jovanović and members of his administration, agents of the Special Police, five of Nedić's ministers, and the staffs of both the Serbian State Guard and the Serbian Volunteer Corps.[181] At the same time, Ljotić sent Ratko Parežanin (Zbor member and the editor in chief of *Naša borba*) with some thirty Volunteers to Montenegro to persuade warlord Pavle Đurišić to withdraw his Chetniks to German-controlled Slovenia, where Ljotić planned to mass Serbian forces under German protection to prepare for a major attack against Croatian territory.[182] On October 6, Nedić and a contingent of officials and notables left Belgrade in a convoy of three automobiles escorted by two German light tanks and Robert Krohnholz, the German general consul in Belgrade. Nedić's entire government, except for his minister of agriculture, reached Vienna five days later.[183]

The German high officers continued to assess the Nedić government as loyal. Toward the end of October, Hermann Neubacher personally visited the Croatian city of Osijek to arrange the safe passage of Ljotić's Serbian Volunteer Corps through Croatian territory to Slovenia.[184] On October 10, only ten days before the liberation of Belgrade, German authorities installed a new Serbian government—the Committee of State Administration for Serbia—composed of collaborators who had remained behind (see appendix B).[185]

In December, 1944, Bishop Nikolaj Velimirović and Patriarch Gavrilo Dožić were released from Dachau through the intervention of Ljotić, and relocated to a tourist resort. In mid-December, they were brought to Vienna as guests of the Third Reich.[186] German troops had already withdrawn from Serbia, and Nedić's government was headquartered at the Grand Hotel in Kitzbühel in Tyrol, about 340 miles from Vienna, in close coordination with Hermann Neubacher.[187] In Vienna, Velimirović and Dožić met with other invited guests from the Nedić government-in-exile, including Nedić, Milan Aćimović, Velibor Jonić, Mihailo Olćan, and Dimitrije Ljotić.[188]

At this time, the Germans were pressuring Nedić to form a new government for Serbia and to supply fifty thousand Serbian troops to fight against

Soviet troops. Nedić agreed in principle to create the army but not to engage the Soviets. He also insisted that any new government must include Gen. Draža Mihailović. Ljotić, however, resolutely opposed the plan to create a new Serbian government for the strategic reason that this would delimit the area of control to only Serbia. Instead, Ljotić envisioned a more ambitious resurrection of a Royal Yugoslavia under King Petar II and extending from Serbia to Slovenia. This plan was supported by Patriarch Dožić and Bishop Velimirović.[189] During the next months, Hermann Neubacher suggested, and Ljotić supported, a plan to name Dožić the president of a new, collaborationist Serbian government-in-exile.[190] According to Dožić's memoirs, however, the position of president was also offered to Velimirović.[191]

In mid-April, 1945, at the request of Ljotić and with the consent of Hitler, Velimirović and Dožić visited the Nazi-controlled Slovenian coast to bless roughly twenty-five thousand Serb and Slovene collaborators who had retreated there under arrangements made by Ljotić.[192] Among them were members of the Serbian Volunteer Corps, the Serbian State Guard, the Serbian Border Guard and Special Police, as well as Chetniks under Father Momčilo Đujić and Dobrosav Jevđević.[193] All had been under direct SS command since December 12, 1944. On April 19, Velimirović and Dožić visited the headquarters of the Serbian Volunteer Corps in Postojna, Slovenia. There, Dožić made a speech emphasizing his happiness to be among "national heroes."[194] When Ljotić died in a car accident on April 23, Bishop Velimirović and Patriarch Dožić jointly conducted the memorial service. Velimirović eulogized Ljotić as "the most loyal son of Serbdom."[195]

Prior to these final months of the war, anti-Nazi resistance in Serbia had been weak.[196] What has been underappreciated, however, is the degree to which resistance in Serbia largely was quelled by Serbian elements. Throughout the German occupation, the Special Police of Belgrade, the Serbian State Guard, the Serbian Gestapo, the Serbian Volunteer Corps, and the Chetniks had sustained a high level of activity against the Partisans. Serbian scholar Milan Borković has argued that Serbian collaboration was essential to the success of the Nazi war effort: "[The] apparatus of the German occupying forces in Serbia was supposed to maintain order and peace in this region and to exploit its industrial and other riches, necessary for the German war economy. But, however well organized, it could not have realized its plans successfully if the old apparatus of state power, the organs of state administration, the gendarmes, and the police had not been completely placed at its service."[197]

Matteo Milazzo, one of the foremost authorities on the Chetniks, also has observed that "from the end of 1941 until the very end of the war, the striking fact about Serbia, in contrast to the remainder of Yugoslavia, was that there was very little serious resistance activity carried out by either Chetniks or the Partisans."[198] For example, during early 1943, there were only about twelve hundred Partisan fighters in all of Serbia proper—although there were undoubtedly a greater number of noncombatant Partisans.[199] According to the postwar testimony of Dragi Jovanović, Belgrade was a quiet city throughout the occupation, due in large part to the effectiveness of his police force.[200]

Tito had publicly solicited Chetnik support in an offer of amnesty on August 17, 1944, and tens of thousands of Chetniks switched sides to the Partisans.[201] After the German withdrawal from Belgrade, Tito again offered amnesty between November 21, 1944, and January 15, 1945, and the Chetniks were once again the major beneficiaries.[202] Cooperation with the Communists meant a de facto rehabilitation of those who had cooperated with the Nazis. For example, the acting head of the Serbian Orthodox Church, Metropolitan Josif, had earlier given his blessings to both the Nedić regime and the persecution of Serbia's Jews. On March 5, 1945, Josif was administering the oath of office to the newly sworn regents of the transitional Yugoslav government, through which legitimacy was transferred from the monarchy to the Communists.

Serbia joined the Allies for the remaining six-and-a-half months of the war—an event thereafter exploited by Serbian propagandists. Even after the Axis defeat in May, 1945, an unknown but undoubtedly significant number of Chetniks obtained their Partisan status through fraudulent testimony. Since Partisan records were often incomplete and proof of active service was often provided by witness testimony, a group of three or more Chetniks could obtain war pension rights by testifying for each other. More significantly, this added a further former collaborationist infusion to the new ruling establishment in postwar Yugoslavia. In the words of Maj. Petar Martinović-Bajica, who served as an officer of the Serbian State Guard and as an intelligence officer for Draža Mihailović:

> Milan Nedić collaborated with the occupier; the Serbian State Guard collaborated; the Serbian Volunteer Corps collaborated; the Chetniks—with a few exceptions—collaborated; I, myself, collaborated, too—[however,] not one of us did it for the sake of himself but for the sake of the Serbian people.[203]

Similarly, Patriarch Gavrilo Dožić, a Serbian spiritual leader much admired in Serbia and in emigration, gave his postwar blessings to the Nazi collaboration of the Aćimović and Nedić governments, whose work he saw as "necessary":

> Concerning the Serbs who worked in the Commissars' Administration of Milan Aćimović and in the government of General Milan Nedić, I completely agree with their difficult task in their work. I know that they carried out work of enormous value that should be respected. It was necessary for the interests of the Serbian people.[204]

Among the Serbian collaborationist forces, none remained more loyal to the Nazi cause to the end than the members of the Serbian Volunteer Corps. Absorbed into the Waffen SS on November 27, 1944, the Serbian Volunteer Corps was renamed the Serbian SS Corps in March, 1945. During the next month, even as Germany's defeat was imminent, they honored Hitler's birthday with a festive celebration—a legacy that postwar emigration publications have taken great pains to conceal.[205]

Chapter Three
Serbian Complicity in the Holocaust

Most of the Jews of Serbia were exterminated during the first seventeen months of German occupation, and the responsibility of the German authorities in executing the "Final Solution" in Serbia has been well documented.[1] Soon after the German occupation of Belgrade, anti-Jewish legislation demanded the registration of all Jews, the wearing of armbands, the confiscation of Jewish property, the restriction of economic pursuits, and the enforcement of hard labor. In mid-August, the Jews of the Banat region were uprooted to Belgrade. At the end of August, 1941, most Jewish males over age fourteen were imprisoned in the Topovske šupe camp in Belgrade under the pretext that Jews were leading the Partisan revolt that had begun in July, 1941, a charge the German authorities knew to be untrue.

Jewish and Gypsy prisoners increasingly were used to fill the quotas for the German reprisal policy, which called for the execution of fifty to one hundred Communists for every German soldier killed. By the end of 1941, most Serbian Jewish males between the ages of fourteen and seventy had been shot by the Wehrmacht firing squads. In October, 1941, the German authorities ordered the construction of Sajmište (Semlin in German), just across the Sava River from Belgrade, for the purpose of concentrating the remaining Jewish women and children.

In December, 1941, over five thousand Jews were transported to Sajmište, where, over the next months, hunger, freezing cold, overcrowding, unhygienic conditions, and disease took their toll. During February, 1942, more Jewish women and children from towns such as Smederevo, Niš, and Šabac were brought to Sajmište, which by that time held roughly sixty-three hundred prisoners, ten percent of whom were Gypsies. Between March and May, 1942, the inmates of Sajmište were exterminated in a gassing van. Approximately seventy-five hundred Jews, half of all Serbian Jews, perished at Sajmište.[2]

The German administrators most responsible for the Holocaust in Serbia were Harald Turner, the chief civilian administrator for Serbia; Felix Benzler, a professional diplomat from the Foreign Office; Wilhelm Fuchs, the chief of the SS *Einsatzgruppe* Security Police for Serbia; and Franz Neuhausen, plenipotentiary for the economy and the military commander for Serbia.[3] In January, 1942, Fuchs was replaced by August Meyszner with Emanuel Schäfer as his deputy. There was a succession of military commanders, and, in 1941 alone, the list included Ludwig von Schröder, Heinrich Danckelmann, Franz Böhme, and Paul Bader. Although the German administrators in Serbia were unable to agree on most issues, they displayed almost "frictionless cooperation" in the extermination of the Jews, particularly with regard to the Sajmište camp.[4]

It is indisputable that the executioners of most of Serbia's Jews were German army personnel or regular police. However, the role of the Serbs as active collaborators in the destruction of the Jews has remained underexplored in the Holocaust literature.[5] According to widely held belief, while the Germans were murdering the Jews of Serbia, the Serbs were helping or saving them. This was certainly true for some.[6] Yet, a large segment of Serbian society willingly and enthusiastically joined in the destruction of the Jews and profited materially from their demise.

Serbian propaganda has constructed as an article of faith the concept of an unambiguous and deeply ingrained historical friendship between Serbs and Jews. An examination of the history of Serbian-Jewish relations, however, reveals a more complex and sinister picture. Serbia's mainly Sephardic Jewish population was descended from those who had fled the Spanish Inquisition to the safety of Ottoman lands. These refugees experienced rather favorable treatment while Serbia remained under Ottoman rule from the fourteenth century until the beginning of the nineteenth century. As a recognized *milet* (non-Islamic religious community in the Ottoman Empire), Jews were free to practice their faith, customs, and traditions, as long as they paid the requisite taxes and submitted to the Ottoman authorities.[7] Throughout most of this period, the Jews lived in the towns among Turks, Greeks, Tsintsars, Armenians, Gypsies, and a variety of foreign merchants, notably Croats from Dubrovnik. Serbs lived in the countryside, and, therefore, contacts between the Jewish town-dwellers and Serbian peasants were infrequent, as the Serbian historian Petrović described: "Economically, as well as ethnically and socially, the towns were almost totally divorced from the Serbian countryside. Being submerged in a primitive form of military feudalism as sharecroppers who rarely saw or needed any money except for the small poll tax they paid, the Serbian peasant population lived a self-contained life in their own villages."[8]

As Ottoman rule began to recede, the Jewish communities of the region lost the religious tolerance, local autonomy, and legal protections they had once enjoyed.[9] The emergence of the Serbian state in the early nineteenth century heralded a particularly difficult time for the Jews. The Serbian insurrection of 1804, led by Đorđe Petrović (better known as Karađorđe, or Black George) was a turning point in this process.[10] Karađorđe—a prosperous pig farmer and livestock trader and the progenitor of the Karađorđević royal family—was a man of violent temper. His brutality was legendary, and the peasants under his command were notorious for terrorizing unarmed civilians.[11] The Jews fared especially poorly. By 1805, the fortress of Smederevo had fallen to Karađorđe's forces and became the capital of his rebel government.[12] Soon, the Jews were expelled from Smederevo, Šabac, and Požarevac, although they had lived for centuries in these rural interior towns, which contained very few Serbian inhabitants.[13] With the capture of Belgrade by the Serbian insurgents in 1806, Jewish homes, stores, and the synagogue in the Jewish quarter were attacked and damaged or destroyed, and Jews were prohibited from residing outside of Belgrade.[14] The persecution of the Jews was alleviated only upon Karađorđe's defeat and the restoration of Ottoman authority in 1813.[15]

In 1815, Miloš Obrenović led a second Serbian insurrection. Through collaboration with the Ottoman authorities and the extensive use of bribery, Obrenović succeeded in establishing Serbia as a semiautonomous state.[16] In 1817, he assassinated his rival Karađorđe in his sleep and sent Karađorđe's head to the Turkish Sultan as a sign of loyalty.[17] During the two periods (1817–39 and 1859–60) when Miloš ruled as prince, the Jews received favorable treatment; but conditions for the Jews deteriorated rapidly on both occasions when Miloš's rule ended.[18]

There were expulsions of Jews from the rural Serbian interior in 1846, and then again in 1861–64, in conjunction with the laws of 1846 and 1861 forbidding Jews to live outside Belgrade.[19] Under the law of October 30, 1856, issued in response to the demands of a growing Serbian merchant class, Jews were forbidden to conduct trade in the interior.[20] This law, signed by Prince Aleksandar Karađorđević, attempted to confine the Jews and their commercial activities to Belgrade.[21] A law dated November 4, 1861, signed by Prince Mihailo Obrenović, the son of Miloš, prohibited the Jews from owning real estate and new shops in the Serbian interior.[22]

The net effect of such legislation was that Serbia's Jews were forced to move to Belgrade or to leave Serbia entirely.[23] On April 27, 1860, the Serbian Ministry of Finance issued a document expressing concern that the Jews were reproducing too quickly and that Serbia would thereby become Jewish. To prevent that, it concluded that the Jews must be expelled from Serbia.[24] Indeed, Serbia's small Jewish population declined precipitously. In 1861, there had been 450 Jewish families (2,475 Jews), most living in the Belgrade ghetto. By 1865, the number had declined to 338 families (1,805 Jews), and, by 1869, only 210 families remained.[25]

British diplomatic correspondence of the late nineteenth century also records the pattern of cruel persecution of the Jews of Serbia. British observers attributed the harsh treatment of the Jews to the Serbs' religious fanaticism, commercial rivalry, and their belief that the Jews were secret agents of the Turks.[26] In January 16, 1865, one month after a series of three highly inflammatory articles in the anti-Semitic journal *Svetovide* (Holy Vision), two Jews were murdered during a pogrom in the town of Šabac.[27] Three months later in Šabac, a sixteen-year-old Jewish girl was forcibly baptized into Serbian Orthodoxy. The governments of England, Italy, and Turkey issued strong diplomatic protests to Belgrade, with a British diplomat noting the "notorious fact that the outrages complained of by the Jews were perpetrated shortly after publication of these articles."[28]

Jewish community leaders submitted letters of protest to the press, but the Serbian government blocked the publication of these responses.[29] In 1867, following a plea from the Jews of Šabac that they be placed under direct British protection, the Paris-based Alliance Israélite Universelle delivered to Lord Stanley of the British Foreign Office a detailed description of the persecution of the Jews of Serbia, causing Lord Stanley to conclude that "the complaints of the Jewish community are too well founded. . . . Servia cannot but suffer in the estimation not only of England, but of all civilized nations from the persecution of an active, industrious, and inoffensive religious community residing in it."[30]

The Šabac Jews' appeal for help engendered a discussion of the persecution of Serbia's Jews in the British House of Commons on March 29, 1867. One member of Parliament reminded listeners that the March, 1856, Treaty of Paris, by which the European Powers had supported the independence of Serbia, required Serbia to uphold "full liberty of worship"; and he observed that the Orthodox Serbs "appeared to understand by this, liberty of worship for the majority" only.[31] The parliamentary discussions revealed uniform British sympathy to the plight of Serbia's Jews and urged continued diplomatic pressure to be exerted upon "the wise and liberal" Prince of Serbia, after which one parliamentarian added the following:

I am afraid it is impossible to deny that the conduct of the Servian people in regard to the Jewish community residing amongst them has been utterly unworthy of a people who reasonably and justly aspire to take their place amongst the civilized communities of Europe. I say the conduct of the Servian people, rather than the Servian Government, because, if I am not misinformed, it is much more a case of popular prejudice and popular bigotry than any intentional impolicy on the part of the Government. I believe that the Government will be willing to do what is fair and reasonable in this matter if they are assured that they can do so without coming too strongly into conflict with popular prejudices.[32]

In Serbia's new and supposedly liberal Constitution of 1869, Article 23 granted equality before the law to every Serb, and Article 28 guaranteed the inviolability of domicile. Article 132, however, reaffirmed the anti-Jewish laws of October 30, 1856, prohibiting the Jews from commerce in the Serbian interior and the law of November 4, 1861, denying Jews the right of domicile outside Belgrade.[33]

The Bishop of Smederevo had argued in favor of religious liberty for the Jews, but the minister of the interior beseeched the parliamentarians not to grant such liberties.[34] The anti-Jewish views prevailed. In 1869, Serbia's Jews appealed to the British government for protection once again.[35] As Jews fled in large numbers from Serbia, the English, French, Italian, and Austrian consuls at Belgrade protested that anti-Jewish laws were retained in the new constitution.[36] In 1871, a British diplomat visited the Jewish community of Belgrade and recorded his findings:

I have accompanied Dr. Levy, the late representative of the Société Israélite at Belgrade to the Jewish quarter, and can hardly believe any poverty can exceed in misery what I have seen there . . . people literally starving by inches from—though most willing to work—being deprived by law of means of earning their subsistence.

The number of Jews of Belgrade is fast diminishing. When two years ago a Report was made respecting them, they numbered 200 families; they now reckon 150, of whom only 20 are in a position to help their poorer brethren; they are mostly located in the most unhealthy part of town, close to the Danube, and are as much shut off from their so-called fellow-subjects as if contact with them would communicate the plague.

Illnesses and fevers, caused by want of nourishment, make greater ravages amongst them than among the other poor of the place. . . .

Some of these poor people would willingly emigrate to the neighboring Austrian provinces [Croatia and Hungary], but impediments are indirectly thrown in their way by the Servian authorities, who pride themselves on the number of immigrants who flock to the country, and like to be able to boast, in their so-called statistics, that there are no emigrants.

I doubt if the Servian Government has ever been in earnest in any of the measures which it has proposed or professed to take in behalf of the Jews; it has passively resisted every pressure put upon it at various times by the majority of the guaranteeing Powers, thinking the support of the mercantile interest of Belgrade, which looks with great jealousy at the Jews, as being of more value.[37]

In 1873, Jews were expelled from Šabac, Smederevo, and Požarevac, and, in 1876, eleven Jewish families were expelled from Smederevo.[38] After the Serbian military captured Niš in 1877, Serbs undertook an ambitious modernization program, widening streets by tearing down buildings owned by Jews and Muslims.[39] Under the Treaty of Berlin of 1878, the European powers required that Serbia grant political and civil equality to all religious minorities as a precondition for its recognition as a sovereign state.[40] Popular sentiment in Serbia, however, strongly opposed Jewish participation in Serbian life, and anti-Semitic tracts fulminated in the popular press.[41] Anti-Jewish sentiment was echoed by such notable Serbian political figures as Nikola Pašić, a veteran statesman, who eventually served as prime minister of Serbia and, later, of Yugoslavia.[42] In 1880, Pašić promised to block the Jews from entering the Serbian countryside, a part of Serbian politics that generally is overlooked by Pašić's biographers.[43]

The Treaty of Berlin required the elimination of anti-Jewish decrees from the Constitution of 1869, but the Serbian traders remained violently opposed to permitting Jews to also trade in the Serbian interior. Therefore, to avoid an embarrassing parliamentary debate on this issue, the *Skupština* (Serbian Parliament) deleted the offensive article from the constitution by acclamation, although the anti-Jewish laws themselves, which were reaffirmed by the deleted article, remained in effect.[44] It was not until the Constitution of January 2, 1889, that the anti-Jewish laws were finally abolished, bringing Serbia into compliance with the treaty obligations.[45] Although, as a result, the legal status of the Jewish community improved, the Serbian view, which held the Jews to be an alien presence, persisted. Jewish participation in Serbian public life remained marginal into the early years of the twentieth century, by which time a total of six Jews were represented in government, education, and the military.[46]

A turning point in Serbian-Jewish relations came in 1903 with the reign of King Petar I Karađorđević (1903–14), which, although initiated in blood, marked Serbia's first encounter with democracy. Peter I succeeded Aleksandar Obrenović, whose murder was engineered by the Black Hand, a secret group composed of Serbian army officers dedicated to the creation of a Greater Serbia.[47] The Black Hand conspired to eliminate Obrenović and restore the Karađorđević dynasty because Obrenović's friendly relations with Austria-Hungary were incompatible with Serbian expansionist goals, which called for annexing Austro-Hungarian lands.[48] The plotters broke into the bedroom of the royal palace, knifed the king and queen to death, hacked off their fingers for the jewelry, and hurled their mutilated bodies from the palace window.

Under the British-educated Petar I, the Serbian kingdom became a constitutional monarchy, with a free press, political parties, and democratic elections, although the monarchy and the military continued to dominate Serbian political life.[49] During this period of relatively enlightened leadership, Petar I was kindly disposed toward the Jews and gave them a reprieve from the last forty-three years of virtually uninterrupted persecution.[50] Nevertheless, anti-Semitic tracts continued to appear in both the lay and religious press. In 1904, a booklet titled *Knjiga o Jevrejima. . . . Kod koga treba da kupujemo?* (Book about Jews. . . . At Whose Store Should We Shop?) warned of the dangers of Jewish domination and advocated the boycott of Jewish businesses.[51] In 1912, an official publication of the Serbian Orthodox Church likewise complained that the Serbian authorities did too little to protect Serbs from the predations of the Jews, who had too many rights.[52]

In many ways, comparison of the treatment of the Jews in Serbia and in Croatia during the nineteenth century offers striking contrasts. During the demise of the Ottoman Empire and the rise of Serbian independence, a period that—with the exception of the two reigns of Prince Miloš Obrenović—saw the persecution of Serbia's Jews, Croatia remained within the Austro-Hungarian Empire. For Croatia's Jews, this period marked the progressive trend toward emancipation—a trend shaped both by Habsburg policy as well as specific developments within Croatia.

Prior to the late eighteenth century, the Habsburg emperors had sporadically enforced anti-Jewish legislation throughout the empire, including in the Croatian lands.[53] However, after Habsburg Emperor Joseph II issued the Edict of Tolerance in 1781, an increasing number of Jews began to migrate to the Croatian provinces.[54] Following an 1839 petition from a delegation of Croatian Jews to the Hungarian Diet at Pressburg (modern Bratislava, Slovakia), the Jews of Croatia were granted the right to live anywhere, build factories, and engage in business and trade, although a "toleration tax"—a daily fee for the privilege of working—was not rescinded until 1846.[55]

In 1859, the Croatian Jews obtained the privilege of employing Christian servants. In 1860, they acquired the right to own real estate throughout Croatian lands. The Jewish community submitted a petition for complete equality to the Croatian *Sabor* (parliament) in 1861 but received no response. However, by 1873, the *Sabor* granted full civil rights to the Jews, and the state treasury disbursed modest funds for the construction of synagogues and schools of religious instruction. With full emancipation, an increasing number of Jews left Bohemia, Moravia, Hungary, and Austria for Croatia, whose Jewish population, 380 in 1840–41 and 850 in 1857–64, swelled approximately to 10,000 in 1870; 13,488 in 1880; and 17,261 in 1890. By the turn of the century, there were 20,032 Jews dispersed among twenty-seven communities in Croatia, while in Serbia there were a mere 6,430 Jews scattered among ten communities.[56] The participation of the Jews of Croatia in Croatian life offered a striking contrast to the situation of the Jews in Serbia:

> The Jews of Croatia are engaged in all occupations, even in agriculture, but especially in trade, wholesale, and retail. The wood industries are flourishing since Jewish business men have taken hold of them and have introduced stave and cane factories; they have also opened the one cotton-spinning and weaving establishment in the province. In professional life there are 30 Jewish lawyers (out of a total of 200), 10 Jewish judges, and about 50 Jewish physicians, either holding official positions or practising privately. . . . Numerous Jews hold offices as town councilors, some even as mayors, and honorary positions in philanthropic and national societies are held by them.[57]

In 1917, the Serbian government undertook its first experiment in using Jews to lobby for Serbian political causes, thereby laying the foundation for Serbia's two-track policy toward the Jews. David Albala, a medical captain in the Serbian Army, was sent to the United States to lobby for Serbia among American Jewry. The official diplomatic letter that accompanied Albala expressed sympathy for the Balfour Declaration of November 2, 1917, and stated that "there is no other nation in the world sympathizing with the plan more than Serbia." Serbian officials, thereafter, placed increasing focus on improving Serbia's image among Jewish communities abroad.[58]

With the creation in late 1918 of the Kingdom of Serbs, Croats, and Slovenes (renamed the Kingdom of Yugoslavia in 1929), the Jewish communities of the former Habsburg lands (for example, Croatia) and former

Ottoman lands (for example, Serbia) were brought together in one country. The fortunes of the Jewish community during the interwar period (1918–41) can be divided into two broad periods. The first, extending through the 1920s, was marked by progress toward social equality for the Jews. The second, from 1930 until the Nazi invasion in 1941, saw increasing apprehension among the Jews, as Yugoslav officials did little to halt—and even played a role in abetting—the growing wave of fascism.

From the beginning of this new kingdom, the Serbian-controlled government discriminated against that segment of the population derived from the former Austro-Hungarian Empire, and this included the Jews. Serbian Jews were regarded as loyal subjects, since about six hundred had fought in the Serbian Army in the First World War. The "foreign" Jews of the former Austro-Hungarian provinces, however, were looked on with suspicion, since some had served in the Austro-Hungarian army during the war. (Of course, Serbs themselves had fought on both sides of the First World War, with Serbs of Croatia, Bosnia, and Vojvodina well-represented in the Austro-Hungarian Army.) Thus, the Belgrade Jews were consistently chosen to represent all Yugoslav Jewry before the king.[59]

The initial optimism among the Jews in the new kingdom was reinforced in 1919 by the formation of the Federation of Jewish Religious Communities. This Belgrade-based organization principally served as an anti-defamation league and worked to secure fair treatment and equal rights for the Jews. During its first decade, a primary focus was to obtain citizenship for the "foreign" Jews. Success was only partial. The government steadfastly refused to grant citizenship to "foreign-born" Jews, but was persuaded to renew regularly their temporary residency permits. Overall, the 1920s were a period of social and economic progress for the Jews in Yugoslavia, notwithstanding a few isolated episodes of anti-Semitic activity. In the 1930s, however, anti-Jewish attacks appeared with increasing frequency in the Yugoslav press.[60]

In 1935 Dimitrije Ljotić, Yugoslavia's leading proponent of Nazi ideology, had founded Zbor, a pan-Serbian pro-Nazi fascist party. The small but highly active organization published and distributed a prodigious number of newspapers, books, and pamphlets, among them the most rabidly anti-Semitic literature printed anywhere in the country. In Vojvodina, an ethnically mixed region that was home to five hundred thousand *Volksdeutsche*, Zbor published a German-language newspaper *Die Erwache* (The Awakening), as well as the Serbian-language *Naš Put* (Our Way). Both publications called for war against the Jews.[61]

In 1936, the Federation of Religious Jewish Communities brought a libel charge against the editor of *Die Erwache*. But the Belgrade court, employing highly questionable legal justifications, found in favor of the accused.[62] Following the publication of the infamous anti-Semitic tract *The Protocols of the Elders of Zion* in Belgrade in 1934, the federation attempted but failed to have the *Protocols* banned, and it was again published in Belgrade in 1939.[63]

By the late 1930s, expressions of anti-Semitism in Serbia were growing more virulent. In January, 1937, Patriarch Varnava (Petar Rosić), the head of the Serbian Orthodox Church since 1930, met with German journalists to express his "vivid interest" in the new Germany and to praise Hitler for leading "a battle which serves all of humanity."[64] Varnava also stressed his sympathy for the Führer's fight against the Bolsheviks. In April, 1937, an official publication of the Serbian Orthodox Church explicitly identified the Jews as the hidden force behind freemasonry, capitalism, and communism, the world's "three great evils":

> Jews are representatives of Masonry, Jews are representatives of capitalism, and Jews are representatives of proletariat revolution. There are no differences between them in their outlook on the world. They are essentially only Jews and nothing else. The Jews are representatives of atheism—for the rest of the world, while they are themselves deeply pious. The Jews are representatives and preachers against private property—for the rest of the world, while they fill their own safe boxes and suitcases with money. They are internationalists for the rest of the world, but they aid only their fellow tribesman. Thus, the enemy is as sly as a serpent and appears in several forms. This is why he is dangerous.[65]

In September, 1938, Anton Korošec, Yugoslav minister of the interior and one of the few non-Serbs to occupy a ministry position, stated that "in Yugoslavia, as everyone can testify, the Jewish question does not exist." To this pronouncement of official policy, he added that Jewish refugees from Nazi Germany were not welcome in Yugoslavia.[66] Three months later, the sole Jew in the Yugoslav Senate, Chief Rabbi Isaac Alcalay, was expelled at the request of Prime Minister Milan Stojadinović. Prince Pavle honored Stojadinović's request that the vacancy be filled with a non-Jew.[67] On October 5, 1940, six months before the Nazi invasion of Yugoslavia, the Yugoslav Royal Government issued two anti-Jewish decrees. One prohibited Jews from the production and distribution of food; the other restricted the enrollment of Jews at universities and high schools.[68] This legislation was initiated by Korošec, who, only two years earlier, as minister of the interior, had denied the existence of Yugoslavia's "Jewish question."[69] Notably, this legislation was not implemented in Croatia.

Throughout the preceding decade, Jewish representatives had appealed to Yugoslav government officials to halt the growing wave of anti-Semitism. They received for their efforts "empty verbal assurances but little concrete support," according to Harriet Pass Freidenreich, the preeminent historian of Yugoslav Jewry in the interwar period.[70] Indeed, the government of Yugoslavia did little to protect its Jews at a time when, as Freidenreich correctly observed, "throughout the 1920s and 1930s the government was essentially controlled by Serbs, and policy reflected their viewpoint."[71] The marginalization of the Jews of Yugoslavia was well in progress before the Nazis struck.

With the German occupation of Serbia, beginning April 12, 1941, anti-Jewish propaganda intensified with the encouragement, but not necessarily the coercion, of the Nazis. Collaborationist newspapers in Belgrade with the largest circulation included *Obnova* (Renewal; editor in chief Stanislav Krakov), *Novo vreme* (New Time; editor in chief Miloš Mladenović), *Srpski narod* (The Serbian Nation; editor in chief Velibor Jonić), and *Naša borba* (Our Struggle; editor in chief Ratko Parežanin). *Obnova* was the successor to the prewar *Politika*.[72] *Naša borba*, which began publication on September 7, 1941, was established at the suggestion of Dimitrije Ljotić, who chose the name as homage to Adolf Hitler's *Mein Kampf* (My Struggle).[73] Most of the newspaper's contributors were well educated and included college students, teachers, lawyers, engineers, physicians, and priests.[74] The editors in chief of each of these newspapers and many of the contributors had championed fascist ideology years before the Nazi invasion of Yugoslavia.[75]

The Serbian collaborationist press published many articles that, in appealing to Serbian nationalism, cited deep-seated grievances against the Jews and advocated revenge. Although these writings echoed the spirit of Nazi ideology, the writers and the themes were entirely Serbian. *Naša borba* and *Obnova* proclaimed that Jews were the ancient enemies of the Serbian people and that the Serbs should not wait for the Germans to begin the extermination of the Jews.[76] An article titled "Borba za čistoću rase" (The Struggle for Racial Purity) vowed that Jews "never again shall be physicians, pharmacists, lawyers, and judges" in Serbia.[77] Still other Serbian writers found in history "proof" that Jews were the saboteurs of Serbian society, as in the following example:

> The Serbs have often written and stood up against the Jews, but they have rarely dug deeply into the past. . . . At the beginning of the eighteenth century, Jews from Central Europe swarmed down on Serbia. By

the eve of Karađorđe's uprising [in 1804] they were already complete masters of the economic situation in the country. In partnership with the Turks they sucked Serbian blood. . . . This is why Karađorđe expelled them from Serbia, and they fled to Bosnia . . . and other areas, in order to return right after Karađorđe's downfall [in 1813].

With the return of the Turks [in 1813], the Jews became a privileged class in Serbia again. They enjoyed: (1) judicial autonomy in civil, trade, and family suits; (2) recognized representation; (3) their own taxes . . . to the benefit of their own community . . . ; (4) dues from ritual slaughter. In other words, they were an exceptionally privileged minority. . . .

Unfortunately, Prince Miloš [Obrenović, whose reign began in 1817] was in partnership with some of the wealthiest Jews, and protected them. . . . In 1841 all of Serbia was in an uproar because the Jews had committed a ritual murder. A pogrom almost took place, but the investigation [of the ritual murder] was stopped, probably by an order from above.

The expulsion of the Obrenović dynasty [in 1842 and the beginning of the reign of Karađorđević] marked the beginning of a new era: the Jews were immediately restrained in Serbia. The National Assembly demanded that Jews should not be free to travel around the country, because they sell bad merchandise, use forged currency, push merchants into debt, etc. This is why the Jews . . . were confined to Belgrade only. They were not . . . given Serbian citizenship, and their foreign citizenship was not recognized; they were proclaimed . . . Turkish citizens, and justice was administered to them in the old way.

Through their connections, the Jews naturally sought Istanbul's and Europe's protection. Austria and other powers interceded for them through their consuls in Belgrade. The European press, already infiltrated by Jews in 1850, helped the Belgrade Jews by condemning the Belgrade government and the ruler of Serbia [Karađorđević]. . . .

. . . Prince Mihailo [Obrenović] after the death [in 1860] of his father, Prince Miloš, was compelled to restore Prince Aleksandar Karađorđević's stern rules on Jews, thus giving them a strong blow. The only concession made by Prince Mihailo was to allow Jewish children to attend Serbian schools. But Prince Mihailo did not yield to any other Jewish demand. . . . This is why [the Jews] hailed the death of Prince Mihailo [in 1868]. . . . The event, however, did not bring them "liberation" (in the sense which they had expected it), because the vice-regency was thoroughly anti-Semitic. All the efforts by the Jews to break through that wall and spread all over Serbia, with the right to settle in the interior, failed. The government did not allow it, knowing the disposition of the Serbian people . . . But the Berlin Congress of 1877 [actually 1878] imposed a Jewish article on Serbia's constitution. Serbia had to give equal rights to the Jews and, to this purpose, change Article 45 of her Civil Law. . . .

This historical material . . . until recently lay forgotten and could not be published anywhere because the Jews everywhere had friends whom they could mobilize to their advantage. . . .[78]

This article, which details and justifies Serbian anti-Semitism, corroborated the reports of persecutions of Serbian Jews in the nineteenth century as found in British diplomatic correspondence.[79]

Zbor was active in publishing tracts such as *Srpski narod u kandžama Jevreja* (Serbian People in the Claws of the Jews), which urged that "Jewry has to be quickly and energetically liquidated, because otherwise the destruction of Christian civilization . . . is inevitable."[80] The following review of this booklet appeared in the collaborationist press:

Milorad Mojić, a well-known Serbian intellectual and volunteer in World War I and in the present one, has written the book *Serbian People in the Claws of the Jews*. This book was ready for printing already in 1940, but could not be published then for political reasons. It has been published these days. We present here a few excerpts from it:

"Our country is a peasant country. About 80% of its population is engaged in agriculture. A huge part of the arable land is in the peasant's hands. . . . The peasant is condemned to toil . . . all his life but to reap little or no benefit. . . . When the peasant's hard work was over, when wheat, corn, and other farm products were ready for sale, the Jews stepped in. They held in their hands the entire trade in farm products and determined their prices. These prices were such that small and medium farmers, who constitute a huge number, did not have enough money left to dress decently and feed their families after paying taxes and other dues, but had to suffer and grieve, while the Jews, who often sold them their own wheat at double price in the spring, so that they could feed their hungry children, earned millions and millions without any effort. Thus, the majority of peasants were the most common slaves of the Jews, tied to the land, condemned to toil and suffer all their lives, only to have the fruit of their labor taken away by their factual masters, the Jews. In this hideous occupation, the Jews strictly adhered to the Talmud, which says: 'Non-Jews have been created to serve the Jews. They have to shovel, plow, sow, harvest, thresh. The Jews have been made to find everything ready.'"[81]

Within six months of the German occupation, Zbor had produced its thirteenth tract, *Zakoni i dela Jevreja* (The Laws and Deeds of the Jews), which was highly praised in the collaborationist press: "With its 80 densely-printed pages, this book is one more convincing and crushing proof of the catastrophic Jewish influence in the world in all areas of human activity and thought. . . . Writing in a very clear way, Mr. Mojić begins with an explanation of the Jewish liturgical books, the Torah, Talmud, and Shulchan Aruch, the truest expression of the Jewish spirit, which contain all the perfidious manifestations of a pagan, accursed thought."[82]

In the destruction of Serbia's Jews, Zbor's military arm, known as the Serbian Volunteer Command (later renamed the Serbian Volunteer Corps), in general proved a highly reliable auxiliary to the Gestapo.[83] The Serbian Volunteer Command sprang from Ljotić's 1st Detachment of Serbian Volunteers, which was organized as a labor brigade in Smederevo and sent to Belgrade in late July, 1941, to support the German authorities. Their activities included searching apartments, guarding imprisoned Communists and Jews, and fighting against Partisans.[84]

On July 27, after 1,200 Belgrade Jews had voluntarily surrendered to the occupation authorities, Ljotić's Volunteers were responsible for dividing them by profession, sending 1,080 to forced labor, and setting aside about 120 as hostages. Two days later, all 120 hostages were executed as a reprisal for the Partisan uprising.[85] On the streets of Belgrade, Ljotić's Volunteers closely worked with the *Volksdeutsche* in capturing mostly elderly Jews, who were then sent to forced labor.[86] After mid-September, 1941, when the Volunteers were armed and became known as the Serbian Volunteer Command, they continued to hunt for Jews in hiding. In February, 1942, for example, *Obnova* praised the 12th Detachment of the Volunteer Command for their capture of seven Belgrade Jews living under Serbian names in the city of Niš.[87]

There were some Jews among the ranks of the Chetniks during the first months of German occupation, but Jewish participation in a resistance that did not actually resist was short-lived.[88] As the Chetniks became overt collaborators, they also began to scour the countryside for Jews in hiding. Often, they murdered the Jews in Chetnik style—which meant torture, throat-slitting, and mutilation.[89] Alternatively, the Chetniks handed their prey over to the German authorities for reward money, after stripping the Jews of whatever money they possessed.[90] Jewish survivors testified that the Chetniks, particularly those under the command of Draža Mihailović, "persecuted Jews mercilessly" and slaughtered them "in a bestial way"—a reference to the similarity between the Chetnik practice of slitting a victim's throat and the methods used in butchering a pig.[91]

Jewish resistance fighters abandoned the Chetniks in favor of Tito's Partisans, deepening the Chetniks' perception that the Jews were among Serbia's principal enemies.[92] Mihailović's Directive no. 1 of January 2, 1943, concerned Chetnik plans to destroy the Partisans in Bosnia and contained a particularly revealing passage: "Partisan units are a motley collection of rascals, such as the Ustashas, the most blood-thirsty enemies of the Serbian people, Jews, Croats, Dalmatians, Bulgarians, Turks, Hungarians, and all other nations of the world. . . . Because of this mixture, the fighting value of the Partisan units is very low, a fact partly due to their poor armament.[93]

Nedić used similar anti-Jewish rhetoric to discredit the Partisan movement. In a speech of December 21, 1943, Nedić called the Partisans a "criminal Jewish-communist band."[94] Indeed, Jews were generally well-received into the National Liberation Army (the Partisans), which offered one of the few avenues of Jewish survival in occupied Yugoslavia. Nevertheless, even the Partisans were on occasion less enthusiastic about receiving Jews into their rank, particularly those detachments with prominent Chetnik elements. For example, when a group of Jewish youths from Sarajevo attempted to join a Partisan detachment in Kalinovik (a town south of Sarajevo that would later serve as a headquarters for Draža Mihailović), the Serbian Partisans turned them back to Sarajevo, where many were captured by the Ustashas and perished.[95]

The Grand Anti-Masonic Exhibition

On October 22, 1941, the *Grand Anti-Masonic Exhibition* opened in Belgrade. The exhibition focused on an alleged Jewish-Masonic-Communist conspiracy for world domination and contained vicious anti-Jewish propaganda.[96] Funded by the city of Belgrade and prepared primarily by Serbs loyal to the Nazis, the exhibition was initially suggested by Đorđe Perić, Nedić's chief of the Section of State Propaganda who had served as a German intelligence agent before the war.[97] The general directors of the exhibition were Perić's State Propaganda colleagues, Lazar Prokić and Stevan Klujić.[98] Both were prominent members of Zbor as well as publishers of the Serbian edition of the Nazi propaganda magazine *Signal*.[99] Klujić was also an agent of the German Security Police.[100] The Jewish section of the *Anti-Masonic Exhibition* was prepared by Professor Momčilo Balić from State Propaganda and a contributor to *Naša borba*.[101]

Collaborationist Serbian newspapers recorded the festive atmosphere of the exhibition's opening day: "The ceremonious opening was attended by representatives of German military authorities with Mr. von Kaisenberg, Area Commander. On behalf of the Serbian government, Ministers Josif Kostić, Dr. Miloš Radosavljević, and Velibor Jonić attended. Dr. Sv. Spanaćević, Assistant of the Minister of Economy, attended in the name of Mr. Dimitrije Ljotić. . . . The Exhibition was opened exactly at noon by Dr. Đorđe Perić, the Chief of State Propaganda. . . . After Dr. Perić, spoke Area Commander von Kaisenberg, who greeted the action of the Serbian National Committee and wished it the greatest success. . . . Colonel von Kaisenberg acknowledged . . . the City of Belgrade which, with a lot of good will and with generous support, made possible the organization and preparation of this very significant exhibition."[102]

Reportedly, tens of thousands of Serbs, including an approving Gen. Milan Nedić, attended the exhibition within its first weeks. As many as eighty thousand visited during its three-month run, which lasted until January 19, 1942. The collaborationist press commented on the enthusiastic public response to the exhibition: "The interest in the Anti-Masonic Exhibition is surprising. People stand in long lines before the ticket office. Everyone would like to see the exhibition as soon as possible. However, it should be pointed out that the public is very undisciplined. It is pushy, and in such a way makes the work of keepers of order and guides difficult. One cannot demand that the small rooms [of the exhibition] accept the whole of Belgrade at one time."[103]

Serbia's pro-Nazi newspapers reinforced the message of the exhibition, observing that the interests of the "Jewish-Masonic internationalists" and that of Serbs have always been divergent, and "therefore, their personal fate cannot move us, for they deserved it."[104] On January 1, 1942, Serbian authorities issued postage stamps to commemorate the *Anti-Masonic Exhibition.*[105] The stamps, by juxtaposing Jewish and Serbian symbols, portrayed Judaism as the source of world evil and advocated the humiliation and violent subjugation of the Jews by the Serbs.

In his 1941 writings, Lazar Prokić, one of the directors of the exhibition, declared that the Serbs would have little compassion for Jewish suffering, for the Jews had brought upon Serbia the March 27 Belgrade coup and the April 6 Axis invasion, and, as Zionists, they comprised a foreign element in Yugoslavia.

> . . . *an indigenous anti-Semitic movement has appeared among the Serbs.* Before April 6, 1941, the Jews suppressed it . . . because they were so strong—financially or in other ways—that they could influence

the authorities as they wished. This anti-Semitism . . . has no connection with the German occupier. Therefore, it was not brought by the occupier. The Jews themselves are to blame for this Serbian anti-Semitism since it is an indigenous Serbian issue. The Serbs do not want to express their support for the Jews. This is as natural as that the Jews did not want to express their support for the Serbs, neither in 1804, nor in 1813, nor 1862, nor 1875, nor 1879, not from 1894 to 1918. . . . [T]hey beat their breast about how they would perish for Yugoslavia, for Serbia, for their "Mother Country"—just in order to get officer epaulets, wages, and privileges. However, when April 6 came, all of them hurried in their cars to the [Adriatic] sea, waiting there for the outcome of the struggle that the Serbs waged with Germany![106]

Early during the German occupation, Nedić's formations, Ljotić's Volunteers, and various Chetnik detachments joined the Nazis and *Volksdeutsche* in desecrating synagogues and Jewish graveyards throughout Serbia.[107] These groups assisted in the manhunts for Jews in fall, 1941. When the Sajmište camp was ready in early December, the Serbian police again helped the Germans, and within three days over five thousand Jewish women and children were transported to Sajmište.[108]

The Nazis had delegated to the Serbian authorities the responsibility of providing food for the camp's prisoners.[109] By this arrangement, the Germans determined the kind and quantity of food to be provided, and the city of Belgrade's Department of Social Welfare was responsible for the purchase and delivery of food to Sajmište. The Serbian authorities, however, routinely provided less food than the Germans had specified. Starvation in Sajmište became so widespread that the Jewish inmates appealed repeatedly to the Serbian authorities "to deliver at least that quantity of provisions that the Germans themselves had approved." The official Serbian response came in Municipal Act no. 1972, dated February 3, 1942, in which Belgrade authorities rejected the Jewish inmates' written request for more food and tersely added, "delivery for the Jewish camp can be made only when all other needs in Belgrade have been met."[110]

One month later, the Final Solution was executed at Sajmište, with the arrival of the mobile gassing van from Germany. Between March and May of 1942, each morning except Sundays and holidays, the van was loaded with Jewish women, children, and the elderly, who were told that they were being resettled. In an act of seeming kindness, the children were even given candy. With a pipe directing the vehicle's exhaust fumes into the sealed compartment which held the victims, the van proceeded along its route through downtown Belgrade, terminating at a burial site at Avala, seven miles southeast of the city. Upon arrival, all were dead.[111]

Although the victims inside Sajmište had no inkling of their fate, outside of the camp, the gassing van could hardly have been a secret to either the Serbian police or the citizens of Belgrade, as the pounding on the van's door and the muffled cries of the dying victims were daily heard issuing from this strange vehicle.[112] Seven thousand Jewish women and children were exterminated, and their clothing was purchased by a Serbian business firm, in accordance with a contractual agreement with the Gestapo office in Belgrade.[113]

Milan Nedić played a decisive role in the persecution and destruction of Serbia's Jews. On September 2, 1941, Nedić promised that he "will act in the strongest way against the Jews and as soon as possible against Freemasons, who should be removed from all public service and gathered in concentration camps."[114] Nedić's own attitude toward Jews is evident in his communications with the German commandant of Serbia. In a letter of February 21, 1942, Nedić requested that the German authorities "give an order for dividing, separating, and moving out these Jewish and leftist elements from the healthy national elements in the detention camp" at Osnabrück.[115] In a follow-up letter to the German authorities, Nedić expanded on his view that the "Jew-communists" in the camps posed the danger of corrupting their fellow Serbian inmates:

> According to information from those officers who have so far come from detention, we learn that in the Osnabrück camp there are around 340 Jews and a certain number of prominent communist officers, mainly reserve but also on active service. They conduct their destructive action ruthlessly in the rooms, barracks, blocks and then in the whole camp. Since many nationally healthy men under the influence of homesickness become apathetic, and in such a way suitable for the destructive influence of the Jew-communists, there is a danger that the healthy elements too will grow discouraged and sink in the water of the communists, in this communal residence. Stating this fact, it is desirable to bring to one's attention that it would be very desirable to separate the Jews and the leftist communists from the common camp and remove them from among the nationally healthy officers. Concerned because of this action, the Serbian government would be very grateful if the authorities of the German Reich undertake effective measures for a separation as soon as possible.[116]

The Belgrade municipal government included a "Section for Jewish Questions" responsible for implementing anti-Jewish decrees of the Gestapo.[117] Assisting the Gestapo was an extensive network of Serbian municipal officials, Serbian police, Nedićites, Ljotićites, and various Chetnik formations, who hunted and captured Jews, Gypsies, and Partisans, often for reward money.[118] In August, 1942, following the virtual extermination of Serbia's Jews, Nedić's government attempted to claim all Jewish property for the Serbian state, and, according to German estimates, confiscated one billion dinars, of which 60 percent was used to pay the Germans' military damages.[119]

The Serbian Orthodox Church and the Holocaust

Prominent clerics within the Serbian Orthodox Church, by openly supporting the Nazis and espousing theological justification for the persecution of the Jews, also bear responsibility for the Holocaust in Serbia. On July 7, 1941, three months after the German occupation of Serbia—and the day the Partisan uprising commenced in Serbia—the Serbian Orthodox Church's Holy Episcopal Synod declared that it "will loyally carry out the laws and orders of the occupying and local authorities, and it will use its influence through its organs for the complete maintenance of order, peace, and submission."[120]

In late October, 1941, in a highly publicized meeting between Milan Nedić and representatives of the Serbian Archbishops Synod, Metropolitan Josif, the acting head of the Serbian Orthodox Church, promised Nedić the church's full support.[121] In November, 1941, Serbian Orthodox priest Dušan Popović condemned the Jews from his Belgrade pulpit: "We have been betrayed and sold out. The worm of betrayal and corruption as embodied by Judaism has penetrated the core of Yugoslavia."[122] During the same period, an article published in *Obnova* stressed that "no matter how much a Jew feigns having integrated with the people in whose midst he lives, even if he has changed faith, he remains first of all and above all a Jew!"[123] On January 30, 1942, Metropolitan Josif officially prohibited conversions of Jews to Serbian Orthodoxy and, by so doing, destroyed for Jews a potential means of survival.[124]

In the eighth month of the German occupation, with the murder of the Jews well underway in Serbia and with anti-Jewish measures well publicized, Serbian economic minister Mihailo Olćan proclaimed that "the Jews have met the fate they deserved." Only moments earlier, Olćan had been blessed by the revered Serbian Orthodox Bishop Nikolaj Velimirović, who had encouraged him to speak his thoughts publicly. Olćan then identified Serbia's principal enemy as "world Jewry" and praised the Germans for having overcome the "disease" of domination by the Jews. He went on to express his gratitude that the powerful sledgehammer of Germany had come down not on the heads of the Serbian people but on the heads of Serbia's Jews instead.[125]

A most striking example of the Serbian Orthodox Church's anti-Semitism combined with historical revisionism is the case of Bishop Velimirović, revered by Serbs as a "true prophet" and viewed as one of the most influential church leaders and theologians after Saint Sava, the founder of the Serbian Orthodox Church in the thirteenth century.[126] To most Serbs today, the bishop is a hero and a martyr, alleged to have survived years of torture in the Dachau concentration camp.[127] Indeed, in late September, 1944, the Germans did bring Velimirović to Dachau, where they had detained many other prominent European clergy and dignitaries as well.[128]

The Nazis held him there for slightly over two months as an *Ehrenhaftling* (honor prisoner). He lived in a special section in private quarters, dined on the same food as the German officers, and went into town under German escort. Prior to his release, Velimirović received medical care in his hospital room at Dachau. Following his release, which was arranged through the intervention of Dimitrije Ljotić, Velimirović was first housed at a tourist resort and then at a hotel in Vienna, where he was provided with further medical care. There is no evidence for the oft-repeated Serbian claim that the bishop was tortured or ill-treated during his internment.[129]

Although Bishop Velimirović must have been aware of the enormous suffering of the Jews at Dachau, his writings from Dachau reflect his contempt for them: "When our Lord was healing the sick on a Saturday, the Jewish elders, much more stupid than the Jewish people themselves, screamed at him for doing it on a Saturday instead of on any other day of the week."[130] From Dachau, Velimirović's writings praised the *Protocols of the Elders of Zion* for clearly identifying the Serbs' true enemy and endorsed Serbian participation in the Holocaust:

Today [Europe] is the main battlefield of the Jew and the Jew's father, the devil, against the Heavenly Father and against his Only-Begotten Son. . . . [The Jews] need first to become legally equal with Christians, in order afterwards to suppress Christianity and to turn Christians into atheists and to step on their necks. All the modern European slogans were composed by Jews, who crucified Christ: democracy, strikes, socialism, atheism, tolerance of all faiths, pacifism, universal revolution, capitalism, and communism. . . . All this is done with the intention of debasing Christ, of destroying Christ. . . . You should think about this, Serbian brethren, and accordingly you should correct . . . your thoughts, desires, and deeds.[131]

In early December, 1944, both Bishop Velimirović and Patriarch Gavrilo Dožić were released from Dachau at the urging of Ljotić, who retained significant influence in Berlin and Vienna.[132] The Germans had previously offered to release Patriarch Gavrilo Dožić if he declared his loyalty to the occupation authorities in Serbia but, according to Nedić's postwar testimony, the patriarch refused this offer because he wanted to retain his authority beyond the borders of Nedić's Serbia to parts of the Independent State of Croatia, Hungary, Bulgaria, and Montenegro.[133]

Ultimately, about 15,000 Jews perished in Nedić's Serbia. This was 94 percent of the Jewish population covering an area that included Serbia proper (11,240), the formerly Hungarian region of Banat (3,800), the Sandžak region (260), and Kosovo (210).[134] Most of these people had been exterminated by the middle of 1942. Among those who remained were several hundred, mainly women and children, who had been hiding in rural Serbian villages and some who had joined the Partisans or had otherwise escaped. However, between 1942 and September, 1944, just before the Germans withdrew from Belgrade, at least 455 of the Jews in hiding were captured by Ljotićites, Nedićites, and Chetniks, who received reward money for every Jew they found. These Jews were transported to Banjica and killed upon arrival. But long before this, in August, 1942, Harald Turner proudly had announced that the "Jewish question" in Serbia had been resolved, and Serbia had become the first country in Europe declared *Judenfrei*.[135]

From the evidence, it is clear that Serb contributions to the German occupation and to the suppression of Partisan resistance were extensive and pervasive. Similarly, the efficient extermination of Serbia's Jews was not the achievement of the Nazis alone. Serbian propagandists have argued that the Serbs' primary role during the Holocaust had been to protect the Jews from harm. To be sure, Jews throughout Yugoslavia were sheltered and saved by virtuous Serbs, Croats, Slavic Muslims, Italians, and others. However, the Serbian recitation of the events of World War II omits important aspects of the Serbian record vis-à-vis the Jews. Under the pro-Nazi government of Milan Nedić, Serbs collaborated with the Nazis in disseminating anti-Jewish propaganda, in plundering Jewish property, in delivering Jews for execution, and in murdering Jews in concentration camps and in the Nazi-supplied gassing van driving around Belgrade.

Indeed, Serbian fascist Dimitrije Ljotić, who had initiated his own collaboration with the Nazis in 1935, had advocated the extermination of Jews for years prior to the Holocaust.[136] Prominent Serbian Orthodox clergy, too, publicly supported the persecution of the Jews. The Chetniks in Serbia, nominally under Draža Mihailović, murdered Jews or knowingly delivered Jews to their death for a cash bounty. Nazi anti-Semitism struck in Serbian society a responsive chord—the Chetnik belief in ethnic purity found at the core of Serbian ultranationalism well before the twentieth century.

Chapter Four
Collaboration and Resistance in Croatia and Bosnia-Herzegovina

Since the end of the Second World War, Serbian historians have promoted the assertion that the Serbs resisted Hitler, while Croats and Bosnian Muslims gave the Axis widespread popular support. The historical record, however, does not support this interpretation. Indeed, the Chetnik movement represented the ideological center of Serbian political culture and enjoyed widespread support among Serbs. The Ustashas, in contrast, were an aberration in modern Croatian history and never attained mass support. Nowhere in Yugoslavia was the resistance as well organized as in Croatia proper, where a small Partisan movement under Croatian Communist leadership—a movement that initially drew its ranks heavily from among persecuted Serbs—transformed into a widely supported, Croatian-dominated resistance.

Prior to the March 27 coup in Belgrade, the Germans had little interest in supporting Croatian political autonomy. Having concluded negotiations with Prince Pavle, Hitler anticipated that Serbian-dominated Yugoslavia would be a reliable ally and would provide food, critical minerals, and a transportation corridor for the Axis war effort. Mussolini had different interests in Yugoslavia, mainly territorial ones. World War I had ended with Italy much enlarged in reward for having joined the victorious Allies, albeit late in the war. Nevertheless, unsatisfied with the acquisition of the Istrian peninsula, several Dalmatian islands, and the major port cities of Zadar and Rijeka, the Italians maintained their longstanding ambition to annex the entire Croatian coast.

Throughout the 1930s, Mussolini encouraged the Italian irredentist movement, which sought to annex Croatian territory. Also, to help prompt the destabilization of Yugoslavia, Mussolini encouraged and supported Croatian separatism, reaching out to both moderate and extremist Croatian elements.[1] Mussolini's designs on Croatian territory may well have remained frustrated were it not for the Belgrade coup of March 27 and the reversal of Hitler's policy toward Yugoslavia. At Hitler's orders, Germany, Italy, Hungary, and Bulgaria invaded. Following a swift campaign, Yugoslavia was divided into German and Italian spheres of influence, and various parts were annexed directly by each of the invaders.

The Axis invasion of Yugoslavia commenced on April 6, 1941. The Wehrmacht reached Zagreb on April 10, two days before they reached Belgrade. Just hours before the arrival of German tanks, Ante Pavelić's deputy, Col. Slavko Kvaternik, was directed by the Germans to proclaim the Independent State of Croatia in the name of Pavelić.[2] To head a collaborationist government, the Germans had approached Vladko Maček, the president of the Croatian Peasant Party and the leading politician in Croatia. Maček, however, refused, as he had refused all previous German proposals to collaborate.[3] Maček's rejection of collaboration, in fact, made possible the ascent to power of Ante Pavelić and his Ustasha regime.

Origins of the Ustasha Movement

At the close of World War I, the Croatian leadership had endorsed the creation of a South Slav state in the anticipation that Serbs, Croats, and Slovenes would achieve equality in a country free of Austrian and Hungarian domination. Moreover, the union with Serbia, a demonstrated military power, appeared to provide a timely defense against imminent Italian plans to annex forcibly the Croatian coast. With some reservations, Croatian and Slovenian leaders accepted rule under a Serbian king, in the belief that their status would be protected by a constitution. The constitution which was offered in 1921, however, was satisfactory only to the Serbs, whose delegates contributed 83 percent of all votes in favor, while the Croats contributed 4 percent.[4]

The assassination of the popular Croatian Peasant Party leader, Stjepan Radić, in June of 1928, ignited widespread civil unrest and revolt among Croats. The royal government, however, responded with even more severe measures, including the suspension of the constitution, the banning of nearly all political parties, the dissolution of the Parliament, the abolition of freedom of speech, the banning of the right to public assembly, the censorship of the press, and the carrying out of still more political imprisonments and murders. The culmination of these measures was the establishment of King Aleksandar's personal dictatorship on January 6, 1929.

Ante Pavelić was the vice president of the Croatian Bar Association and a delegate to the Parliament in Belgrade when he witnessed Radić's assassination. Pavelić himself was marked for murder by the Yugoslav Secret Police, and, days after King Aleksandar imposed the royal dictatorship, Pavelić fled to Hungary.[5] Determined to achieve Croatian independence through any means, including armed struggle and terrorism, Pavelić and Gustav Perčec formed *Ustaše-Hrvatska revolucionarna organizacija* (Ustasha-Croatian Revolutionary Organization). The name Ustasha was derived from *ustati,* meaning to stand up.[6]

After short-lived attempts to organize Ustasha units in Hungary, Pavelić and several hundred Croatian émigrés established themselves in paramilitary training camps in Italy in 1930, under the patronage and control of Mussolini. Money, weapons, and explosives primarily were supplied by Italy and Hungary.[7] Historian Menachem Shelah summarizes the relationship between Pavelić's Ustashas and Mussolini: "The Ustaše members became an auxiliary arm in furthering Benito Mussolini's policy in the Balkans and the Middle East. When the Italians were interested in unrest in Yugoslavia, they dispatched Ustaše terrorists, and when they wanted quiet, they shut them in camps and placed obstacles in their way."[8]

On October 9, 1934, King Aleksandar Karađorđević was assassinated during a state visit to Marseilles, France, by Vladimir Černozemski from the Internal Macedonian Revolutionary Organization. Behind the conspiracy, however, were Italy and the Ustashas.[9] European public outrage followed the assassination, and the Ustashas became a political liability for Mussolini, who thereafter kept Pavelić and his followers largely confined to their camps.

Throughout the 1930s, some Ustashas returned home to cultivate support for a movement that was illegal, as were virtually all political parties in Yugoslavia. Intellectuals were conspicuously rare among Pavelić's early followers, 95 percent of whom were peasants, laborers, or sailors, with little or no formal education.[10] At home, the Ustashas concentrated their recruitment efforts in the most impoverished mountainous regions. They appealed to the popular discontent caused by government corruption, high taxation, and the routine beatings of citizens by the Serbian Gendarmes. For example, in western Herzegovina, known through the centuries for its production of high-quality tobacco, popular unrest erupted after King Aleksandar imposed a royal monopoly on the crop and forced the local peasantry to sell it all to the government at a fraction of its market value. For this already poor and barren region, the economic strain was unbearable, and when smuggling ensued, the *financi* (customs police) and Royal Gendarmes—virtually all Serbs—responded with beatings, torture, and summary executions. In 1932, Ustasha organizers instigated a series of armed attacks on the police and Royal Yugoslav Army garrisons, resulting in mass arrests, which affected a few Ustashas and their sympathizers but were mostly aimed at innocent Croats.

Although Ustashas were often imprisoned with Communists during the 1930s, and although both perceived the Yugoslav state as their common enemy, the Communists had little success in recruiting the Ustashas to their cause.[11] Toward the late 1930s, the Ustasha movement acquired a strong anti-Communist ideology, primarily infused by Pavelić, who had adopted the views of his patron governments, Italy and Hungary. By 1937, all relations between the Ustashas and the Communists had been severed. The Ustashas continued to attract some adherents, so that on the eve of the Axis conquest of Yugoslavia there were approximately twenty thousand sympathizers at home and perhaps one thousand or so avowed Ustashas abroad.[12] The movement's ideology was defined by its militant commitment to Croatian independence, extreme anti-Communism, hatred of the Serbs, and willingness to embrace terrorism to achieve their goals.

By early March, 1941, Mussolini had concluded that Pavelić and his followers were of no further value, and he informed Pavelić that the Ustasha exiles would have to cease their activities altogether. After Hitler decided to invade Yugoslavia, however, Mussolini and Pavelić concluded a secret agreement by which most of the Croatian coast would be ceded to Italy in exchange for Mussolini's political support. Initially, Nazi leaders opposed Mussolini's plan to install Pavelić to power, but after Maček's refusal to collaborate, Hitler accepted Mussolini's recommendation of the Ustasha leader.[13] On April 15, 1941, Pavelić and some two hundred uniformed Ustashas from the camps in Italy entered Zagreb, riding in Italian tanks under the cover of night.[14]

The Ustasha Regime

Mussolini had hoped to extend Italian control over the entire Croatian puppet state. Toward this end, Italy legally established the Independent State of Croatia as an Italian protectorate. In obedience to Mussolini, Pavelić requested that King Victor Emmanuel III of Italy reign over Croatia. The king, however, named his nephew, Prince Aimone of Savoy, "King Tomislav II of Croatia" after the first Croatian king, crowned in the year 925. This nominal king never set foot officially in his supposed kingdom, and Italian aspirations for control over the puppet state were frustrated when the Germans insisted on partitioning the Independent State of Croatia into German and Italian zones of occupation.[15]

Within their zone of occupation, the Italians often wrested civil and military authority from the Ustashas, at times even extending their influence beyond the demarcation line into the German zone.[16] Within the German occupation zone, German troops were stationed throughout all important towns, and German military commanders interfered in the internal affairs of the nominally independent state to the extent of appointing local civil authorities.[17] Throughout all of occupied Yugoslavia, the German authorities seized control over banking, trade, industry, mining, and transportation and, further, obtained liens on strategic mineral and agricultural resources in areas under Italian, Bulgarian, and Hungarian occupation.[18] The *SS Einsatzgruppe,* mobile SS units that included the Gestapo and a special anti-Jewish department, organized Nazi police activities throughout German-occupied Yugoslavia. Its central command was based in Serbia (Belgrade), with satellite offices in the Independent State of Croatia (Zagreb, Osijek, and Sarajevo); in Vojvodina (Novi Sad), annexed by Hungary; and in Macedonia (Skopje), annexed by Bulgaria.[19]

The day after Pavelić arrived in Zagreb, a Ustasha government of ministers was established. The real seat of power, however, was the *Glavni Ustaški Stan* (GUS), or the Main Ustasha Headquarters, the central managing authority of the Ustasha Party (see appendix B).[20] Headed by Pavelić, GUS had been formed in Italy during late March, 1941, in anticipation of the takeover in Croatia. During the first two months of Ustasha rule, GUS formulated the ideology and policies for the Ustasha state and, thereafter, essentially functioned as a rubber stamp for Pavelić's decisions.[21]

Pavelić's regime, following the rhetoric of its Axis sponsors, declared war on Communists and other "undesirable elements." Following a GUS decree of April 22, 1941, the regime began to purge Serbs, Jews, and Gypsies from government service, the military, mass media, business, and the professions. Pavelić's early success in rounding up Communists and Socialists was aided particularly by the cooperation of the prewar Yugoslav police authorities, who handed over their police files to the Ustasha authorities intact.[22]

The Ustasha massacres began on April 27–28, 1941, with the arrest and execution of 176 Serbs near Bjelovar. On May 5, 1941, Pavelić ordered the conversion of Orthodox Serbs to Catholicism, and the Ustashas carried this out with threats of deportation, confiscation of property, and death.[23] In a meeting at Berchtesgaden during early June of 1941, Hitler encouraged Pavelić to accept the transfer of Slovenes into Croatia—a plan never carried out by the Nazis—and to deport Serbs from Croatia to Serbia. Admonishing Pavelić that too much tolerance can be damaging, Hitler suggested that Pavelić should conduct "fifty years of a nationally intolerant policy."[24]

Over the next six months, the Ustashas deported nearly 120,000 Serbs to Serbia, in addition to which some tens of thousands fled. An estimated 250,000 Orthodox Serbs, under Ustasha coercion or to avoid persecution, converted to Roman Catholicism.[25] Genocidal massacres accounted for tragic losses in the Serbian population in the Independent State of Croatia.

As it became apparent that their persecutions of Serbs were stimulating the growth of both the Partisan and Chetnik movements, the Ustashas attempted an accommodation with the Serbs. On May 28, 1942, the Bosnian Chetniks and the Ustasha state authorities concluded the first of several formal agreements by which the Croatian military would supply Chetnik forces; Chetniks wounded in campaigns against the Partisans would receive care in Croatian military hospitals; and the widows and orphans of Chetniks who died while fighting against Partisans would receive the same financial assistance provided to the surviving family members of Croatian soldiers.[26] As late as 1944, wounded Chetniks could be transported from the Independent State of Croatia to the Belgrade Military Hospital, or even to Germany, for medical treatment.[27] These agreements covered about ten thousand of the roughly fifteen thousand Bosnian Chetniks within the German occupation zone. Within the Italian occupation zone, the Chetniks were already functioning largely as Italian auxiliaries in anti-Partisan and anti-Ustasha activities.

Notwithstanding the Ustasha-Chetnik agreements, the Chetniks, whose political character and military objectives were essentially anti-Croat rather than anti-Axis, pursued their war against the Croats by any means possible. Chetnik activities ranged from sabotage and massacres of civilians to large-scale battles.[28] With Ustasha persecutions having stimulated unrest and resistance among the Serbian population, the Ustashas attempted to accommodate the Serbs by establishing an autocephalous Croatian Orthodox Church in June, 1942. Although the establishment of a Croatian Orthodox Church was technically in accord with the Orthodox theory that a separate state should have a separate church, it was, understandably, condemned by the Serbian Orthodox Church and received little support from the Orthodox clergy.[29]

The anti-Jewish policies of the Ustasha regime were enacted swiftly. On April 30, 1941, following prodding from the German Embassy, the Ustashas enacted anti-Jewish legislation in imitation of the Nazi Nuremberg laws of September, 1935.[30] The Ustashas' version of the laws defined who was a Jew, but with an innovation: protection was extended to Jews in mixed marriages and their offspring, and a number of wealthy Jews, who pledged their loyalty to the Ustasha regime, were protected as "honorary Aryans."[31] Jewish property was confiscated, and collective fines were imposed on the Jewish communities. The civilian police, which included many *Volksdeutsche,* participated in the mass arrest of Jews, ordered by Pavelić on June 26, 1941.

By the end of June, several hundred Jewish families from Zagreb were imprisoned in concentration camps on the island of Pag or at the Jadovno camp in the Velebit Mountains. The Ustashas committed brutal murders at these camps, which were dismantled in August, 1941, when the area was handed over to the Italians.[32] In July, the Jews from the smaller communities throughout Croatia were ordered to Zagreb, from where they were sent to various camps. Pavelić then ordered the destruction of synagogues. In the towns of Bosnia-Herzegovina, the arrests of the Jews began in early August; in Sarajevo, the arrests were completed by November. Most of these victims were imprisoned at Jasenovac, the largest Ustasha concentration camp, which operated from August, 1941, until April, 1945. There, Jews, Serbs, and Gypsies, as well as Croats and Muslims opposed to the Ustasha regime, were murdered.

Of the forty thousand Jews living in the territory of the Independent State of Croatia, about thirty thousand would perish: twenty thousand at the Jasenovac concentration camp, some hundreds in the Slano and Metajna camps on the island of Pag, and seven thousand at Auschwitz.[33]

Italian Treatment of the Jews

In the German occupation zone of the Independent State of Croatia, most Jews perished in the Holocaust, while, in the Italian occupation zone, most Jews survived, reflecting the influence of the respective occupying forces on Jewish survival.[34] The prewar Jewish population in the Italian-occupied zone had been little more than 500, but Italian-controlled areas became a relative haven for the Jews. Roughly 6,000 escaped the German occupation zone of Croatia and Bosnia-Herzegovina to head for the Italian sector.[35] The cities of Split, Dubrovnik, Sušak, and Mostar, all under Italian control, became vital transit points for Jewish refugees.[36] By 1942, the Italian authorities had confined some 6,500 Jews to concentration camps, variously in the Italian occupation zone, the annexation zone, or in Italy proper; but they generally refused to murder or deport the Jews, despite repeated German and Ustasha demands. In mid-1943, in response to continued German pressure, the Italian authorities moved 3,577 Jews from the Italian occupation zone to a single camp in the annexation zone on the island of Rab. Since some Jews remained in annexed Split while others were interned in Italy proper, the Italians had effectively concentrated the Jews in what was then uncontested Italian territory.[37]

Only in exceptional instances did the Italians fail to protect the Jews. On June 12, 1942, in the Dalmatian port city of Split, a mob, which included Italian soldiers, devastated the synagogue, attacked the Jews inside, and looted sixty Jewish homes. In the coastal town of Sušak, 200 Jewish refugees from western Europe were arrested by Italian forces and handed over to the Ustashas, who killed them. Similarly, on another occasion, the Italian military command in Dubrovnik permitted the transport of 27 Jews to Ustasha hands; they were later killed.[38]

The most notable incident, however, occurred at the end of 1942 in the Italian-occupied part of the Kosovo province. The area's inhabitants included a number of Jewish escapees from Austria, Czechoslovakia, and Nedić's Serbia, as well as 400 Jews native to the province. In an uncharacteristic move, Italian authorities delivered to the Germans all of the nonnative Jewish refugees, who were murdered at a Serbian concentration camp (there is some question over whether the camp was Sajmište or Banjica). The native Jews were transported to Albania, also under Italian occupation, where many survived.[39] In the two Ustasha camps—Slano for males and Metajna for females—on the island of Pag, Italian military authorities watched as the Ustashas tortured and murdered the inmates.[40] Notably, the local residents of Pag, all Croats, requested that the Italian military commander protect the inmates, mostly Jews and Serbs.[41]

Italian protection of the Jews in their occupation zone lasted until the capitulation of Italy on September 9, 1943, after which time the protection of the Jews largely devolved to the Partisans. For example, after Italy's surrender, the Partisans captured the island of Rab and evacuated nearly all of the Jews: 1,820 went to Partisan-controlled villages in Croatia, 1,350 joined the Partisans, 250 went to Allied-controlled southern Italy, and some 200 comprising women, children, the elderly, and the sick remained behind.[42] In early 1944, the Germans invaded the island and deported the remaining Jews to Auschwitz. Similarly, when German authorities extended their occupation to the formerly Italian-controlled port city of Split, some Jews fled to the nearby mountains and joined the Partisans. Some 400 that remained were deported to concentration camps in two stages: in 1943, all adult men and some women were sent to a Serbian-operated concentration camp in or around Belgrade (there is some discrepancy whether it was Banjica or Sajmište), and, in 1944, the remaining 300 women and children were sent to Jasenovac.[43] All perished.

Of the 82,500 Jews who lived in prewar Yugoslavia, 15,000 survived the Holocaust.[44] Nearly 10,000 of the survivors came from the territory of the Independent State of Croatia, where approximately 40,000 Jews had lived before the war. That roughly 25 percent of the Jews from the Independent State of Croatia survived the Holocaust is largely attributable to the Italians and also to the Partisans. Indeed, among the Jewish survivors from the Croatian puppet state, an estimated two-thirds had been interned at some point in Italian concentration camps. At the close of the war in 1945, about one-third of all Jewish survivors from Yugoslavia had fled abroad; many others remained in or had passed through Italy. At least 4,556 Jews throughout Yugoslavia joined the Partisans. The majority of these (2,621) had joined following their liberation from Italian concentration camps. Seventy percent of all Jewish Partisans survived the war.[45]

Resistance

Most Croats, including Communist sympathizers, had supported the break-up of Yugoslavia, which they identified with the oppression and brutality of more than two decades of Serbian rule. The initial popular support for the creation of the Independent State of Croatia, nevertheless, was not synonymous with support for the Ustashas. Within their first weeks of power, the Ustashas saw their unpopularity rapidly increase, as their lawless behavior—murders, persecutions, and robberies committed in the name of the Pavelić regime—became general public knowledge.[46]

The Croats' contempt for the Ustashas was even furthered when, less than six weeks after taking power, Pavelić signed the Rome Agreements of May 18, 1941.[47] Devised in secret while Pavelić was still in Italy, this agreement ceded to Italy most of Dalmatia—an integral part of the Croatian homeland since early medieval times.[48] Moreover, when the public learned that an Italian duke would be imposed as the king of Croatia, support for the Ustashas virtually collapsed.[49] Most Croats viewed the Rome Agreements as nothing less than treason.

Soon after the Ustasha regime assumed power, Hitler recognized how unpopular and poorly organized the Ustashas were but continued to support them because he viewed them as the only reliable collaborators in the so-called Independent State of Croatia.[50] Notorious for their brutality, the Ustashas were strongly opposed by a large majority of Croats.[51] The German estimate of support for the Ustashas was two percent of the population.[52] By October, 1941, the Ustashas' massacres had stimulated so much unrest and insurgency that a German officer made yet another approach to Maček to offer him the leadership of Croatia. Again, Maček refused. Five days later, Maček was arrested by the Ustashas and taken to the Jasenovac concentration camp. After five months of detention there, he and his family were moved to house arrest at their family home, where they remained until the collapse of the Ustasha regime.[53]

Among the Croats, one of the earliest and strongest resistance movements began in Dalmatia, largely the result of the local population's outrage at having been sacrificed by Pavelić to Italy. The Italians brutally subdued the locals (Croats) in the territories being annexed, and the effect on the population was compounded by Chetnik atrocities. The Chetniks, throughout a vast portion of Yugoslavia, were engaged in a murderous campaign against non-Serbian civilians. The wholesale slaughter was being conducted in accordance with the Chetnik plan for an ethnically homogenous Greater Serbia and was additionally fueled by Ustasha massacres. Since the Chetniks' enemies included both Ustashas and Partisans, the Italians found the Chetniks to be useful proxies. Croatian resistance in Dalmatia, formed in response to Italian and Chetnik campaigns of terror, became the core of the Croatian Partisan resistance movement.[54] It is noteworthy that, after the Partisan uprising in Serbia was crushed in late 1941, causing Tito to withdraw his forces to eastern Bosnia, Dalmatian Partisans were transferred there to protect Tito's High Command.[55]

Organized Croatian resistance to the Ustasha regime began more slowly outside of Dalmatia, despite marginal support for the Ustashas. Unlike the Serbs, the Croats had no tradition of guerrilla warfare. Also, the resistance movement in Croatia was initially confounded when the respected leader, Vladko Maček, called for pacifism and obedience to the new authorities in his last proclamation, issued on the day the Ustasha government took power. Moreover, during the earliest months of Pavelić's regime, many Communists were compelled, because of the Molotov-Ribbentrop Pact of 1939, to view the Nazis as allies, not enemies. This Communist policy was quickly swept away by Hitler's invasion of Russia on June 22, 1941. Indeed, the first Partisan uprising in Yugoslavia commenced on that day, when forty Croatian Communists—three women among them—from Sisak staged an uprising in the Brezovica woods between Sisak and Zagreb.[56] Although this Partisan uprising in Croatia was the first of its kind in Yugoslavia, it was ignored in official Yugoslav historiography. The uprising that was recorded as the first occurred two weeks later in Serbia and was led by Tito.[57]

Although the Serbian insurgency in the Independent State of Croatia was undoubtedly stimulated by the Ustashas, Serbs in Croatia and Bosnia had begun to arm themselves and commit atrocities against non-Serbian civilians, even before the Axis invasion of Yugoslavia. According to German intelligence, armed Chetnik formations had begun to arrive in Croatia during the early part of March, 1941.[58] These "imported" Chetnik detachments had came to reinforce existing formations or to start new ones. During the first weeks of the Croatian puppet state, these Serbian Chetniks claimed the lives of hundreds of Croatian and Muslim civilians in a series of massacres, mostly in Herzegovina. The perpetrators were, in at least some cases, members of the Royal Yugoslav Army.[59] Such Chetnik attacks were, in effect, an extension of the Serbian nationalist view, which saw former Habsburg lands as the domain of a conquered enemy and the Croats as inherently disloyal to Yugoslavia, simply by virtue of their having claimed a national identity other than Serbian.

The Ustasha campaign of terror against Serbs had the effect of helping Tito and the Communist leadership build a successful Partisan movement during 1941 and 1942. As Serbs fled from Ustasha terror, many joined the Chetniks, whose brutality mirrored that of the Ustashas. Others joined the better-organized Partisans, and the allegiances of many switched back and forth between the Chetniks and Partisans, depending on whose strength prevailed locally. Serbian Partisans tended to view the organization as exclusively Serbian and generally rejected the inclusion of non-Serbs. Furthermore, Serbian Partisans often raided the villages of their Croatian neighbors in retaliation for earlier Ustasha attacks. Thus, in certain regions, it proved difficult for the movement, in the beginning, to attract Croats to its ranks.[60]

In the beginning, when the Partisan movement was small in number, Serbs comprised the majority of the rank and file in Croatia and Bosnia-Herzegovina. By 1943, when the movement further expanded, the majority of Partisans in Croatia were Croats (no figures for the ethnic breakdown of the Partisans in Bosnia-Herzegovina are available).[61] By the end of 1943, Croatia proper—which contained about 24 percent of the Yugoslav population—had provided more Partisans than Serbia, Montenegro, Slovenia, and Macedonia, which, combined, made up 59 percent of Yugoslavia's population (see table 2).[62] Overall, from 1941 to 1945, the Partisans of Croatia were 61 percent Croat and 28 percent Serb, the rest comprising Slovenes, Muslims, Montenegrins, Italians, Hungarians, Czechs, Jews, and Volksdeutsche.[63]

As some Croatian Peasant Party leaders became increasingly prominent within the Partisan movement in Croatia (Peasant Party president Vladko Maček himself distrusted and rejected the Communist-led Partisans), and as the number of Croatian Partisans grew, Serbian Partisans became discontented. In efforts to reassure the Serbs, Andrija Hebrang, leader of Croatian Partisans, emphasized in his speeches the Serbian sacri-

Table 2. Growth of the Partisan movement in Yugoslavia, 1941–44 (in thousands)

	Late 1941	Late 1942	Sept. 1943	Late 1943	Late 1944
Bosnia-Herzegovina	20	60	89	108	100
Croatia	7	48	78	122	150
Kosovo	5	6	6	7	20
Macedonia	1	2	10	7	66
Montenegro	22	6	10	24	30
Serbia (proper)	23	8	13	22	204
Slovenia	1	19	21	25	40
Vojvodina	1	1	3	5	40
TOTAL	80	150	230	320	650

Note: Partisan strength peaked at 800,000 in April, 1945, by which time the majority of Yugoslavia was under Partisan control.

SOURCES: Strugar (1969), pp. 69, 219, 318; Anić et al. (1982), pp. 69–86, 113, 199, 209, 279, 301, 332, 348–49, 368, 378, 387, 457, 468, 536–40. Data analysis by Henry L. de Zeng IV.

fices in the war and the importance of cultural and political equality for both Serbs and Croats. The Croatian Peasant Party, furthermore, established a newspaper, Srpska riječ (The Serbian Word), in the summer of 1943. Its editor, Rade Pribičević, came from the Independent Democratic Party, a Serbian party with some history of cooperation with the Croatian Peasant Party.[64]

In January, 1944, the Croatian Peasant Party faction within the Partisans took the further step of establishing a Serbian Club, intended to represent the interests of Serbs in the Partisan movement. Pribičević presided over an executive council that was composed mainly of Communist Party members. Some Serbs, however, remained so troubled over the Croatian prominence in the Partisan movement of Croatia that, as late as May, 1944, several hundred Serbian Partisans in Kordun defected to the Germans.[65]

The Croatian Partisan movement achieved a remarkable level of organization. On June 13–16, 1943, with considerable territory under Partisan control and the establishment of hundreds of National Liberation Committees, a session of the Partisan political leadership was convened in the name of the Sabor (Croatian Parliament). This session was designated Zemaljsko antifašističko vijeće narodnog oslobođenja Hrvatske (Countrywide Antifascist Council for the People's Liberation of Croatia), known by its Croatian acronym ZAVNOH.

Milovan Djilas, not noted for his pro-Croat views, attended this session and recorded his impression: "Nowhere was a power structure as conspicuous and as real as on this liberated territory. It was evident not only in the better dress and food of the staffs and agencies, but also in the official, bureaucratic mode of operation. ZAVNOH . . . had every appearance of an assembly and a government. . . . All kinds of schools were operating; agencies exchanged reports and circulars."[66]

The second session of ZAVNOH was held October 12–15, 1943. The Croatian Peasant Party participated as an independent party. In his speech, Božidar Magovac, the secretary of the Croatian Peasant Party, defined the fundamental principles of his party: harmony between Croats and Serbs; brotherhood among Slovenes, Croats, Serbs, and Bulgarians; complete and unrestricted right of national self-determination; a government by a majority of the people; guaranteed human rights regardless of citizenship; complete equality for women; freedom of meeting; freedom of the press; freedom of association; freedom of religion and education.[67]

The opening speech was delivered by Moša Pijade, a high-ranking Partisan of Serbian Jewish extraction. Reflecting on the widespread participation of the intelligentsia in the Partisan movement in Croatia, he somberly noted the near nonexistence of such a movement in Serbia. More striking, however, than Pijade's assertion that only a small number in Belgrade had joined the resistance was his statement that the Gestapo prison in occupied Belgrade was run by the same "criminals and executioners" who had run the notorious prison Glavnjača under royal Yugoslavia.[68]

The steady growth in the number of National Liberation Committees in Croatia reflected the widening base of popular support for the Partisan movement. At the end of 1941, there were 677 such committees; at the end of 1942, there were 1,609; and, by the end of 1943, there were 4,596 committees at the local, district, and regional level.[69] The Croatian Partisans under Hebrang had attained a broad public mandate, representing not only a resistance movement but a healthy Croatian national movement.

According to official Yugoslav accounts, by May of 1944, the Partisan movement under ZAVNOH auspices could claim 1,350 primary schools with 90,000 students and more than 2,300 teachers, 30 high schools, and 20 publishing houses, which produced 270 journals and bulletins.[70] At this time, the ten-member presidency of the ZAVNOH included three representatives of the Croatian Peasant Party, two from the Communist Party, two from the Serbian-led Independent Democratic Party of Pribičević (which had cooperated with the Croatian Peasant Party before the war), and three independents with no party affiliation.[71]

For most of the war, especially between late 1941 and late 1944, the activities of the Partisans, arguably the strongest and most effective anti-Nazi resistance in occupied Europe, were primarily in the occupied Independent State of Croatia. The Partisan presence in Serbia, on the other hand, was much weaker and less aggressive. In June, 1942, six months after the failed Partisan uprising in Serbia, Tito was informed that a total of 852 Partisans existed throughout all of Serbia.[72] Later, Maj. H. B. Dugmore, a British liaison officer with the Partisans in eastern Serbia from November, 1943, to June, 1944, reported to his superiors that the number of Partisans in Serbia had risen from 1,700 to over 13,000 during this period.[73] Even the more generous Yugoslav figures for the number of Partisans in occupied Serbia tell a similar story: until German forces were driven from Belgrade by the advancing Red Army, the Partisan movement in Serbia remained numerically weak and static—Serbia contributing roughly 10 percent of all Partisans—in contrast to its steady growth in Croatia and Bosnia-Herzegovina (the Independent State of Croatia). (See table 2.)

A Multisided War

The puppet Independent State of Croatia served as the battleground for a multisided war, involving Partisans, *Domobrani* (Home Guards), Ustashas, Chetniks, German Nazis, and Italian Fascists. It is instructive to compare the situation in the Ustasha state with other parts of occupied Yugoslavia.

For Serbs, the choice over whether to ally themselves with either the Communist-led Partisans or ultranationalist Chetniks was determined by which formation first arrived in the area looking for "volunteers." Often, whole Serbian villages switched in their loyalties between Partisans and Chetniks. For Croats, had the option been available, most would have supported the return to power of Croatian Peasant Party leader Vladko Maček, who deplored Ustasha atrocities and distrusted and rejected the Communists.

Relationships among the Ustashas, Chetniks, Home Guards, Italians, Germans, and Partisans were complex. The Italians, aspiring to control the entire Independent State of Croatia, were displeased at the prominent role that the Germans assumed in the Croatian capital. In the Rome Agreements of May 18, 1941, Italy had already annexed a part of the Dalmatian coast, but it coveted still more territory and wanted to limit Zagreb's claim to Italian-occupied territory. It was in Italy's interest to undermine the authority of the Ustashas in the Italian occupation zone. At the same time, the Italians were plagued by the Partisan insurgency. The Italians, therefore, found it convenient to support the Chetniks against both Partisans and Ustashas.

Depending on the local situation, unusual alliances could emerge. For instance, in May, 1942, in the vicinity of Knin, just inland from the Dalmatian coast, Ustashas and Chetniks attempted to collaborate in fighting against the Partisans.[74] As part of this short-lived agreement, the Ustashas supplied the Chetniks with food, money, and arms, as well as some Home Guards ordered to assist the Chetniks.[75]

Not far from Knin, however, the Chetniks committed atrocities against the civilian populations of Dalmatia, Herzegovina, and western Bosnia, ostensibly in retaliation for the earlier killings of Serbs in these and adjacent areas in 1941 but most essentially in accordance with the longstanding Chetnik plan for the creation of Greater Serbia.[76] Chetniks from Herzegovina under the command of Maj. Petar Baćović, one of Mihailović's top officers, burned seventeen villages in Croatia, tortured and killed three Catholic priests, and killed all males over the age of fifteen during a rampage while en route to the Croatian coastal town of Makarska.

Such atrocities directed against the Croats exacerbated civil unrest and stimulated rebellion, undermining Italian interests. In October, 1942, Italian army general Mario Roatta, commander of the Second Italian Army, sent a telegram to Chetnik warlord Col. Ilija Trifunović-Birčanin demanding that Chetnik violence against civilians in Croatia and Bosnia-Herzegovina cease: "I request that Commander Trifunović be apprised that if the Chetnik violence against the Croatian and Muslim population is not immediately stopped, we will stop supplying food and daily wages to those formations whose members are perpetrators of the violence. If this criminal situation continues, more severe measures will be undertaken."[77] Italian protests did little to mitigate Chetnik terror, however; and, in fact, Italian policy did much to encourage it.

The multisided war being fought within the Independent State of Croatia created for Germany a military burden. Hitler attempted to solve the problem by subordinating the Croatian army to German command. After meeting with Hitler in September, 1942, Pavelić accepted this demand, and from then on he could no longer order Croatian troop movements without explicit German approval.[78] By early September, 1943, there were 262,326 regular Croatian army troops (the Home Guards), all ultimately under German command, and in September, 1944, Croatian forces peaked at 312,000 (see table 3).[79] The Home Guards, however, were notoriously unreliable as collaborators with the Germans and the Ustasha regime. Distinguished by their poor morale and unwillingness to fight, the Home Guards often secretly assisted the Partisans, and, ultimately, large numbers of them defected to the Partisans.[80] Generally, their military and strategic value was small, and they were not connected with atrocities or persecutions. The voluntary Ustasha militia and Pavelić's Personal Guard, responsible for

Table 3. Collaborationist armed formations in Yugoslavia, 1941–45

	Peak strength	
Independent State of Croatia		
Domobran (Home Guard) under Croatian command	160,027	Sept., 1944
Domobran components in the German Wehrmacht	62,632	Sept., 1944
Ustasha Militia & Pavelić's Personal Guard	70,000	Sept., 1944
Gendarmerie	15,000	Sept., 1944
regular uniformed city and town police	5,000	Sept., 1944
7th SS "Prinz Eugen" Division[a]	21,102	Dec., 1942
13th SS "Handžar" Division	17,000	Apr., 1944
Chetniks (Greater Serbian)	20,000	Sept., 1944
Serbia		
Serbian State Guard and Border Guard	21,000	Sept., 1943
Serbian Volunteers Corps	9,886	Aug., 1944
Chetniks	60,000	Sept., 1944
Serbian Gestapo	145	Dec., 1942
Volksdeutsche police	6,000	Oct., 1943
Volksdeutsche militia	7,500	Sept., 1943
Russian Defense Corps	11,197	Sept., 1944
Montenegro		
Chetniks (Greater Serbian)	15,000	Sept., 1944
Kosovo[b]		
Albanian Gendarmerie (under Italians)	1,000	Sept., 1943
Albanian Territorial Militia (under Germans)	8,000	Jan., 1944
Bali Kombëtar Militia (under Germans)	8,000	Sept., 1944
21st SS "Skanderbeg" Division (under Germans)	6,500	May, 1944
Macedonia		
Kontraćeta (Greater Bulgarian group)	200	Aug., 1944
Internal Macedonian Revolutionary Organization	(small)	
Bali Kombëtar Militia (Greater Albanian)	(small)	
Chetniks (Greater Serbian)	8,000	Sept., 1944
Slovenia		
Blue Guard (Slovene Chetniks) (under Italians)	6,049	Aug., 1943
White Guard (Village Guard) (under Italians)	6,500	Aug., 1943
Slovene Domobran (Home Guard) (under Germans)	12,000	Dec., 1944
Slovene Littoral National Guard (under Germans)	2,000	Aug., 1944
Wehrmannschaft des Steirischen Heimatbundes[c]	3,000	Aug., 1944

[a]Initially *Volksdeutsche* and Croats; later, mainly *Volksdeutsche*.
[b]These forces also operated in western Macedonia, annexed to Albania.
[c]Militia of the Styrian Homeland Union, consisting of *Volksdeutsche*; 66,000 to 105,000 belonged, but only the cited number were armed.

SOURCES: N.A., microcopy T-501, roll 253, frame 283; T-311, roll 194, frame 974; Strugar (1969), pp. 182, 262; Neulen (1985), p. 239; *Zbornik dokumenata* (1979), p. 540; Kreso (1979), p. 182; Bender and Taylor (1972), pp. 6–23; Colić (1977), pp. 61–79 (esp. p. 68); Littlejohn (1985), p. 264; Borković (1979a), p. 198. Data analysis by Henry L. de Zeng IV.

nearly all World War II atrocities attributable to Croats, numbered 70,000 at their peak in September, 1944.[81] Without the direct support of Adolf Hitler, however, the Ustasha regime could not have stayed in power for even months.

The Ustasha state officially proclaimed the Muslims to be "the flower of the Croatian nation." However, as among the Croats, only a minority of Muslims supported the Ustasha movement. The majority remained opposed to or neutral toward the Ustashas and tried to stay clear of the fighting.[82] The Bosnian Muslims quickly became disillusioned with the Pavelić regime and the general lawlessness that prevailed. In the summer and fall of 1941, Bosnian Muslim clergy and intellectuals from six major cities and towns—Sarajevo, Tuzla, Banja Luka, Bijeljina, Mostar, and Prijedor—issued resolutions condemning the atrocities being committed in the Independent State of Croatia by both Ustashas and Chetniks. These resolutions called for the protection of innocent lives, punishment of the perpetrators of crimes, religious tolerance, and material assistance for the victims, especially for orphans. The Sarajevo resolution, for example, unambiguously condemned the persecution of Jews and Serbs.[83]

Under genocidal attack by Chetniks, some Muslims joined the Ustashas and some joined the growing Partisan movement, while others tried to negotiate directly with the Germans for protection and autonomy.

In the fall of 1942, Heinrich Himmler conceived of an SS division composed of Bosnian Muslims. This plan found support from Hajj Amin Al-Husseini, the Grand Mufti of Jerusalem, who had found the Nazis' program of Jewish extermination so inspirational that he tried to persuade the Axis powers to extend it to the Middle East and North Africa.[84]

In March, 1943, Husseini flew from Berlin to Sarajevo, where he spoke publicly in favor of the Handžar SS Division and inspected its troops, an event well-publicized by the Germans.[85] Husseini's prestige as an Islamic leader helped the division's recruiting efforts. But the more immediate stimulus to recruitment came from German assurances that the new military formation would be employed in the defense of Muslim communities, which had endured nearly two years of Chetnik attacks on their civilians. These promises to the recruits were never fulfilled. The recruits, mainly Muslims and some Croats, were trained in occupied France and deployed in northeastern Bosnia, eastern Croatia, and the adjoining Hungarian-occupied portion of Vojvodina, where they fought against Partisans and conducted reprisals against Serbian civilians. The officers were composed mainly of Germans and *Volksdeutsche*. The formation attained a maximum strength of 21,000, which soon came to include increasing numbers of *Volksdeutsche*.[86]

Notably, a group of recruits in training for the Handžar Division was responsible for the only mutiny that occurred within an SS unit. On September 17, 1943, in Villefranche-de-Rouergue, approximately five hundred recruits, mostly Bosnian Muslims and some Croats, undertook an armed rebellion against the Germans. Some one hundred fifty rebels were killed immediately, and others were court-martialed and executed by the Germans. Every year since 1944, on September 17, Villefranche-de-Rouergue has commemorated "the revolt of the Croats," and a road leading to the cemetery bears the name "Avenue des Croates" (Slavic Muslims being identified as Croats of the Islamic faith). After the war, in an effort to blur the ethnic identity of the mutineers, the Yugoslav government requested that the French government remember this anti-Nazi insurrection of 1943 as "the revolt of the Yugoslavs" instead of as "the revolt of the Croats"—a request which the French refused for the sake of "historical truth."[87] Ultimately, the Handžar SS Division proved short-lived, and growing distrust of the Germans emerged, as the Germans and Chetniks more openly cooperated. By the fall of 1944, the Handžar SS Division was essentially nonfunctional, and Muslims increasingly joined the Partisans.

Despite the complexity of events in Axis-occupied Yugoslavia, Serbian popular mythology has simplified the picture by having emphasized the collective guilt of the Croats for atrocities committed during the war and, in contrast, the collective innocence of the Serbs.[88] Ignored in this picture are the pro-Nazi activities of the Nedić government, of many parts of the Chetnik movement, and of much of the Serbian Orthodox clergy. At the same time, the Serbian popular retelling of the war history generalizes the Ustasha movement as one that included the whole of the Croatian people, when, in fact, it constituted a fringe element of Croatian society. That the overwhelming majority of Croats rejected the Ustashas—and that the Croats provided an essential core of the Partisan resistance movement—also is ignored.

Furthermore, when comparing Serbia's role in the Holocaust to that of Croatia, Serbian propagandistic logic absolves Serbians by arguing that Serbia was an "occupied" country and, therefore, bore no responsibility for crimes committed against the Jews in its territory; Croatia, on the other hand, was "independent," and, therefore, Croats must collectively shoulder responsibility.[89] In truth, both Serbia and Croatia were occupied by Axis troops. Moreover, the so-called *Independent State* of Croatia throughout the war had more Axis occupying troops on its soil than did Serbia (see tables 4–9). The reasons that the Independent State of Croatia was neither an independent nor a proper state are well summarized by the historian Aleksa Djilas:

> [The Independent State of Croatia] was created by the Germans and
> Italians after their victory over Yugoslavia; the Ustashas who ruled it

Table 4. Axis occupation forces in Yugoslavia (in thousands)

	Late 1941	Late 1942	Sept. 1943	Late 1943	Late 1944	Apr. 1945
Bulgarian	45	60	81	80	—	—
German	90	181	312	357	450	400
Hungarian	15	14	14	13	—	—
Italian	330	325	337	—	—	—
TOTAL	480	580	744	450	450	400

SOURCES: Colić (1988), p. 86; N.A., microcopy T-821, roll 474, frames 857–80; Anić et al. (1982), pp. 111, 468, 536–40; Strugar (1969), pp. 69, 123–24, 187, 221; Piekalkiewicz (1984), p. 304. Data analysis by Henry L. de Zeng IV.

Table 5. Axis occupation forces by republic (in thousands)

	Late 1941	Late 1942	Sept. 1943	Late 1943	Late 1944	Apr. 1945
Bosnia-Herzegovina	40	64	115	100	270	160
Croatia	182	210	257	77	100	160
Macedonia	30	38	55	69	—	—
Montenegro	50	50	50	20	30	—
Serbia[a]	113	128	145	134	—	—
Slovenia	65	90	122	50	50	80
TOTAL	480	580	744	450	450	400

[a]Including Vojvodina and Kosovo.

SOURCE: "Nemačke, italijanske, bugarske i mađarske snage na teritoriji Jugoslavije u toku NO rata" [German, Italian, Bulgarian, and Hungarian Forces on the Territory of Yugoslavia during the National Liberation War] in: *Vojnoistorijski glasnik* [Military-Historical Herald], Belgrade, vol. 3, 1952: no. 2, pp. 78–109, no. 3, pp. 58–110, no. 4, pp. 75–77, no. 5, pp. 82–106, no. 6, pp. 80–93; vol. 4, 1953: no. 1, pp. 72–94, no. 2, pp. 82–99, no. 3, pp. 85–99, no. 4, pp. 68–98. Data analysis by Henry L. de Zeng IV.

never had the support of the majority of the Croatian people; their method of ruling was terroristic and genocidal, and therefore incompatible with any concept of legality or constitutionality; the [Independent State of Croatia] was obliged to pay for the upkeep of foreign armies on its territory and to make trade agreements with Germany and Italy; it had no independent foreign policy; it gave large parts of its territory (Dalmatia) to a foreign power (Italy); an enormous number of its inhabitants were totally opposed to it—not only all persecuted "minorities" (Serbs, Jews, and Gypsies) but also many Croats and Mus-

Table 6. German occupation forces in Yugoslavia by republic (in thousands)

	Late 1941	Late 1942	Sept. 1943	Late 1943	Late 1944	Apr. 1945
Bosnia-Herzegovina	10	54	100	100	270	160
Croatia	2	30	70	77	100	160
Macedonia	—	2	5	20	—	—
Montenegro	—	—	—	20	30	—
Serbia[a]	73	80	90	90	—	—
Slovenia	5	15	47	50	50	80
TOTAL	90	181	312	357	450	400

[a]Including Vojvodina and Kosovo.

SOURCES: N.A., microcopy T-312, roll 462, frames 8049630–955; T-501, roll 352, frame 367; T-501, roll 253, frame 1333; T-78, roll 413, frame 6381187; T-311, roll 190, frames 1–750; T-77, roll 1423, frame 292; T-77, roll 867, frame 3614322; Tessin (1965–80); Schramm (1961–65); *German Anti-Guerrilla Operations* (1954); Mitcham (1985); "Nemačke, italijanske, bugarske i mađarske . . ." (see table 5 for the full citation). Data analysis by Henry L. de Zeng IV. Estimates for the regional distribution of German forces may contain a margin of error as great as 20 percent, due to the highly mobile nature of German military operations in the Balkans.

Table 7. Italian occupation forces in Yugoslavia by republic (in thousands)

	Late 1941	Late 1942	Sept. 1943	Late 1943	Late 1944	Apr. 1945
Bosnia-Herzegovina	30	10	15	—	—	—
Croatia	180	180	187	—	—	—
Macedonia	—	—	—	—	—	—
Montenegro	50	50	50	—	—	—
Serbia[a]	10	10	10	—	—	—
Slovenia	60	75	75	—	—	—
TOTAL	330	325	337	—	—	—

[a]Kosovo only.

SOURCES: N.A., microcopy T-821, roll 474, frames 857–1150; *Le Operazioni delle Unità Italiane in Jugoslavia* (1978); "Nemačke, italijanske, bugarske i mađarske . . ." (see table 5 for the full citation). Data analysis by Henry L. de Zeng IV.

lims; it could not, even with the mobilization of its own forces, control large parts of its own territory.[20]

As in Serbia, the puppet government of the Independent State of Croatia was installed by the Axis occupiers. The origins of the Serbian and Croatian collaborationist governments, however, offer a striking contrast. In

Table 8. Bulgarian occupation forces in Yugoslavia by region (in thousands)

	Late 1941	Late 1942	Sept. 1943	Late 1943	Late 1944	Apr. 1945
Bosnia-Herzegovina	—	—	—	—	—	—
Croatia	—	—	—	—	—	—
Macedonia	30	36	50	49	—	—
Montenegro	—	—	—	—	—	—
Serbia[a]	15	24	31	31	—	—
Slovenia	—	—	—	—	—	—
TOTAL	45	60	81	80	—	—

[a]Serbia proper, excluding Vovjodina and Kosovo.

SOURCES: Mitrovski et al. (1971), pp. 51–52, 60–62; *Order of Battle and Handbook of the Bulgarian Armed Forces* (1943), p. 69; "Nemačke, italijanske, bugarske i mađarske . . ." (see table 5 for the full citation). Data analysis by Henry L. de Zeng IV.

Table 9. Hungarian occupation forces in Yugoslavia by region (in thousands)

	Late 1941	Late 1942	Sept. 1943	Late 1943	Late 1944	Apr. 1945
Bosnia-Herzegovina	—	—	—	—	—	—
Croatia	1	1	1	1	—	—
Macedonia	—	—	—	—	—	—
Montenegro	—	—	—	—	—	—
Serbia[a]	14	13	13	12	—	—
Slovenia	—	—	—	—	—	—
TOTAL	15	14	14	13	—	—

[a]Vojvodina only.

SOURCES: Mirnić (1968), pp. 7–70; Council of the Order of Vitéz (1977); Strugar (1969), pp. 69, 123–24, 187, 221; "Nemačke, italijanske, bugarske i mađarske . . ." (see table 5 for the full citation). Data analysis by Henry L. de Zeng IV.

Serbia, the collaborationist leadership was largely a direct continuation of a part of the prewar political mainstream. Serbian intellectuals and men of influence publicly urged collaboration with the Nazis, and the collaborators in Serbia operated with significant public support. This was especially true during 1941 and 1942, when the Holocaust in Serbia was carried out. Remarkably, many prominent Serbs who had urged cooperation with the Nazis remained prominent and influential even in postwar Yugoslavia (see appendix A). In Croatia, the mainstream political leadership, represented by Vladko Maček, refused to collaborate with Hitler. The Ustasha leadership itself came from the émigré political and social fringe. Most Croats rejected the Ustashas, whose regime could not have remained in power without Hitler's support.

That Serbian popular support for the Chetniks was widespread while Croatian support for the Ustashas was marginal reflected historical and cultural differences between the two countries. In Serbian popular culture, since at least the time of the 1804 uprising, the guerrilla who avenged the 1389 Battle of Kosovo by mutilating his non-Serbian victims with a knife was celebrated as a hero. Indeed, sadistic Chetnik-style violence, driven by this romantic national mythology, had played an essential role in the creation of the modern Serbian state and its successive territorial expansions. The Croatian historical experience, however, was quite different. The Kingdom of Croatia, united with the Kingdom of Hungary in 1102, remained an integral part of the Hungarian crown and, later, of the dual Austro-Hungarian monarchy, with the political center of gravity shifting to Vienna and Budapest. Although de facto foreign rule generated significant discontent in Croatia, particularly with the rise of national consciousness during the nineteenth century, Croatian politicians emphasized remedies in accordance with the rule of law, rather than through armed rebellion.

When joining the new Yugoslav state in 1918, Croatia unexpectedly traded national suppression under Habsburg rule for systematic state terror under the royal Serbian regime. Throughout the entire period of Royal Yugoslavia, the Croats, overwhelmingly represented by the Croatian Peasant Party, continued to press for legal solutions to the oppression imposed by Belgrade. Prior to the rise of the Ustashas, nothing synonymous to the Chetniks existed among the Croats, for whom the practice of state terrorism was without precedent.

From the beginning of the war, the Croats played a major role in the Partisan movement. The multiethnic Partisan movement within Croatia and Bosnia-Herzegovina (the Independent State of Croatia) grew to be the most formidable resistance in occupied Europe, while the resistance in neighboring Serbia from late 1941 until mid–1944 remained weak. It is precisely the weakness of Serbia's resistance and the widespread nature of Serbia's Axis collaboration that postwar Serbian propaganda has undertaken to conceal.

The Question of War Casualties

Serbian propagandistic assertions rely greatly on the claimed numbers of Serbs killed by the Ustashas during the Second World War. Indeed, in postwar writings, Bishop Nikolaj Velimirović, who, in his sermons did not hesitate to support Nazism and foment anti-Semitism, pro-claimed the genocide of Serbs as eclipsing that of the Jews.[91] Figures overestimating the number of Yugoslav and, specifically, Serbian victims started to appear in Western literature at the close of World War II—long before actual losses could be known. Since this time, most quoted figures have relied on the same erroneous information, citing the same question-able sources and neglecting genuine data and scholarship on this subject.

The writings of one Edmond Paris, for example, a shadowy figure quoted frequently by Serbian apologists, linked Jews and Serbs as Holo-caust victims and, furthermore, implied that the Serbs had somehow even surpassed the Jews as innocent victims of genocide during the Second World War. According to Paris, "The greatest genocide during World War II, in proportion to a nation's population, took place, not in Nazi Germany but in the Nazi-created puppet state of Croatia. There, in the years 1941–1945, some 750,000 Serbs, 60,000 Jews and 26,000 Gypsies—men, wo-men, and children—perished in a gigantic holocaust."[92] The number of Serbian victims in Croatia that Paris alleges happens to exceed the actual number of Serbs who died in all of Yugoslavia during World War II (dis-cussed below). Although the number he cites for Jewish losses is approxi-mately correct for all of Yugoslavia, Paris attributes all Jewish losses to Croatia, as though the Holocaust had never touched Serbia.[93] Similarly, the Gypsy losses for all of Yugoslavia were attributed solely to the Croatian puppet state.[94] Nevertheless, despite such unsound scholarship, these kinds of sources have been quoted for years in official U.S. government publica-tions, various Jewish publications, and periodicals.

A broad range of figures representing the number of war victims in Yugoslavia can be found quoted by Western governments, the press, and in historical literature. The estimated number of Yugoslav war victims has ranged from one million to more than two million. The figure cited most frequently is 1,706,000 for total mortality, including one million Serbs. This figure is based on estimates released by the Yugoslav government, which knew that the numbers were inaccurate.[95] Nevertheless, in 1991, one major American television network's news broadcast reported that the number of Serbian victims had reached two million in Croatia alone, ex-ceeding Yugoslavia's own claimed losses for the entire country.[96] Such erro-neous figures have been accepted in many Western circles, largely as a result of their repetition and because bona fide research in this area has received little attention.

A careful observer can trace the origin of the inflated figures for Yugo-slavia's war victims to Tito's own pronouncements. As early as May, 1945, Tito stated publicly that Yugoslavia had lost 1.7 million of its population during the war. No source was offered. In fact, the first postwar population census in Yugoslavia was not conducted until March, 1948, and its results were not analyzed until 1951, a fact noted by researchers in the U.S. Bureau of Census as early as 1954.[97] Yet the Yugoslav government reiterated these figures and broadly disseminated them to the West on the occasion of the 1947 meeting of the Allied Reparations Committee in Paris.

How these figures were generated became clear only in 1989, following revelations by the individual who actually produced them. That person was Vladeta Vučković, then a twenty-four-year-old sophomore at the Institute of Statistics in Belgrade. In March, 1947, he was ordered to calculate the number of war victims in Yugoslavia in order to provide information requested by the Allied Reparations Committee for war reparations claims against Germany. Vučković was instructed that "the number should be significant, but based on scientific statistics." Vučković understood that Yugoslavia was interested in the largest possible number of war victims. With less than two weeks to complete this task, Vučković extrapolated an estimate of total demographic losses over the entire territory of Yugoslavia, finishing his work in ten days.

The 1.7 million figure included not only war-related deaths, but also what the country's population would have been if there had been no war, and included the calculated number of unborn children and losses due to emigration and disease. Within days after Vučković had generated this figure, the Belgrade newspaper *Borba* on March 26, 1947, proclaimed that Yugoslavia had endured 1.7 million war-related deaths. Subsequently, the Yugoslav regime presented the 1.7 million figure as war-related and, in 1948, submitted it to the Allied Reparations Commission in Paris.[98]

By 1963, the Yugoslav government, in official correspondence with Germany, had already revised its war losses to 950,000.[99] Germany subsequently requested verifiable data for the purpose of war reparations, and, in 1964, the Yugoslav authorities conducted a detailed, nationwide survey. The results yielded fewer than 600,000 victims of war. These data were provided to Germany and declared a Yugoslav state secret, since they were approximately one-third of the number originally claimed.[100] This 1964 war reparations survey and its concealment are discussed in a scholarly journal published by the North American Society for Serbian Studies: "The statistical count of the total number of persons killed in the Second World War in Yugoslavia is to this day the subject of passionate controversies. . . . [The] Yugoslav government has created this situation, first by making unsubstantiated claims and later, by keeping the figures of war victims a secret."[101]

According to the suppressed 1964 Yugoslav government census,

Table 10. World War II losses according to the 1964 Yugoslav war reparations census

Location	Mortality	Nationality	Mortality
Bosnia-Herzegovina	177,045	Albanians	3,241
Croatia	194,749	Croats	83,257
Kosovo	7,927	Hungarians	2,680
Macedonia	19,076	Jews	45,000
Montenegro	16,903	Macedonians	6,724
Serbia (proper)	97,728	Montenegrins	16,276
Slovenia	40,781	Muslims	32,300
Vojvodina	41,370	Serbs	346,740
Unknown	1,744	Slovak	1,160
		Slovenes	42,027
		Turks	686
		Unknown	16,202
TOTAL	597,323	TOTAL	596,293

SOURCE: Željko Krušelj and Đuro Zagorac, "Sporna knjiga mrtvih" [The Contested Book of the Dead], *Danas*, Zagreb, November 21, 1989, pp. 24–25. The figures exclude Axis collaborators. The totals by location and nationality show a discrepancy of 1,030.

597,323 Yugoslav citizens died in all of Yugoslavia, of which 346,740 were Serbs and 83,257 were Croats. These figures, submitted for the purpose of reparations, excluded foreigners and Axis collaborators.[102] (See table 10.)

Credible figures for war victims in Yugoslavia can be found in several sources. In their 1954 study, Mayers and Campbell of the U.S. Bureau of Census cited 1,067,000 war losses throughout Yugoslavia.[103] This range of losses was corroborated in 1985 by Serbian scholar Bogoljub Kočović, who calculated total losses for Yugoslavia at 1,014,000.[104] Of these, 487,000 were Serbs and 207,000 were Croats. In Croatia proper (including the Jasenovac camp, where Serbian sources generally claim 750,000 Serbs alone perished), 125,000 Serbs and 124,000 Croats died from all causes. In Bosnia-Herzegovina, 209,000 Serbs, 79,000 Croats, and 75,000 Muslims died. In Serbia proper and Vojvodina, 147,000 Serbs died (see table 11). Unlike the 1964 Yugoslav census, this study included foreigners and Axis collaborators. In his introduction, Kočović anticipated his critics:

> Very soon it dawned upon me that the major obstacle to my work would be the myths created over four decades about the number of victims; myths by now deeply implanted in the soul of the people of all religions, political beliefs and nationality; myths, which by repetition became a "reality." There will be many who will reject my study because it does not conform to their beliefs. . . . Many [Serbs] are looking

Collaboration and Resistance

Table 11. World War II losses (by place of origin) according to Kočović
(in thousands)

	Serbs and Montenegrins	Croats	Muslims	Jews	Others	TOTAL
Bosnia-Herzegovina	209	79	75	10	9	382
Croatia	125	124	—	17	29	295
Kosovo	4	—	—	1	5	10
Macedonia	7	—	1	6	11	25
Montenegro	45	—	4	—	1	50
Serbia (proper)	114	1	5	8	13	141
Slovenia	—	—	—	1	34	35
Vojvodina	33	3	1	17	22	76
TOTAL	537[a]	207	86	60	124[b]	1,014

[a]Includes Serbs (487,000) and Montenegrins (50,000).
[b]Includes Albanians (6,000), Germans (26,000), Gypsies (27,000), Hungarians (5,000), Slovenes (32,000), Macedonians (7,000), and others (21,000).
SOURCE: Kočović (1985), pp. 65, 70, 79, 89, 93, 99, 120, 124–25, 172–83.

for spiritual food for their positions in their anti-Croatianism. . . . There exists a "deeply" rooted opinion, I would say myth, that there were at least one million, if not more, Serbs killed [and] that the Serbs were practically the only ones who had real victims.[105]

In close agreement with the conclusion drawn by Kočović was an independent study by Croatian scholar Vladimir Žerjavić, whose initial research was supported by the Jewish community of Zagreb.[106] This study also included foreigners and Axis collaborators. Total losses throughout Yugoslavia were calculated to be 1,027,000, of which 530,000 were Serbs and 192,000 were Croats. In Croatia proper, 131,000 Serbs and 106,000 Croats died from all causes. In Bosnia-Herzegovina, 164,000 Serbs, 64,000 Croats, and 75,000 Muslims died. In Serbia proper and Vojvodina, 187,000 Serbs died. These data, summarized in table 12, do not differentiate among various causes of death. For example, throughout Yugoslavia, Serbs were killed by Germans, Italians, Croats, Albanians, Muslims, Hungarians, Soviet forces, Allied air attacks, the typhoid epidemic, and, especially in Serbia and Montenegro, by other Serbs.

The causes of some 320,000 Serbian losses in the Independent State of Croatia were elucidated by Žerjavić: 82,000 Serbs were among Partisans killed; 23,000 were Axis collaborators; 34,000 were civilians in battles between Ustashas, Chetniks, and Partisans; 45,000 were killed by Germans; 15,000 by Italians; 25,000 by the typhoid epidemic; 48,000 by Ustashas at

Table 12. World War II losses (by place of death) according to Žerjavić (in thousands)

	Serbs	Monte-negrins	Croats	Muslims	Jews	Others	TOTAL
Bosnia-Herzegovina	164	—	64	75	9	4	316
Croatia	131	—	106	2	10	22	271
Kosovo	3	—	1	2	—	17	23
Macedonia	6	—	—	4	—	7	17
Montenegro	6	20	1	4	—	6	37
Serbia (proper)	142	—	—	13	7	5	167
Slovenia	—	—	—	—	—	33	33
Vojvodina	45	—	6	—	7	25	83
Abroad	33	—	14	3	24	6	80
TOTAL	530	20	192	103	57	125[a]	1,027

[a]Includes Albanians (18,000), Germans (28,000), Gypsies (18,000), Hungarians (2,000), Macedonians (6,000), Slovenes (42,000), and others (11,000).

SOURCE: Žerjavić (1992), p. 168.

the Jasenovac concentration camp; and 28,000 by Ustashas at other camps, prisons, or massacre sites. In addition, 20,000 Serbs were transported to the German-Serbian Sajmište camp near Belgrade.[107] The total mortality figure at the Jasenovac camp was approximately 83,000, apportioned as follows: 48,000 Serbs (plus or minus 3,500), 13,000 Jews, 12,000 Croats and Muslims, and 10,000 Gypsies. Thirty-one thousand Croats and Muslims also perished in Ustasha concentration camps throughout the Independent State of Croatia (see table 13).[108]

Similarly, Žerjavić analyzed the causes of 142,000 Serbian losses in Serbia proper and found that 34,000 Serbs were killed in civilian locations by Germans (21,000), Bulgarians (11,000), and Chetniks (2,000). Serbs also died as Partisans (39,000), as collaborators (23,000), and in concentration camps (46,000).[109]

Because the official Yugoslav figures for war losses had been so misleading and a source of controversy, Žerjavić's study, like Kočović's earlier investigation, offered the possibility to approach the issue of war losses rationally and objectively.

The Belgrade government was aware from the outset that the original claims of 1.7 million war victims were false. However, since inflated figures served Yugoslavia's interest in anticipated war reparations from Germany, the fiction was perpetuated. In 1964, when census data, which excluded foreigners and collaborators, demonstrated one third of the original claimed war victims, the resulting figures were made a state secret and re-

Table 13. Estimated civilian losses of Croats, Bosnian Muslims, and Serbs
in the Independent State of Croatia (in thousands)

	Serbs	Croats	Muslims
In concentration camps, prisons	93[a]	19	12
In villages, towns	124	43	25
TOTAL	217[a]	62	37

[a]Includes approximately 20,000 Serbs who were transferred to and perished at
the Sajmište camp, under German-Serbian administration.

SOURCE: Žerjavić (1992), pp. 70–72, 77.

main so at the time of this writing. For many Serbs, inflated war losses,
especially the alleged 700,000 to 800,00 at the Jasenovac concentration
camp in Croatia, remain integral to the mythology surrounding the Serbian
war record.[110] The continued falsification of these losses, however, can no
longer be uncritically accepted.

Chapter Five
Serbian Historical Revisionism and the Holocaust

Since the end of World War II, for reasons of state and personal interests, the Serbian leadership has projected an image of Serbia's role in the war that is often in serious conflict with the historical record. In creating this image of wartime Serbia, the country's alleged loyal alliance with the West, uncompromising resistance to the Axis, and innocence pertaining to war crimes have been stressed. Recently, there also have been efforts to rehabilitate the war-era reputation of the Chetnik movement as well as of the Nedić regime.

Serbia's revision of Second World War history perhaps has been most thorough in meting out responsibility for the Holocaust in Serbia. This discussion on the Serbian rewriting of the Holocaust will explore the process of historical revisionism, revealing its political ends and its relationship to recent trends within intellectual and political circles of the Serbian establishment, including the revival of nationalistic anti-Semitism so prevalent during World War II.

Historical revisionism in Serbia began even before the end of the Second World War. Only days after the Partisan victory in Serbia, the Belgrade newspaper *Politika* (formerly *Obnova;* resurrected as a Communist organ) proclaimed Serbia's unbroken legacy of love for the Jews:

> It was not by accident that all the Jews in Serbia called themselves Serbs of Moses' faith. And it was not a miracle of religious and racial tolerance that all the Serbs regarded the Jews as citizens having the same rights as the Serbs themselves. Every Serb . . . knew that it was more

important to be a good man than a bad Serb. This is why there has never been any anti-Semitism among the Serbs, except when the Germans ordered it. . . . Even then, all the Jews could see the sincere love of the Serbian people. . . . The Serbs . . . regarded it as their civic duty to hide their Jewish fellow citizens.[1]

In this tribute to Serbia's virtually exterminated Jewish population—really more a tribute to supposed Serbian religious tolerance—exists the essence of the revisionism that is at the center of Serbia's World War II mythology. This mythology has been so consistently disseminated that it has become accepted as conventional wisdom, even among some respected Jewish scholars.[2]

The denial of Serbia's own anti-Semitic tradition and complicity in the Holocaust yielded several benefits to Serbs individually and collectively. It deflected attention from the collaborationist backgrounds of the many Chetniks who had joined the victorious Partisans after accepting Tito's offer of amnesty, announced in August, 1944. Downplaying Serbia's pro-Nazi history, in turn, increased Serbian political power and facilitated the postwar Serbian drive for hegemony in the new Yugoslavia. The pattern of historical revisionism became more firmly established in the postwar era, when the dissemination of information about Yugoslavia was once again controlled mostly by Serbian authorities.[3]

It has been a pattern of Serbian propaganda to convey to the Jews the impression that Serbs have been and remain their only friends among the peoples of former Yugoslavia.[4] In 1994, the following description of the SS Handžar Division appeared in a Jewish publication in an apparent attempt to turn Jewish sympathy away from the Bosnian Muslims, who have been the major victims of Serbian aggression since 1992: "It was the Grand Mufti who organized the Hanjar SS squads that roamed through the Balkans, mainland Greece and the Greek Islands—rounding up Sephardim."[5]

The Grand Mufti, however notorious a Jew-hater and supporter of Hitler, did not initiate the idea of a Bosnian Muslim SS division, nor did he organize it, although he did visit Sarajevo to speak publicly in its favor. The idea for the SS division originated with Heinrich Himmler in the fall of 1942. It was deployed almost exclusively in northeastern Bosnia, eastern Croatia, and the adjoining part of Vojvodina, but never in Greece. The officers of the Handžar Division were mainly Germans and *Volksdeutsche,* a few Croats, and one Muslim. With time, the soldiers also were increasingly composed of *Volksdeutsche.* Their activities were directed almost exclusively against the Partisans, not the Jews, most of whom had already met their tragic fate by the time the Handžar SS Division was conceived in March, 1943.

It is worth repeating that Handžar Division recruits, in 1943, became the only SS members to mutiny, and by so doing undertook the first significant act of resistance in occupied France. The French referred to the insurrection as the "revolt of the Croats." After the war, the Yugoslav government requested that the French remember it as "the revolt of the Yugoslavs."[6] Indeed, the celebration of a "Yugoslav" anti-Nazi movement that obscured the resistance efforts of non-Serbs was a form of historical revisionism in postwar Yugoslavia.

Serbian propagandists also have failed to mention the incorporation, at the end of the war, of Serbian forces—including the Chetniks, Serbian State Guard, and Serbian Volunteer Corps—into an SS formation. Even in the war's final months, when Axis forces were facing imminent defeat, Ljotić's followers had remained devoted to Hitler. With overflowing adoration, the Ljotićites celebrated what would be Hitler's last birthday (he committed suicide some ten days later), praising the Führer as a missionary, as the leader of the world anti-Communist struggle, and as nothing less than a half-divine being.[7]

Serbian propaganda also suggests boldly that Serbs had been singled out for the same persecution as the Jews. To support this claim, Serbian sources often reiterate that the German authorities had ordered the shooting of a hundred Serbs for every German soldier killed during the failed anti-Nazi uprising in Serbia in 1941.[8] That Serbians were victims of the German reprisal policy is indisputable; however, it must be stated that such claims without further qualification are misleading. In fact, the order to shoot fifty to one hundred *Communists* for every German soldier killed was issued by Field Marshal Wilhelm Keitel on September 16, 1941, as a general policy to be followed throughout occupied Europe.[9] Serbian propagandists also fail to note that, when Keitel's order was applied in Serbia, it was directed against Jews and Gypsies rather than against Serbs.

On October 26, 1941, Harald Turner issued order number 44/41, specifying that the subjects for retaliations should be primarily Jews and Gypsies, because they were regarded as "unreliable elements" and especially because "the Jewish element" had taken significant part in the leadership of the Partisans.[10] Thus, in late 1941, German soldiers shot two thousand Jewish prisoners and two hundred Gypsy prisoners.[11] Indeed, in his postwar testimony, SS colonel Wilhelm Fuchs, chief of the *Einsatzgruppe* for Serbia prior to January, 1942, stated: "I often gave Jews to be shot in order to save Serbs."[12]

In the late 1980s, Serbian emissaries began to reach out to Israel in an attempt to distance Serbia from Yugoslavia's anti-Israeli policy of the prior three decades. Particularly with regard to the Arab-Israeli conflict, Yugoslavia consistently had favored the interests of the Arab states at Israel's expense. The shift in Belgrade's attitude toward Israel was signaled by a manifesto issued in 1986 by Belgrade's leading Serbian intellectuals. This document, known as the Memorandum of the Serbian Academy of Science and Arts, portrayed Serbs as the most victimized and oppressed people in Yugoslavia, and it concluded that the Serbs' suffering demanded a compensation: the borders of Serbia must be redrawn so that all Serbs throughout Yugoslavia can live in an expanded Serbia.[13]

Adding legitimacy to the central argument of the Memorandum, Serbian intellectuals argued that the Serbs' right to their "Promised Land" of Greater Serbia rested on no less a moral foundation than the right of the Jewish people to the State of Israel, since both peoples were history's victims. In an open letter to Jewish writers in Israel, one Serbian author proclaimed that "every foot" of Kosovo (populated by a peaceful Albanian majority for centuries) had become "Jerusalem," that Serbian and Jewish suffering were indistinguishable, and that Serbs were really "the thirteenth, lost, and the most unfortunate tribe of Israel."[14]

In 1987, a government-sponsored Serbian-Jewish Friendship Society was formed in Belgrade. Part of its function was to proclaim the spiritual kinship of Serbs and Jews as eternal friends and as victims of Nazi persecution.[15] The principal purpose of the society, however, was to facilitate the establishment of full diplomatic relations between the Belgrade regime and Israel, as described by the society's founder and spokesperson, Klara Mandić:

> The first point in the program of the Serbian-Jewish Friendship Society is unconditional re-establishment of diplomatic relations between Yugoslavia and Israel. The first great step was made by the Week of Serbia in Israel. It was very difficult. It was necessary to overcome 25 years of pathological hatred of Israel, dictated by Josip Broz Tito and executed by the darkest segment of our past—the foreign policy of the Socialist Federative Republic of Yugoslavia. It was not simple. In the beginning we got consent from Mr. Slobodan Milošević who had understood all that and who completely agreed with the idea. And, now, one had to get consent from Israel. It was not so simple but the consent was gotten from Israel, too. Mr. Slobodan Milošević had appointed my friend Dušan Mihajlović as my assistant. Four hundred forty Serbs and about ten of us, Jews, departed to Israel.[16]

Noteworthy was the role of Serbian president Slobodan Milošević, named by the U.S. government for prosecution as a war criminal in the Balkan blood bath, which he helped initiate and orchestrate.[17] It was with Milošević's support and under his direction that the Serbian-Jewish Friendship Society, a lobby consisting almost entirely of Serbs, made repeated visits to Israel beginning in June, 1990. They established roughly two dozen "sister cities," linking Serbian (not Yugoslav) and Israeli culture through activities ranging from sports to commerce.[18] As the wave of Serbian emissaries to Israel grew, even Crown Prince-in-exile Alexander visited Israel to plead the case of commonality between the two cultures. During the Persian Gulf War, when Iraqi missiles landed in Israel, Mandić brought the mayors of fifteen Serbian cities to Israel in an expression of solidarity, even as the Belgrade regime continued to staunchly support and militarily supply its ally, Iraq.

In 1988, a Serbian émigré publication titled *Srbi i Jevreji* (The Serbs and the Jews) was issued in Australia, because, according to the editors' remarks, it was the right "political moment" to publish this work.[19] The principal author of *The Serbs and the Jews,* Laza Kostić, was a commissar in Milan Aćimović's Nazi-collaborationist government, a signatory to the "Appeal to the Serbian Nation," and a postwar defender of Mihailović's Chetnik movement. On his feelings toward the Jews, Kostić wrote: "I am a fanatical friend of the Jews in general and of the Serbian ones in particular."[20]

The two editors of the posthumously published book possessed equally intriguing political pedigrees. Radiša M. Nikašinović had recently printed a book titled *Literarni pabirci* (Literary Gleanings) by Laza Prokić, a prominent member of the Zbor movement, a publisher of the Serbian edition of the Nazi propaganda magazine *Signal,* and one of the principal organizers of the 1941 *Anti-Masonic Exhibition* in Belgrade.[21] The other editor, Ilija M. Pavlović, was a former officer in Nedić's Serbian Border Guard.[22]

The Serbs and the Jews typically reiterates the Serbs' historical love for the Jews, as follows:

> . . . The Serbs are one of the rare peoples in the world who have lived with the Jews in peace and . . . love throughout the whole history of their settlement in our lands. . . .

> . . . The Serbs never persecuted the Jews, never carried out any demonstrations against them. Not one anti-Semitic text has ever appeared in the press, and hatred against them was not spread orally either. . . .

... There was no more tolerant country toward the Jews. Considerably later, many other countries copied the so-called "emancipation of the Jews" from the Serbs. . . .

... Never did Nedić's government or [Aćimović's] Government of Commissars even contemplate participation in any aspect of the extermination of the Jews by the Germans. . . .[23]

The book argues, however, that the Jews had betrayed the friendship and trust extended by the Serbs. Kostić complains of the "ingratitude of the Jews toward General Nedić who was saving them and at no moment organized persecution against them."[24] Numerous instances of alleged Jewish duplicity are cited in *The Serbs and the Jews;* for example, "At the end of 1943, our government in London sent through Switzerland one million Francs to the movement of General Mihailović to whom, as it seems, money never arrived. The mediator was some former attorney called Anić from Sarajevo, who had had another name before that. He was a Jew."[25]

One section of the book discusses the 340 Jews detained along with Serbs in the Osnabrück camp for Yugoslav officers. Milan Nedić himself, it may be recalled, had written to the Germans to express his concern that the Jewish officers were contaminating the Serbian "healthy national elements" imprisoned there. In his book, however, Kostić maintains that the Osnabrück Jews' lack of support for the Serbian nationalist cause represents a betrayal of trust. Kostić quotes the recriminations of one Maj. Miodrag Đorđević, apparently himself interned at Osnabrück: "Our Jews in the Osnabrück camp, excepting thirteen of them, assisted the Partisans. Moreover, they were among the main organizers of the Partisan action in the camps. . . . When food arrived from the sad country of Serbia that suffered from famine, the Jews were not discriminated against. They received the same meals as the Serbs did. The Serbs were magnificent then as they have been on many occasions in their history. And what happened? Col. Brana Pantić informs us that after the war, out of the 300 Jewish officers imprisoned in Germany, not even one . . . joined the Serbian nationalist movements. Not a single one. . . . This hurts the Serbs a lot. . . ."[26]

It is noteworthy that Colonel Pantić—who, according to the major, reported the lack of Jewish enthusiasm for the Serbian nationalist cause—had participated directly in Draža Mihailović's negotiations with the Germans in mid-November, 1941.[27] For these allegations of Jewish betrayal, Kostić finds corroboration in a letter from one Capt. Đorđe Kostić of Toronto, a former prisoner in the Nuremberg camp: "[The imprisoned Jewish officers] had no kind word for us: Greater Serbianism, hegemony, lack of culture, imperialist demands, the suppression of the Macedonian and other peoples ... I see that you [Kostić] are preparing a book about the Jews and the Serbs. Please, do not be misled by individual good examples. Most of them were against us ... no one among the Jews was with the nationalist Serbs, while many of them were with the Partisans."[28]

In Kostić's chapter titled "The Relationship between the Serbs and the Jews after World War II," the author broadly condemns the Jews for failing to "cooperate" with the Serbs: "After World War II one had to expect the most intimate friendship, mutual respect, and closest cooperation between the two ethnic groups that have always been in good relationship and that experienced the war with similar sufferings by the same enemies. However, the events have denied those expectations. Rather than a strong rapprochement, just the opposite occurred with unpleasant if not hostile acts. . . . But we can state with pride that it was not the Serbs who demonstrated their indignation toward the Jews, but the latter toward the Serbs."[29]

Were it not for widespread Jewish ignorance of the anti-Semitism often found in Serbian nationalistic thought, the Serbian campaign for Jewish support would be unsuccessful. From the outset, however, the Serbian propaganda campaign directed at Jewish opinion, especially in Israel, has been characterized by deliberate falsification and cynical manipulation. By the summer of 1991, when Serbian-led forces under the direction of Milošević were executing their program of ethnic cleansing in Croatia, a flurry of diplomatic activity between the Belgrade regime and Israel ensued—and moved in the direction of full relations. Nevertheless, even as the Serbs have attempted to disavow the prior "errors" in Yugoslavia's stance toward Israel, the uncomfortable fact remains that these policies were largely of Serb design.

As had been the first Yugoslavia (1918–41), postwar Yugoslavia was ruled from Belgrade. To be sure, foreign policy was formulated by Yugoslavia and not "Serbia" per se, but there is little question that the decision-making machinery was firmly in the hands of the Communist Party, and that the party was primarily in Serbian hands. Several factors contributed to the reassertion of Serbian dominance in postwar Yugoslavia, but one of the most critical may have been the earlier termination of the war in Serbia.

Fully six months before the German occupation had ended in Croatia, Bosnia-Herzegovina, and Slovenia, German forces had already withdrawn from Serbia. During those six months, the Partisan movement in Serbia, which had been less than thirty thousand strong throughout most of the war, swelled by hundreds of thousands (see table 2). Since Belgrade was destined once again to become the political center of Yugoslavia, an abundant supply of new Serbian Partisans found themselves generously represented in the still newly forming Yugoslav administrative structure. However, since many of these late-joining Partisans had Chetnik roots, they tended to view the Communist Party as a vehicle for the restoration and exercise of Serbian hegemony.

Although Tito attempted to achieve a balance of power among national groups in postwar Yugoslavia, Serbian dominance remained an unquestionable fact of Yugoslav life. Through the Communist Party, Serbs exerted disproportionate control over the treasury, police, courts of law, mass media, industry, commerce, agriculture, education, trade unions, medicine, sports organizations, literature, film, and theater. Promotions in nearly all fields of endeavor were facilitated by and often restricted to party membership. Even religious organizations, officially unconnected to the Communist Party, had their party informants. Most important for the management of foreign policy, Serbs represented the dominant element in the national banking system (and, therefore, in international commerce), the diplomatic corps, and the Yugoslav military officer corps, intelligence services, and secret police.[30]

Although the Yugoslav government initially took a friendly stance toward Israel, as did Stalin's Soviet Union, for that matter, official policy progressively became hostile as the Nonaligned Movement, led by Yugoslavia, India, and Egypt, took shape. In 1955, when Prime Minister Ben-Gurion of Israel sought admission for his country to the Nonaligned Movement, Belgrade denied the request in order to strengthen ties to Arab countries.[31]

For years, the Belgrade government supported and trained PLO terrorists, when that organization was most actively committed to the total destruction and dismemberment of the state of Israel. Beginning in the early 1970s, Yugoslav youths were permitted to join Yassir Arafat's Special Operations Group and Abu-Nidal's Fatah Revolutionary Council, and many of these youths were later recruited by the Yugoslav intelligence service. In 1986, the official Yugoslav media denounced Israel as a "terrorist state," noting that "terrorism is nothing new in the activities of Israel on the international scene," since "the Jewish state itself arose in a violent way."[32] Similar accusations appeared in an official, English-language Yugoslav journal:

Israel bears a very heavy responsibility. As Israel and the Jewish lobby still exercise a dominant influence over the media of information in the Western world concealing the real consequences, the total number of Palestinian, Lebanese, Syrian and other Arab victims who have lost their lives in recent years owing to Israeli bombings, terrorist actions, reprisals and punitive expeditions is still largely unknown. Such an aggressive Israeli policy has been holding, during the past two decades, the whole of the Middle East in a state of permanent crisis and chaos ... Israel has got involved in armed operations of "state terrorism" (bombing of reactors in Iraq, airborne commando raid on Entebbe in Uganda, bombing of Tunisia, aggression in Lebanon, kidnappings, reprisals).[33]

Immediately after the murder of Leon Klinghoffer aboard the *Achille Lauro* in 1985, the terrorist responsible for the attack, Abu Abbas, was welcomed in Belgrade. From the late 1980s, Abu-Nidal maintained a large terrorist infrastructure in Yugoslavia, in coordination with Libyan, Iraqi, and Yugoslav intelligence services.[34] Moreover, since the dissolution of Yugoslavia, Belgrade has continued to cultivate relations with Israel's sworn enemies, Iraq and Libya, who in turn have staunchly backed Belgrade. During the 1991 Persian Gulf War, as Iraqi missiles landed in Israel, Belgrade supported Iraq, with whom it had an active arms sales and servicing relationship, in the same fashion that Iraq had supported Belgrade with rocket launchers, jet fighters, and oil.[35] Indeed, during the Persian Gulf War, the government of the Republic of Croatia protested to Belgrade that the Iraqi planes were flying from the military air base in Zagreb. Serbia has been instrumental in supplying chemical weapons, weapons technology, and equipment—including key components of Iraq's nuclear weapons program—for the rebuilding of Iraq's military infrastructure.

It is reasonable to presume that Serbia's anti-Israeli policy has been driven primarily by several strategic considerations: maintaining the trade of military hardware for oil from Middle Eastern countries; keeping a friendship with certain extremist Arab regimes; and preserving Yugoslavia's pivotal position within the Nonaligned Movement by supporting the policies of various anti-Western nonaligned Arab states.

However, it is precisely because Serbian propaganda consistently claims an unwavering friendship with the Jews and with Israel that Serbia's record must be scrutinized. Indeed, disturbing anti-Semitic rhetoric has resurfaced recently in mainstream Serbian institutions such as the Serbian Orthodox Church and the official news media. For instance, the January 15, 1992, issue of *Pravoslavlje* (Orthodoxy), the official publication of the Serbian Orthodox Church, carried an article titled "Jevreji ponovo raspinju Hrista" (The Jews are Crucifying Christ Again).[36] In this polemic, "treacherous" and "surreptitious" Israeli politicians are said to be constrained from openly expressing their "pathological" hatred of Christians, because "they know that Christian countries gave them the state." The article also alleged that Serbian Orthodox nuns were frequently beaten in Israel. After the intervention of the Belgrade Jewish Community, the editor in chief of *Pravoslavlje* was forced to resign, but remained a member of the editorial board.[37] The issue of *Pravoslavlje*, however, was not withdrawn from sale or circulation. When Russia extended diplomatic recognition to Croatia and Slovenia in February, 1992, the official Belgrade-based news agency, *Tanjug,* blamed "the activity of the Jewish lobby at the highest level of leadership of Russian diplomacy."[38]

From the outset of the war against Croatia and Bosnia-Herzegovina, the American and European Jewish communities were careful not to take sides, since Jews were neither the cause nor the targets of the war and taking sides could endanger one or more of the Jewish communities in Yugoslavia.[39] If anything, there was a palpable sympathy for the Serbian side, largely attributable to the belief that, during World War II, the Serbs had protected Jews, while the Croats had killed Jews.

General anti-Croatian sentiment among various Jewish organizations went so far as to dampen any outcry against the Yugoslav People's Army for its barbarous siege and destruction of the town of Vukovar over a three-month period. The event had received extensive coverage by the international media, and the transportation of Croatian civilians to "prisoner of war" camps in Serbia was observed by European Community monitors and representatives of the International Red Cross. Jewish organizations concerned themselves primarily with humanitarian relief operations and remained distinctly apolitical, until August, 1992, following the revelations of Serbian-run death camps and deportation trains in Bosnia-Herzegovina. Morally outraged, many American Jewish leaders demanded an end to Serbia's death camps and called for aid to Serbia's victims.[40] In response, newspapers and television in Belgrade condemned the Jews of the world as enemies of Serbia.[41]

Indeed, in an interview aired on National Public Radio in May of 1993, a twenty-two-year-old law student from Belgrade justified Serbia's war, using words that echo the theme of the 1941–42 *Anti-Masonic Exhibition*: "This war is . . . the last resort of white Europe, patriotic Europe, a nationalistic Europe . . . fighting against [the] Judeo-Masonic new world order, against [the] Judeo-Masonic United Nations, against the melting pots, a new world that is built by United Colors of Benetton, by example, Rockefeller World Center, and all those, you know, communo-capitalists."[42]

Ironically, in no other country has the Serbian propaganda campaign for Jewish sympathy been more successful than in Israel. Although the news of Serbian-run death camps in 1992 was first reported in tones sympathetic to the victims, Israeli moral outrage was soon blunted by an effective pro-Serbian lobby.[43] At the center of the pro-Serbian propagandist movement in Israel have been a number of columnists and commentators, some of Yugoslav-Serbian origin.[44] Following the initial reports of Serbian-run death camps, columnist and television personality Yosef "Tommy" Lapid, originally from Novi Sad in the Vojvodina province of Serbia, protested: "In Bosnia and Herzegovina no extermination camps and no proof of mass murder have been found, things which the Croats and Muslims have accused the Serbs. The Serbs have offered to turn over all prisoner camps which they have set up to U. N. supervision. It seems that another chapter in the war has been completed, in which the Serbs are the victors at the military front while their rivals are the victors at the propaganda front."[45]

Within months, several articles appeared in various Jewish publications, all similarly alleging that the Palestinian Arabs descended from Bosnians and, thus, concluding that the solution to the "Palestinian problem" is that the Palestinians return to Bosnia.[46] Factually, in 1878, when the Austro-Hungarian empire occupied Bosnia-Herzegovina, the Bosnian Muslims' apprehension of living under Christian rule stimulated a wave of emigration, and a second wave of emigration followed Austria's annexation of Bosnia-Herzegovina in 1908. These Bosnian Muslim refugees resettled in Ottoman lands. The overwhelming majority migrated to modern Turkey, while smaller numbers settled in Syria, Lebanon, Jordan, and Palestine. In 1878, some Bosnian Muslim families arrived in Caesarea (Palestine), where they built two mosques and established a colony near other Muslim colonists from Morocco, Algeria, the Crimea, the Caucasus, and Turkestan.[47] Initially speaking only their Slavic language, the Bosnians assimilated into the local Arab population. During the 1948–49 war, some Bosnian descendants left, presumably for neighboring Arab states, while some remained. Their descendants live in a number of villages in northern Israel, a heritage reflected in the Arab surnames Bushnaq and Boshnak.

Despite the questionable historical accuracy of claims that "most" Palestinians originated in Bosnia, such arguments have been recycled repeatedly in the media. When Israel decided in February, 1993, to accept 101 Bosnian Muslim refugees, protest letters flooded the press. One such letter, by Gershon Kaponi, national chairman of the Association of Yugoslav Immigrants, cited the World War II Handžar SS Division and asked: "Who can guarantee that the same 101 refugees are not children or grandchildren of those Bosnians who killed Jews 48 years ago?"[48]

Revisionism and the Holocaust

Among those propagating such ideas has been journalist Raoul Teitelbaum, also an émigré from Serbia. Writing for the daily *Yediot Aharanot* under the pen name Yisrael Tomer and appearing in public symposia and on Israeli television, Teitelbaum has staunchly defended the position of the Belgrade regime and reminded his fellow Israelis that the Jews' adversaries and Serbia's enemies were Muslims. To reinforce an association between Bosnian Muslims and Palestinian Arabs, Teitelbaum cited the SS Handžar Division, organized with the help of the notorious Grand Mufti of Jerusalem during World War II.[49] If Teitelbaum's rhetoric seemed similar to that emanating from Belgrade, then it may be significant to note that, in the spring of 1989, the official Belgrade news agency, Tanjug, had enlisted Teitelbaum as its correspondent in Israel.[50]

The notion that Serbian atrocities in Croatia and Bosnia-Herzegovina in the 1990s can be justified by Serbian grievances dating back to World War II has been critiqued eloquently by Professor Igor Primoratz of Hebrew University in Jerusalem, also an émigré from Belgrade:

> The response in Israel to the war of devastation, genocide, and "ethnic cleansing" waged by Serbia on Croatia and Bosnia-Herzegovina has, with very few exceptions, been quite different from that of both the international community and world Jewry. It has been one of understanding, sympathy, and support for Serbia and indifference to the fate of its victims, if not outright hostility to them.
>
> This is true of Israel's political establishment, of the overwhelming majority of media commentators, and of the majority of ordinary citizens with whom I have talked on the subject. Throughout, a central theme constantly recurs. I call it the World War II Argument. It goes like this:
>
> • The current war in ex-Yugoslavia must be understood as the direct continuation of what happened in Yugoslavia in World War II.
> • In those years, the Croats and Moslems were on the side of the Nazis, and helped them exterminate the Jews. The Serbs fought against the Nazis, and helped and protected the Jews.
>
> The Croats and Moslems *are* Nazis. Accordingly, they richly deserve whatever they are getting today, and there is no reason for us Jews to feel any sympathy for them. The Serbs, on the other hand, were anti-Nazis, freedom fighters and friends of the Jews. That entails a "historical obligation" on our part to understand their cause and stand by them today. . . . The argument has been used by every activist of the Serbian lobby in Israel, on practically every occasion.[51]

Although nearly all of the Yugoslav immigrants who have taken public stances on the war have defended Serbia, the Association of Yugoslav Immigrants generally has attempted to remain neutral; while deploring the violence in Croatia and Bosnia-Herzegovina, its official statements have never identified Serbia as responsible for any particular wrongdoing.

Some Jews of non-Yugoslav origin have also adopted a strongly pro-Serbian stand. The writings of Teddy Preuss, a journalist and frequent visitor to Belgrade, passionately portray the Serbs as the Jews' truest ally and defends the Serbs against their critics.[52] Preuss absolves Serbs of all responsibility for Yugoslavia's anti-Israeli posture from the 1950s to the 1990s—both under and after Tito—by attributing the control of the state machinery to a "Croatian-Slovenian mafia." However, the power in the multinational Yugoslav state, which underwent violent disintegration in the 1990s, was firmly in the hands of the dominant nation, the Serbs, notwithstanding Tito's own mixed Croatian-Slovenian parentage.[53]

Implicit in the pro-Serbian argument offered by many Israelis is the notion that Jewish survival in Yugoslavia during World War II was attributable largely to Serbian good will. Nevertheless, it remains a peculiar fact that most of the 7,578 Yugoslav Jews who emigrated to Israel between 1948 and 1952 did not originate in Serbia, but in Croatia or Bosnia-Herzegovina.[54] Indeed, 94 percent of Serbian Jewry did *not* survive the war, while those Jewish survivors of Ustasha horrors had much to remember and tell.

After the Partisan victory in Serbia—as war was still raging in neighboring Croatia and Bosnia-Herzegovina—Serbs had resumed their courtship of what remained of the devastated Jewish community in Belgrade. Serbs claimed to have been victims of Nazi atrocities alongside the Jews, and the symbol of Serbian victimization became Jasenovac. Indeed, about 50,000 Serbs, over 20,000 Croats, Muslims, and Gypsies, and nearly as many Jews had perished there.[55] Yet, Serbian losses at Jasenovac were inflated to 700,000, as the Serbian political and intellectual leadership came to recognize the political and propagandistic value derived from identifying Serbs and Jews in the post-Holocaust era.

Nevertheless, it is ironic that in Israel—the country uniquely founded on the ashes of the Holocaust—the public's moral outrage over Serbia's policy of frank genocide has been successfully blunted to the point of near nonexistence. It is further ironic that Serbia, which has a history of persecuting Jews, has courted the sympathy of Jews amid a genocidal war against non-Serbian nationalities and minorities. In portraying Jews and Serbs as comparable victims of Holocaust, Serbian propaganda has used contemporary events to insist that Jews as well as Serbs are endangered by Croats and Slavic Muslims.[56] The Serbian-Jewish Friendship Society has played a significant role in disseminating this message. Founded in Belgrade in 1987 with the support of the Serbian government, the society is headed by Klara Mandić, whose activities provide an insight into the Serbian influence on Jewish opinion.

In early 1992, Mandić released to the American Jewish press a fraudulent but chilling account of Croats murdering an elderly Jewish woman, Ankica Konjuh.[57] This provocative article, which described in detail the mutilation of the victim's body, appeared in many Jewish newspapers immediately prior to Mandić's speaking tour of the United States. Citing the incident as evidence of rising Croatian anti-Semitism, the article concluded, "Who among us will be next?" Even as she released this story to the press, however, Mandić knew that Ankica Konjuh was neither a Jew nor had she been killed by Croats. According to eyewitness testimony, Ankica Konjuh, a sixty-seven-year-old Croat, was one of 240 civilians massacred in a campaign of "ethnic cleansing" by Serbian forces after the last armed Croatian defenders were driven from the area.[58] On December 23, 1991, the Federation of Jewish Communities of Yugoslavia met in Belgrade and demanded in writing that Mandić no longer misrepresent Ankica Konjuh as the first Jewish victim of the war.[59]

Nevertheless, on February 20, 1992, when Mandić lectured at the Hillel House of George Washington University in Washington, D.C., she provided the rabbi with a copy of the misleading article without further comment. In her lecture, she began with the assertion that anti-Semitism simply has never existed in Serbia and predicted the imminent repetition of the Holocaust in Croatia. Mandić described herself as an "eyewitness" to the war, speaking on behalf of "endangered" Jews of Croatia. Since the outbreak of the war, however, she has had no contact with any of the nine Jewish communities of Croatia, nor has she had a working relationship with any official Jewish organization within any part of former Yugoslavia.[60]

Although Mandić bills herself as a "Jewish leader," Jews are conspicuously absent from her organization: approximately one half-dozen Jews were to be found among its thousands of claimed members, a fact that she has publicly acknowledged.[61] Indeed, from the inception of Mandić's organization, Jewish intellectuals in Belgrade have been wary of its propensity for manipulation by the Serbian government.[62]

Mandić's portrayal of Croatia's Jews as "endangered" has been consistently contradicted by Jewish leaders within Croatia, American Jewish visitors to Croatia, and on-site observers from the American Jewish Joint Distribution Committee. A consensus has emerged that there is no state-sponsored anti-Semitism in Croatia; the rights of the Jewish minority are respected; and anti-Semitic incidents are rare. A notable anti-Semitic attack occurred during August, 1991, within two months of the Serbian-controlled Yugoslav People's Army invasion of Croatia, when the Jewish cemetery and Jewish Community Center in the Croatian capital, Zagreb, was bombed. Within days of the bombing, Croatian civic, religious, and political leaders, as well as tens of thousands of citizens, demonstrated in the streets of Zagreb to express solidarity with the Jewish community. The Croatian government promptly assisted the Jews in repairing the damages and, furthermore, committed itself to rebuild a synagogue, destroyed during World War II, in its original location in the center of Zagreb.

As it turned out, the bombing was an attempt to turn Western opinion against Croatia, and the perpetrators were members of the Yugoslav Air Force intelligence service carrying out an operation code-named "Opera." This information was revealed during the trials that accompanied the purges of the Yugoslav Army in 1992–93. Those responsible for the bombing, however, were not found guilty of any wrongdoing by the court in Belgrade.[63] Reported in the Belgrade press, the story received no coverage from international news organs.

Nevertheless, at her George Washington University debut, Mandić cited the Zagreb bombing incident as conclusive evidence of Croatian anti-Semitism. Yet, when Mandić was asked to comment on the Serbian-dominated Yugoslav Army's shelling of the synagogue of Dubrovnik in Croatia, she emphatically denied that the attack had ever occurred. Contradicting Mandić's "eyewitness" testimony, is Mirjam Ferera, a member of the president's council of the Jewish Community of Dubrovnik and a concentration camp survivor, who described the Yugoslav Army attack and the resultant damages to the second oldest surviving synagogue in Europe.[64] In light of the contradicting testimony, Mandić's presentation leaves one with the inescapable impression that she is distinctly more concerned with Serbian public relations than with Jewish well-being. In fact, Mandić's February, 1992, speaking tour of North America was not arranged by any legitimate Jewish organization, but rather by Wise Communications, a Washington-based public relations firm representing Jugopetrol, the Serbian-controlled oil company that is a thinly veiled proxy for the Belgrade government. Mandić's public relations venture on Capitol Hill exposure was assisted also by Rep. Helen Delich Bentley of Maryland, who had been Serbia's leading advocate in the U.S. Congress.[65]

Klara Mandić's efforts at exploiting Jewish sensitivity to the Holocaust to win support for Serbia have been reflected in the activities of the California-based Jewish-Serbian Friendship Society of America, an offshoot of Mandić's organization. The society's newsletter asserts that both Jews and Serbs were victims of the Croats during World War II, and it contains accounts of Ustasha atrocities, some of which are more fiction than fact.[66] The society's selective recounting of history, however, omits any mention of the Holocaust in Serbia; Serbian genocide against Jews, Croats, Gypsies, and Slavic Muslims; and Serbian collaboration with the Nazis. The Jewish-Serbian Friendship Society professes its concern for Jewish well-being, yet has offered no protest as Jewish community centers, synagogues, and cemeteries in Croatia and Bosnia-Herzegovina have been bombed and shelled by Serbs, at times indiscriminately and at times intentionally. In 1993, when a Jewish cemetery was desecrated in Šabac—a Serbian town, which during World War II was the site of a concentration camp for Jews—the Federation of Jewish Communities of Yugoslavia, a respected and legitimate voice for Jews in Serbia, protested this act of vandalism. The Serbian-Jewish Friendship Society remained silent.

The aims of the society are derived presumably from Serbian opposition to Nazism, linking Serbs to Jews; but it has been strikingly indifferent toward the Serbian concepts of racial purity that are reminiscent of Nazi ideology. One such proponent of racial purity and *Lebensraum* for Serbs is Chetnik warlord and political leader Vojislav Šešelj. In June, 1991, weeks before the Serbian-dominated Yugoslav Army invaded Slovenia and Croatia, Šešelj boasted that his forces would not kill Croats with knives but would instead gouge out their eyes with rusty spoons, so that the victims would die of tetanus.[67] Later, in 1991, when his Chetniks drove Croatian civilians from their homes in a rampage of murder, looting, and rape, Šešelj openly declared his guiding principle: "We want no one else on our territory and we will fight for our true borders. The Croats must either move or die."[68] Šešelj is a Serb of significant influence: he heads the Serbian Radical Party, which won 27 percent of the popular vote during the elections of December, 1992—compared with Serbian president Slobodan Milošević's 40 percent—giving Šešelj the second largest block of seats in the Serbian Parliament at that time.[69]

A folk hero among Serbs, Šešelj rose to political prominence, boosted by his connection to yet another revered Serb, the Orthodox priest Momčilo Đujić. Father Đujić, it may be recalled, was a World War II Chetnik warlord, whose Nazi-assisted escape to safety at the end of the war was arranged by Dimitrije Ljotić. Indeed, after the war, Đujić described himself as a "spiritual seedling" of Ljotić.[70] It was this same Father Momčilo Đujić who, on June 28, 1989, personally promoted Šešelj to the rank of *vojvoda*, or Chetnik warlord.[71] In his instructions, Đujić ordered Šešelj "to expel all Croats, Albanians, and other foreign elements from the holy Serbian soil," promising that he would leave his refuge in the United States and return to the fatherland only if Šešelj was able "to cleanse Serbia of the last Jew, Albanian, and Croat."[72]

Another Chetnik militia, the White Eagles (a name reminiscent of the pro-Nazi Zbor youth group that went by the same name in the 1940s) under the command of Mirko Jović, has pursued a goal of Serbian racial purity, and its anti-Semitism is undisguised in its publications. In 1994, for instance, *Srpska narodna obnova* (Serbian National Renewal), the political wing of Jović's militia, issued an "informational bulletin" under the title, "The Jewish Vampire Ball." It stated, "There are not enough words to describe all their deceit, deviancy, and crimes against the holy Church of Christ, that is, the Orthodox Church and its believers," and characterized the Jews as "the sons and servants of the devil" as well as "killers, thieves, tricksters, wanderers, and vermin." The article further accused the Jews of having been responsible for inventing AIDS "in their monstrous laboratories."[73]

The Chetnik warlord Siniša Vučinić openly suggested that all Jewish depositors in the failed Belgrade Dafiment Bank should have their property confiscated, attributing to the Jews the bank's failure in 1994.[74] Vučinić typifies the close relationship between the revival of Serbian ultranationalism and anti-Semitism. As the head of *Srpski sokolovi* (Serbian Falcons) Chetnik militia, Vučinić promised to "liquidate U.N. soldiers in Belgrade," and as the founder of the "Zbor" movement, which emerged in April, 1992, he promised to take away properties from "wealthy Jews."[75]

One popular Chetnik paramilitary leader known as "Captain Dragan," whose *Knindže* (Knin ninjas) militia is notorious for rape, torture, and looting in some of the earliest "ethnic cleansing" operations in Croatia, has had connections with the Serbian-Jewish Friendship Society.[76] For nine months he lived with Klara Mandić, turning her Belgrade home into his command office.[77] Mandić became a member of the board of directors for the Captain Dragan Fund, which supports the war activities of his militia group. Captain Dragan, in turn, has been known to sport a Star of David around his neck and boast of his membership in the Serbian-Jewish Friendship Society.

Recently, Serbia has publicly rehabilitated several of its World War II–era collaborators. In 1992, a monument to the sometime Nazi collaborator Draža Mihailović was erected with great ceremony and mass attendance at

Ravna Gora, the Chetnik leader's headquarters. The *Antisemitism World Report 1993*, published by the Institute of Jewish Affairs in London, offered this description of the "attempted rehabilitation of World War II fascists" in Serbia: "In 1992, there were unofficial attempts to rehabilitate Dmitrije Ljotic, who was a theoretician of anti-Semitism and whose troops aided the Nazis in the extermination of Serbian Jewry, and Milan Nedic. . . . The Serbian Orthodox church continued to publish antisemitic books written by Bishop Nikolaj Velimirovic, who was a prominent theologian, anti-Communist and anti-Semite. In all three cases, no mention was made of the anti-Jewish sentiments of the individual concerned."[78]

The celebration of Serbian fascists and Nazi-sympathizers of the Second World War as heroes has been ongoing within the Serbian émigré community for years. Until his death in 1956, Serbian Orthodox Bishop Nikolaj Velimirović, who remained highly respected among Serbian emigrants, continued to bless Dimitrije Ljotić, Milan Nedić, and Draža Mihailović as "the three great Serbian martyrs"; and in his correspondence, the bishop noted with satisfaction that similar liturgies were held for the three men in Serbian Orthodox Churches in Chicago and London as well.[79] Like the "martyrs" he blessed, Bishop Velimirović himself remained devoted to Greater Serbia and preached the concept: "[My] children, this country you were born in is small. However, it is not your whole fatherland, but only one part of your future fatherland. It is only one floor of that building whose plan all of us carry in our minds."[80]

Indeed, the Serbian Orthodox Church has played a continuing role in the rehabilitation of World War II–era Serbian fascists. In 1994, Serbian Orthodox Patriarch Pavle, while officiating at a memorial service for Milan Nedić and Toma Maksimović (a relatively minor player in Nedić's government), justified the actions of the two men as "the only way to save the Serbian people from the revenge of the occupiers" and asked for "indulgent understanding for them, these maligned individuals."[81]

More than three decades after his death, Bishop Velimirović and his world view have remained an inspiration to Serbian emigrants. On May 31, 1992, following UN condemnation of Serbia as an aggressor, a floridly anti-Semitic sermon by Bishop Velimirović was broadcast in Serbian during the weekly Serbian Hour on Cleveland public radio (WCPN-FM). The announcer indicated that the following words were offered "in place of our commentary on events in our fatherland and the condemnation of the Serbian people as the aggressor." Velimirović's sermon follows in its entirety:

There are events in the history of the human race, which, like a great bell, ring every day in the ears of those who are not deaf and summon their conscience to alarm. One such event, which for thousands of years already has disturbed the human conscience, is the narrower choice between Jesus Christ and Varavvas, or Barabbas, as the Western heretics [Catholics and Protestants] pronounce it. It was Pontius Pilate, a Roman polytheist, who was both the president and proposer of this election, the voters were the Jews, monotheists. Pilate attempted everything in order to free Jesus, for he could find no fault in him. His final attempt was offering the Jews the choice of either Jesus or Barabbas. He reasoned logically, not one charge against Jesus was proven, whereas all the charges against Barabbas were proven and were obvious. Barabbas had earned death as a rebel and a bloodsucker. Pilate hoped that the conscience of the Jewish elders was not entirely burned out and that they would be able to rise above personal malice and wickedness and prefer a just man to a criminal. Pilate also surely thought that the choice would be for Jesus, because of the greatest holiday, on whose eve this choice was to be carried out, because, for what purpose is the great holiday, if not to cleanse and revive man's conscience? A monotheistic people—the holiday of Passover—the righteous man Jesus. Pilate believed that in a few minutes, by the liberation of the righteous man Jesus, he would please his wife Claudia, who had begged him not to spill the blood of this righteous man, and so the polytheist Pilate cried to the monotheist Jews: "Who do you want me to release to you? Barabbas or Jesus?" But to the exceeding surprise of the polytheist Pilate, the monotheistic Jews cried out with a single voice: "Barabbas! Barabbas!" Pale and confused by such a choice, Pilate asked one other question of that irrational and conscienceless Satanic rabble, polytheist to the monotheists: "What am I to do with Jesus?" To this, the monotheists began to howl like hungry jackals: "Crucify him! Crucify him!" And the polytheist Pilate washed his hands of the blood of the righteous man. And the jackals in human skin once again began to bark rabidly: "His blood is on us and on our children!"—which happened and which happens to the present day. Barabbas was set free, and the Son of God, the Messiah and Savior of the world, was driven to Golgotha and crucified on the cross. And while the greatest righteous man under the sun and above the sun expired in torment on the cross, Barabbas treated his voters [the Jews] to drinks in the beer halls of Jerusalem. This is truly the great bell, which every day disturbs the conscience of humanity. Everyone asks himself, "How could that have happened?" And we ask ourselves, "How can that also happen this very day?" For, do you not see, Brethren, that today as well, Barabbas wins elections, and Jesus loses? The cause of the gloomy tragedy of today's humanity can be explained with a single word: for they chose Barabbas in place of Christ. For they have become Barabbases, rather than being Christians. Their goals are barbarian. Their methods, too, are barbarian. Their goal is to elevate themselves and their people to the skies, and to trample all other people and peoples like mud. And their methods are the same as those of that first Barabbas: secret conspiracy, falsehood, rebellion, and blood.[82]

No further commentary followed. More recently, on February 13, 1994, the Serbian Hour broadcast another attack on the Jews. The featured guest was Ognjen Mihailović, a journalist from Serbian-occupied Bosnia-Herzegovina who is a descendant of Chetniks. After threatening that Bosnian Serbs would launch missiles against civilian targets in Italy, and after comparing former U.S. secretary of state Lawrence Eagleburger to a Nazi, Mihailović turned his attention to the Jews:

> Here, in America, watching TV, I obtained many insights. One of them will be very painful for our people when I arrive over there [Bosnia-Herzegovina]: All Jewish intellectuals are absolutely against us. I think it is their great error. When I return there I am going to inform the whole *Republika Srpska* [self-declared Serbian Republic within Bosnia-Herzegovina] about that. I assure you that I have the power to do that. I do not know whether, after that, waves of anti-Semitism would take place. It is not my problem at all. My nation should be informed that the Jews are totally against the Serbs; that this time they simply forgot all their graves and all their concentration camps in which they suffered together with Serbs. All because of, so to say, everyday politics, because of their personal attempts at negotiation with the Arabs—those are only attempts because there can be no agreement. The Arabs will not stop until they exterminate them.
>
> I think that the Serbian-Jewish friendship has been ended, once and for all. This is unfortunate for the Jews because we, the Serbs, could be a good connection with everything in the East, with all those Orthodox Christian countries where anti-Semitism has existed. Anti-Semitism has never existed among us Serbs. We might be friends of the Jews as we are friends of the Russians, from whom—we must recognize it—the Jews suffered a lot. In a way we might . . . reconcile these two nations to smooth the situation. However, that has been finished now.

These inflammatory statements, broadcast in the Serbian language, were never rebutted or questioned on the air. Indeed, the Serbian emigration, which has played a key role in supporting Belgrade's war effort through intensive lobbying abroad, has produced virtually no dissenting voices.[83] And to all of this, the Serbian-Jewish "Friendship" Society has remained conspicuously silent.[84]

Afterword

At the end of the twentieth century, a fierce war is again being fought in the Balkans. The war is driven partly by the Serbian goal of creating an ethnically homogeneous Greater Serbia—a central national aim since it was first formulated by the Serbian ideologue, Garašanin, in 1844. Historically, this objective has been accomplished through seeking the patronage of larger powers and by Serbian aggression, in which a policy of genocide has been employed to eliminate non-Serbs from coveted lands. Belgrade's emphasis on expansion has been evident since even before 1878, when Serbia gained full and formal independence from Turkish rule. Nevertheless, critical scrutiny of Serbia's record has occurred only rarely.

Serbian nationalist aims were fulfilled partially in Tito's Yugoslavia. Political power was once again centralized in Belgrade, but, in order to consolidate power, Tito had included in his Communist government some prominent Serbian pro-Nazi elements. This afforded the opportunity for many former Serbian collaborators to occupy positions of influence in postwar Serbia and bury their pro-Nazi past (see appendix A). Thus, when sociologist Dinko Tomašić observed in 1948 that the ruling Communists in Yugoslavia had successfully institutionalized a pattern of deceit, his books, although highly praised by his colleagues in the United States, were banned in Yugoslavia by Tito.[1] As the Yugoslav politician and writer Milovan Djilas would remark wryly in 1988, "The hardest thing about being a Communist is trying to predict the past."

Within postwar Yugoslavia, much of the documentation that would reveal the sequence of historical events was suppressed, while the interpretation of history was tailored to suit contemporary ideologies. Therefore, a broad antifascist movement was attributed to wartime Serbia, while denying Serbia's collaboration with the Nazis. Nazi collaboration in other parts of Yugoslavia, particularly Croatia, was emphasized and resistance minimized. This revised, pro-Serbian view of the war was disseminated abroad by a public relations network that included Yugoslav embassies and consulates, businesses, and various professional forums. Western perceptions of Yugoslav history were shaped accordingly.

In the 1990s, in order to influence Western policy makers and blunt international outrage, Serbia's information campaign has promoted its war effort as justifiable. One essential feature of Serbian propaganda has been to portray Serbia's enemies, especially the Muslims and Croats, as a threat not only to the Serbs, but to European civilization. Thus, Belgrade has claimed an "Islamic threat" in Bosnia-Herzegovina, where religious fundamentalism has never existed, and has accused Croatia of fascism, when in truth the resistance movement during the Second World War was strongest in Croatia.

An intriguing aspect of the propaganda campaign has been an attempt to equate the supposed victimization of present-day Serbs with that of the Holocaust Jews. In promoting the image of Serbian spiritual kinship with the Jews as fellow victims, Belgrade has concealed Serb willingness to collaborate with the Nazis in the extermination of Serbia's Jews. Since the late 1980s, Serbia has sought Jewish support for a war in which the policy of "ethnic cleansing" so tragically echoes Nazism.

What has been most remarkable about Belgrade's propaganda campaign has been its persistence in portraying Serbs as the defenders of Western interests and values in the region and as martyred victims in war, even as the Serbian population overwhelmingly has embraced a resurgence of fascist principles and has elected the leadership responsible for directing Serbia's calculated program of genocide. It would appear that Belgrade's image-molding has been largely effective. The Belgrade government and the rebirth of fascism that it represents have been mostly tolerated, and even supported, by Russia as well as by certain Western governments.[2]

As has been discussed, historical revisionism is an essential component of Serbia's drive toward its national goals of territorial conquest and the elimination of unwanted populations. Of course, historical revisionism concerning the totalitarian history of twentieth-century Europe is hardly new, as trends in France and Russia bear witness. For example, the former president of France, François Mitterand, whose personal résumé had emphasized only his involvement in the resistance, was ultimately compelled to admit his involvement in pro-Nazi collaboration. In the former Soviet Union, more than twenty million people were murdered by the state, although not a single political functionary has been brought to trial for these Stalinist crimes.[3] Nevertheless, with the rise of Russian ultranationalist sentiment since the late 1980s (to a large degree fostered by the Communist authorities), there has been a distinct trend toward the rehabilitation of Josef Stalin and a surge of public attacks on Masons, Jews, and other minorities.

Revisionist trends in Europe increase the probability of repeating the grievous errors of the past. Developments in Serbia are especially worrisome, for history has recorded that wars in the Balkans, where competing spheres of international influence intersect, are significant events with far-reaching consequences. The tragedy resulting from Serbia's aggression in the 1990s has been compounded by the passivity of American policy and positively abetted by the international community's appeasement of genocide and fascism—even at a time when the consequences of Neville Chamberlain's appeasement of Adolf Hitler remain a part of living memory.

A Warning Concerning the Disappearance of Documents

There is compelling evidence that some documents cited in this work, particularly primary source materials, have already been and are being systematically removed from library collections in the United States and abroad. For example, several key issues of the Serbian collaborationist newspapers *Obnova* and *Novo vreme* were missing from the Library of Congress in Washington, D.C. The missing issues of August 13, 14, and 20, 1941, contain the pro-Nazi "Appeal to the Serbian Nation" and document the public reception to the Appeal.

Materials in the greatest need of protection include the following Serbian language publications printed in Cyrillic: wartime Serbian newspapers, such as *Obnova, Naša borba,* and *Novo vreme;* wartime and prewar publications of the Serbian Orthodox Church, including *Glasnik pravoslavne crkve* (Herald of the Orthodox Church) and *Glasnik srpske pravoslavne patrijaršije* (Herald of the Serbian Orthodox Patriarchate).

More current materials which have disappeared from such collections as that of the Library of Congress include issues of the Serbian Orthodox Church's periodicals that carry its new nationalistic program of 1989 as well as issues of the Belgrade daily *Borba* from the 1980s, carrying World War II Chetnik documents of atrocities committed against the Muslim community.

Librarians are urged to protect these works by microfilming and safeguarding the originals and to be watchful for patterned disappearances.

Appendix A

SIGNATORIES TO THE APPEAL

The following is a translation of the complete list of the 545 signatories to the "Appeal to the Serbian Nation." Part of the list appeared in the Belgrade newspaper *Novo vreme* on August 13, 1941, and the rest was published the following day. Seventy-three of the signatories were recognized in postwar Yugoslavia with entries in *Mala enciklopedija Prosveta* [Prosveta's Little Encyclopedia], the Serbian equivalent of *Who's Who*. Twenty-eight became members of the prestigious Serbian Academy and Sciences during the Communist era. Twelve of the signers received high state honors from the postwar Yugoslav government for opposing fascism (an observation first noted in Vuković [1991], pp. 52–56).

An asterisk indicates the seventy-three signatories honored in postwar Yugoslavia. High state honors received are indicated in brackets.

1. Dr. Jovan, bishop of Niš
2. Nektarije, bishop of Zvornik and Tuzla
3. Valerijan, bishop of Budimlja and the vicar of His Holiness the Patriarch
4. Dr. Kosta Kumanudi, former president of the National Assembly
5. Dr. Miroslav Spalajković, retired member of the National Assembly
6. Aleksandar Cincar-Marković, former minister of Foreign Affairs
7. Josif Kostić, senator and retired army general
8. Petar V. Kosić, army general

9. Dr. Velizar Janković, retired minister
10. Dragutin Pećić, former minister
11. Aleksandar Mijović, former minister
12. Milan Aćimović, former minister
13. Dr. Svetislav Popović, former minister
14. Dušan Letica, former minister
15. Dimitrije Ljotić, former minister
16. Rista Jojić, former minister
17. Dr. Lazar Marković, former minister
18. Žika Rafajlović, former minister
19. Đura Janković, former minister
20. Spasoje Piletić, former minister
21. Panta Jovanović, former minister
22. Vojislav Đorđević, former minister
23. Vasa Jovanović, former minister
24. Dušan Pantić, former minister
25. Ugrin Joksimović, former senator
*26. Dr. Jovan Radonjić, senator and member of the Serbian Royal Academy
27. Momčilo Janković, attorney and former member of the National Assembly
28. Tasa [Tanasije] Dinić, colonel and former member of the National Assembly
29. Đura Kotur, former senator
30. Jovan Radulović, former member of the National Assembly
31. Milan Stoimirović-Jovanović, former member of the National Assembly
32. Dragomir Stojadinović, former member of the National Assembly
*33. Dr. Aleksandar Belić, president of the Serbian Royal Academy of Sciences
*34. Engineer Petar Micić, university president
35. Rusomir Janković, president of the Court of Cassation
36. Milan N. Jovičić, president of the Appellate Court
37. Dragiša Leovac, deputy president of the State Council
38. Milivoje Purić, president of the Main Control
39. Dr. Milan Radosavljević, governor of the National Bank
*40. Toma Rosandić, sculptor and president of the Academy of Fine Arts
*41. Dr. Aleksandar Jovanović, president of the Economic-Commercial School

*42. Petar Konjović, president of the Musical Academy
43. Dr. Miloslav Stojadinović, vice president of the Belgrade Municipality
44. Nikola Belović, president of the Merchants' Youth
45. Dr. Jovan Mijušković, vice president of the Chamber of Physicians
46. Vlada Ilić, president of the Chamber of Industry
47. Mihailo L. Đurić, president of the Chamber of Trade
48. Milan Stojanović, purse maker and president of the Craftsmen's Chamber
49. Engineer Dušan Glišić, president of the Engineers' Chamber
50. Ivan M. Milićević, vice president of the Belgrade Municipality
51. Boško Bogdanović, retired assistant of the minister of education
*52. Veljko Petrović, writer and member of the Serbian Royal Academy of Sciences
*53. Đoka Jovanović, sculptor and member of the Serbian Royal Academy of Sciences
54. Ranislav Avramović, retired assistant minister
*55. Dr. Laza Stanojević, university professor
*56. Dr. Svetomir Ristić, professor at the Teachers' College
57. Velibor Jonić, professor
58. Dr. Mihailo Ilić, university professor
*59. Dr. Ljubomir S. Dukanac, university professor
60. Radivoje Nikolić, retired state adviser
61. Dr. Miloš Radojković, university professor
*62. Dr. Miloš Moskovljević, professor at the Teachers' College
63. Radoje Janković, retired minister
64. Miloš Lazarević, retired minister
65. Branko Lazarević, retired minister
66. Dr. Milan Horvatski, assistant minister
67. Mirko Kosić, university professor and former member of the National Assembly
68. Nikola Stanarević, director of the Postal Savings Bank
*69. Dr. Milan Kašanin, writer and museum director ?
70. Dr. Svetislav Stefanović, writer
71. Engineer Milosav Vasiljević
72. Dr. Stevan Ivanić, assistant minister
73. Engineer Stanislav Josifović, assistant minister
74. Buda Cvijanović, assistant minister
75. Aleksa Matanović, state adviser
76. Dragiša Zdravković, state adviser

77. Dobra Petković, member of the Main Control
78. Dr. Kosta Luković, writer and journalist
79. Jovan Tanović, journalist and president of the Politika Publishing House
*80. Jovan Tomić, university professor
*81. Dr. Branko Miletić, university professor
*82. Dr. Ivan Arnovljević, university professor
83. Engineer Đorđe Mijović, university professor
84. Dr. Relja Popović, university professor
85. Vladimir-Velmar Janković, writer
86. Đorđe Perić, journalist
*87. Sima Pandurović, writer
88. Ratko Parežanin, journalist
89. Damnjan Kovačević, writer
90. Dr. Viktor Novak, university professor
91. Engineer Darko Petrović
*92. Dr. Milan Budimir, university professor [July 7 Prize]
93. Dr. Ljubiša Vulović, university professor
*94. Dr. Voja Mladenović, professor at the Teachers' College
95. Teofan Ristić, assistant professor at the Economic-Commercial School
96. Engineer Milorad Dimitrijević
97. Dušan Vasić, archpriest
98. Milorad Mihailović, archpriest
99. Božidar Prokić, judge of the Appellate Court
100. Milan Božić, judge of the Appellate Court
101. Dr. Đorđe Pešić, president of the *Jugoras* (Yugoslav Workers Trade Union)
102. Aleksa Pop Mitić, merchant
103. Rada Dimić, industrialist
104. Radomir Puljević, merchant
105. Lazar Petrović, merchant
106. Nikola Simić, merchant
107. Mihailo S. Švabić, director of the Mortgage Bank of the Merchants' Fund
108. Milivoje Kostić, exporter
109. Svet. J. Jelić, director of the Export Bank
110. Dimitrije Bogojević, director of the Merchant Bank
111. Jovan S. Obradović, director of the *Dunav* Insurance Company
112. Ilija Bogdanović, builder
113. Milutin Popović, delegate

114. Engineer Drag. Petrović
115. Engineer Jovan Milosavljević
116. Miodrag Kuzmanović, attorney
117. Franja Galijan, attorney
118. Slobodan D. Subotić, attorney
119. Engineer Drag. Savčić
120. Vlad. A. Bogdanović, president of the Union of Caterers
121. Dr. Branimir Maleš, head of the ministry of education
122. Vladimir Vujić, writer
123. Petar J. Odavić, writer
124. Svetozar Spanaćević, journalist
125. Ljubomir Aleksić, head of the ministry of education
126. Stevan Stanković, secretary of the Academy of Fine Arts
127. Siniša Kordić, writer and director of the High School
128. Milan Nedeljković, director of the School For the Applied Arts
129. Mihailo Popović, archpriest
130. Ilija M. Paranos, director of the *Diris* (organization for supplying food in Belgrade)
131. Momir Veljković, manager of the National Theater
132. Momčilo Milošević, manager of the State Printing House
133. Dr. Jovan Gašić, main secretary of the Belgrade Stock Market
134. Dr. Cvetko Gregorić, main secretary of the Union of Industrialists
135. Nikola Petrović, merchant
136. Nikola Živković, merchant
137. Atanasije Urošević, merchant
138. Marinko Grujičić, exporter
139. Petar Mladenović, director of the Clerks' Bank
140. Dr. Josip Špoljar, insurance company director
*141. Dr. Miloš Trivunac, dean and university professor
*142. Dr. Mihailo Radovanović, professor at the Teachers' College
143. Dr. Pavle Vujević, university professor
*144. Dr. Borivoje G. Milojević, university professor
145. Dr. Milan Marković, assistant university professor
146. Dr. Stanko Škerlj, university professor
*147. Dr. Vukić M. Mičević, associate university professor [July 7 Prize]
*148. Dr. Dimitrije Antić, university professor
149. Dr. M. Vidaković, university professor
150. Dr. Filip Medić, professor at the Teachers' College
*151. Dr. Slobodan Popović, university professor

152. Dr. Milan Todorović, university professor
*153. Dr. Radivoje Kašanin, university professor [July 7 Prize]
154. Dr. Dimitr. Stefanović, university professor
*155. Dr. Drag. Aranđelović, university professor
156. Dr. Vankić, professor at the Teachers' College
157. Milutin Jovanović, bank director
158. Vasa Petrović, bank director
159. Milan Divjak, industrialist
160. Đorđe Anđelković, printer
161. Dragutin Urošević, merchant
162. R. Jovanović, exporter
163. Ljubomir Saračević, exporter
164. M. Krsmanović, archpriest
165. Dr. Branislav Krstić, director of the Female Teachers' Academy
166. Engineer Andra Popović
167. Engineer A. Petrović
168. Sergije Baltić, private office worker
169. Dr. Dušan Uzelac, director of the National Bank
*170. Dr. Miloje Stoiljković, university professor
171. Dr. Đoka Slijepčević, assistant university professor
172. Dr. Jovan Đorđević, university professor
173. Stevan Jovanović, head of the ministry of education
174. Panta Aranđelović, head of the *Ban* administration (governor of the Banovina)
*175. Dr. Jovan Erdeljanović, university professor
*176. Dr. Milutin Milanković, university professor and member of the Serbian Royal Academy
*177. Dr. Toma Živanović, university professor
178. Dr. Đorđe Tasić, university professor
*179. Dr. Miodrag Ibrovac, university professor [July 7 Prize]
180. Đurđe Stojanović, private office worker
181. Nikola B. Jovanović, secretary-general of the Association of Actors
*182. Vladeta Dragutinović, member of the National Theater
183. Engineer Dušan Đorđević, opera singer
*184. Nikola Cvejić, opera singer
185. Dr. Adam Bogosavljević, senior adviser of the ministry of education
186. Mihailo Vončina, merchant
187. Stevan Škorić, president of the Association of Dairy Salesmen
188. Jezdimir Milosavljević, merchant

189. Dušan Lazić, merchant
190. Rista Rakočević, school superintendent
191. Todor Dimitrijević, school manager
192. Miodrag Janković, school manager
193. Vladan S. Lapčević, school manager
194. Dragan Dodoš, merchant
195. Aleksandar Bogojević, bank director
196. Dimitrije Milosavljević, merchant
197. Dr. Velimir Mihailović, manager of the State's General Hospital
198. Dr. Nikodije Blagojević, ward chief of the State's General Hospital
199. Dr. Miodrag Marković, physician
200. Engineer Svetozar Matijašević
201. Engineer Nikola Lalić
202. Engineer Vasa Todorović
203. Dr. Miodrag Vračević, physician
204. Dr. Žika Marković, physician
205. Dr. Vlastimir Ivković, physician
206. Dr. Milica Mićić-Ivanić, physician
207. Dr. Sima Ilić, physician
*208. Dr. Milan Vlainac, university professor
209. Dr. Nikola M. Popović, university professor
*210. Dr. Vojislav Mišković, university professor
211. Dr. Sava Janković, *Privatni Docent* (distinguished graduate recognized as teacher at a university)
212. Miodrag M. Matić, manager of the main telegraph
213. Nikola Radovanović, deputy director of the post office, telegraph, and telephone
214. Velja Pavlović, inspector
215. Čeda Radojković, vice governor of the National Bank
216. Slavko Teokarović, industrialist
217. Milan Janošević, merchant
218. Branislav Janošević, merchant
219. Luka Soldatović, merchant
220. Drag. A. Štula, industrialist
221. Branko Stojanović, merchant
222. Milo Seferović, senior adviser
223. Engineer Petronije Jokić, adviser
224. Dr. Ž. Miladinović, senior adviser
*225. Dr. Lazar Mirković, university professor
*226. Dr. Borivoje Ž. Milojević, university professor

227. Dr. Ljubomir Bajalović, professor at the Economic-Commercial School
228. Engineer Dragomir Jovanović, university professor
*229. Dr. Ivan Đaja, university professor
230. Dr. Ilija Pržić, university professor
*231. Dr. Dušan Popović, university professor
*232. Dr. Milosav Lutovac, professor at the Economic-Commercial School
233. Dr. Mil. V. Jović, professor at the Economic-Commercial School
234. Dr. Simeon Gaćeša, professor at the Economic-Commercial School
235. Dr. Fehim Barjaktarović, university professor
236. Dr. Jovan Lovčević, university professor
*237. Dr. Dušan Glumac, university professor
238. Svetislav Petrović, professor at the Teachers' College
*239. Dr. Branislav Stanojević, university professor
*240. Dr. Milan Fotić, university professor
241. Dr. Vladimir R. Petrović, professor
*242. Dr. Miloje M. Milojević, professor at the Musical Academy
243. Dr. Radoslav Brašovan, university professor
*244. Dr. Dušan Borić, university professor
245. Dr. Gojko Ružić, university professor
246. Dr. Milan Vladisavljević, university professor
247. Dr. Jovan J. Tucaković, university professor
*248. Dr. Branislav Šljivić, university professor
249. Božidar Stojković, professor at the Teachers' College
*250. Dr. Ilija Đuričić, university professor
*251. Dr. Radoslav Grujić, university professor
*252. Dr. Rastislav Marić, university professor
253. Dušan Milojković, ministry chief
254. Stanoje Protić, member of the main control
255. Vlad. Bublik, insurance bank director
256. Spasoje Spasojević, merchant
257. Živko Šajnović, merchant
258. Jovan Kostić, senior inspector of the National Bank
259. Anton Vošić, merchant
260. Petar Mladenović, merchant
261. Bor. Janković, member of the Maričić & Janković firm
262. Mil. Stekić, member of the Todor Mraović firm
263. Andra Žeželj, inspector

264. Branko Radulović, ministry adviser
265. Vasa Jovanović, vice president of the Industry Chamber
266. Boža M. Vićentijević, attorney
267. Dr. St. Nižetić, physician
268. Dr. Bora Popović, physician
269. Dr. Dobrivoje Maksimović, physician, ward chief of the State's general hospital
270. Sveta Jovanović, post office manager
271. Ilija P. Zarzević, post office manager
*272. Dr. Miloš Radojčić, associate professor at the university
*273. Engineer Đorđe Dimitrijević, associate professor at the university
274. Dr. Nikola Konstantinović, professor at the School of Economy and Commerce
275. Dr. Laza Kostić, professor at the School of Economy and Commerce
276. Borivoje Josimović, school supervisor
277. Todor Lilić, professor
278. Dimitrije Popović, high school director
279. Nikola Popović, professor
280. Spasoje Prica, high school director
281. Nikola Kuzelj, professor
282. Živojin Đorđević, high school director
283. Darinka Stojanović, high school director
*284. Engineer Branislav Kojić, associate professor at the university [July 7 Prize]
285. Dr. Rista Pesarić, associate professor at the university
286. Engineer Miloš Martić, associate professor at the university
287. Panta Šobajić, high school director
288. D. L. Spasić, insurance company director
289. Miloš Petrović, merchant
290. T. Tutunović, merchant
291. Radoslav Pavlović, teacher
292. Dušan S. Tomić, associate professor at the university
293. Stevan Stevanović, associate professor at the university
294. Sima Milutinović, engineer
295. Aleksandar B. Damjanović, associate professor at the university
296. Jordan Petrović, engineer
297. Dušan J. Vitas, engineer
298. Dr. Miloš Misirlić, physician
*299. Dr. Vladimir Čavka, physician [AVNOJ Prize]

300. Dr. M. Jovčić, physician and head of the department
301. Dr. Cupara Stevanović, assistant professor
302. Jovan Popović, engineer
303. Laza Safkov, engineer
304. Dr. Stevan Vasojević, physician
305. Dr. Milovan Bakić, physician
306. Dr. Petar Martinović, physician
307. Velislav Tomašević, engineer
308. Milutin Maksimović, engineer
309. Pavle Đorđević, engineer
310. Dr. Jovanka Magovčević, physician
311. Dr. Pavle Tucaković, physician
312. Dr. Pavle Radosavljević, physician
313. Dr. Dušan Gregorić, physician
314. Dušan Kostić, engineer
315. Jelena Đorić, engineer
316. Bogdan Lalković, engineer
*317. Stevan Hristić, professor at the Musical Academy
*318. K. Manojlović, professor at the Musical Academy
319. Engineer Simeon Korečki, assistant professor at the university
320. Radivoje Gajić, school supervisor
321. Bogdan Potkonjak, school director
322. Darinka Mitranović, high school director
323. Kosta Nikolić, high school director
324. Katarina Jovičić, high school director
325. Miomir Sikobad, high school director
326. Pavle Vujić, law student
327. Mladen Vuković, law student
328. Momčilo Knežević, student of veterinary medicine
329. Milan Vesović, engineering candidate
330. Vekoslav Mandić, student
331. Mijo Pušić, worker
332. Ljubomir Maksimović, graphic worker
333. Ljubomir Milenković, machine worker
334. M. Kolarić, merchant
335. Ranko Stanovjević, merchant
336. Milan Mojić, merchant
337. Vasa Vasiljević, merchant
338. Dragutin Miličević, merchant
339. Mil. S. Milošević, teacher
340. Drag. Milanović, school director

341. Rastimir Jevčević, teacher
342. Srbisav Petrović, teacher
343. Stevan Petrović, teacher
344. Dragan Grbić, school director
345. Vlad. Piščević, law student
346. Dušan Bukovajac, student
347. Žarko Čakić, law student
348. Miladin Jevtić, mechanic
349. Milorad Đurišić, worker
350. Milan M. Mikić, graphics worker
351. Jevta P. Kolaković, worker
352. Dušan Ćirić, shoemaker
353. B. Tadić, merchant
354. D. Marković, teacher
355. Drag. Mitrović, teacher
356. Milan Popović, musician
357. Franja Požarković, private employee
358. Branko Divjak, worker
359. Dragan Dodoš, worker
360. Dr. Pavle Vulasović, physician
361. Dr. Sava Šaulić, physician
362. Dr. Bojan Pirc, physician
363. Dr. Vladimir Korostovec, physician
364. Predrag Anić, teacher
365. Milan Šalinac, school director
366. Drag. Đorđevic, school director
367. Aleksandar Popović, teacher
368. Tihomir Jevtić, teacher
369. Đorđe P. Jelačić, school director
370. Čeda Vuković, merchant
371. M. Radivojević, merchant
372. Dr. Nadežda Stanojević, physician
373. Dr. Milorad Čortanović, physician
374. Vitomir Milenković, post office director
375. Dušan Brkić, merchant
376. Marko Lazarević, merchant
377. Živadin S. Bogdanović, civil servant
378. Dr. Vlad. Piletić, head of the medical department
379. Cvetko Cvetković, senior adviser
380. Dr. Nikola Belosavić, physician
381. Dr. St. Novaković, physician, head of department

382. Ratomir Miličević, economist
383. Ljuba Marković, merchant
384. Čedomir Nešković, worker
385. Vasa Mučibabić, worker
386. Vojislav Jelenković, worker
387. Toša Anđelković, worker
388. Aleksandar Nikolajević, worker
389. Milorad Vujičić, worker
390. Ljubomir Šmeglić, worker
391. Mile Jovanović, merchant
392. Pavle Žarić, merchant
393. Petar Berisavljević, engineer
394. Đura Ilkić, entrepreneur
395. Mića Dimitrijević, journalist
396. Toša Miletić, merchant
397. Branko Karanović, industrialist
398. Milan Kremanac, lawyer
399. Dragiša Stefanović, industrialist
400. Dušan Đurić, retired naval officer
401. Aleksandar Damjanović, engineer
402. Dr. Dimitrije Gostimirović, physician
403. O. Roš, economist
404. Milivoje Dimitrijević, restorer
405. Jovan Petrović, merchant
406. Sava Đurašinović, printer
407. Vera Matić, jeweler
408. V. Polić, merchant
409. Sava Sarić, merchant
410. R. D. Todorović, merchant
411. S. B. Cvijanović, bookseller
412. Anton Grubor, bookbinder
413. Jovan Živadinović, bookseller
414. Ilija Mihajlović, former president of the National Assembly
415. Srećko S. Tešić, retired president of the Main Control
416. Dr. Milutin Jovanović, former member of the National Assembly
417. M. M. Vujović, engineer
*418. Dr. Stevan Marković, university professor emeritus
419. Milivoje S. Jevremović, pharmacist
420. Đorđe Terzić, attorney
421. Spasoje Tajsić, pharmacist

422. Boža M. Savić, industrialist
*423. Dr. Čedomir P. Simić, university professor [AVNOJ Prize]
424. Pavle M. Vasić, engineer
425. Dragoljub R. Petrović, director
*426. Dr. Gojko Grđić, assistant professor at the Economic-
     Commercial School
*427. Nikola Najdanović, engineer
428. Nenad Lancoš, engineer
429. Milutin Božić, ministry adviser
430. Dr. Ž. Miletić, assistant of minister
431. Dr. Stojan Dedić, assistant university professor
*432. Nikola Banašević, university professor
*433. Engineer Bogić Knežević, university professor [July 7 Prize]
*434. Živojin Đorđević, university professor
435. Dr. Branislav Demetrović, assistant professor at the Economic-
     Commercial School
436. Živojin Piperski, architect
*437. Milo Milunović, painter
*438. Ilija Kolarović, associate professor at the Academy of Fine Arts
     [July 7 Prize]
*439. Mihailo S. Petrović-Petrov, painter [July 7 Prize]
*440. Nedeljko Gvozdenović, associate professor at the Academy of
     Fine Arts [July 7 Prize]
441. Omer Kajmaković, former member of the National Assembly
442. Milorad D. Mojić, journalist
443. Dragutin D. Moderčin, attorney
444. Dr. Velimir Ž. Danilović, physician
445. Aleksandar Nedeljković, attorney
446. Milutin Vidović, attorney
447. Aleksandar Đuričić, druggist, M.A. in pharmacy
448. Branko Nedeljković, engineer
449. Milovan Đ. Popović, journalist
450. Aleksandar M. Lazarević, attorney and former member of the
     National Assembly
*451. Dr. Vladimir Vujić, university professor
*452. Dr. Aleksandar Radosavljević, university professor
453. Dr. Milorad Milošević, university professor
454. Bora Đorić, attorney
455. Slobodan Dobrosavljević, engineer
*456. Dr. Jovan Dimić, associate university professor
457. Dr. Milan Zelić, physician

458. Dr. Milorad Pavlović, physician
459. Mihailo S. Đorđević, renter
460. Ljubomir Milušević, furrier
*461. Ivan Tabaković, professor [AVNOJ and July 7 Prize]
*462. Mihailo Tomić, professor
463. Milorad Mihailović, secretary of the School For the Applied Arts
464. Svet. M. Lazarević, engineer
465. Slobodan V. Petrović, engineer
466. Dr. Milivoj Čokorda, assistant university professor
467. Đuro Filipović, assistant university professor
468. Kosta Trajković, attorney
469. Spiro Š. Narandžić, journalist
470. Stanko C. Blažić, merchant
471. Bor. Karapandžić, teacher
472. Zvonimir Jakovljević, typographer
473. Dr. Kostić Marinković, physician
474. Dušan Đorđević, craftsman
475. Miroslav Zeleni, artisan
476. Radivoje Ljubinković, high school teacher
477. Milivoje Stanković, theology student
478. Ilija M. Dinić, merchant
479. Pavle Gregorić, industrialist
480. Dušan Ninković, attorney
481. Dušan L. Marković, attorney
*482. Milenko Šerban, teacher
*483. Svetolik Lukić, teacher
484. Ljubomir N. Radović, bookseller
485. Milivoje Pandurović, renter
486. Nasuf Gačović, high school teacher
487. Ljubiša Mirčić, medical school student
488. Žarko Živković, private office worker
489. Milutin Podboj, theologian
490. M. Radosavljević, surveyor
491. Đ. M. Petrović, architect
492. Ljubomir Todorović, engineer
493. Vlad. Todorović, engineer
494. Jordana Siprić, philosophy student
495. Milovan Kostić, graduate philosopher
496. Momčilo T. Novković, law student
497. Olga Aksentijević, philosophy student

498. Nebojša M. Mandić, law student
499. Čedomir Ninković, butcher
500. Vera Mandić, schoolgirl
501. Drag. S. Tomić, theology student
502. Branislav B. Kostić, technology student
503. Boris Bavdek, typographer
504. Dragoljub Hmeljak, worker
505. Vojislav Savkić, worker
506. Luka Dabić, merchant
507. Mihailo Đurović, merchant
508. Vujica Radosavljević, merchant
509. Kuzmanović and Perić, merchants
510. Dragoljub Jevtić, merchant
511. Dragomir Radivojević, quilt maker
512. Radomir Pantelić, merchant
513. Vasa Popović, tailor
514. Stanko Brakulić, merchant
515. Mihailo Milivojević, mechanic
516. T. Siljanović, coffee bar owner
517. Vlada Vrbaški, merchant
518. Ilija A. Brocan, storekeeper
519. Jela Vasiljevića, coffee bar owner
520. Leontije Ivanović, butcher
521. Bezisten Petković, butcher
522. Marko Stojšić, flower seller
523. Uroš Jakovljević, sausage maker
524. Sava Ružić, fruit vendor
525. Dobrosav Ristić, fruit vendor
526. Andra Andrejević, butcher
527. Vladimir M. Jovanović, butcher
528. Lazar Đ. Radojčić, fruit vendor
529. Dušan Radovanović, sausage maker
530. Dragomir Dimitrijević, fruit vendor
531. Jordan Jovanović, fruit vendor
532. Ljubomir Zdravković, fruit vendor
533. Kosta Stefanović, fruit vendor
534. M. Antonović, merchant
535. Mika Bračinac, butcher
536. Radovan M. Aćimović, fruit vendor
537. Krsta V. Krstić, merchant
538. Nikola Stefanović, fruit vendor

539. Jovan Stefanović, coffee bar owner
540. Pera Skrobonja, worker
541. Slobodan Stojanović, worker
542. Mihailo N. Lazarević, mechanic
543. V. Kredlić, manager
544. Dragan Simić, surveyor
545. Miodrag M. Gosić, bookkeeper, etc.

Appendix B

MEMBERS OF COLLABORATIONIST GOVERNMENTS

Aćimović's Government of Commissars, April 30, 1941

Commissar	Commissariat	Prior Position(s)
Milan Aćimović*	president, interior	minister of the interior
Momčilo Janković	justice	member, National Assembly
Dušan Letica	finance	minister of finance
Laza Kostić	transportation	university professor
Dušan Pantić	post office	minister
Jeremija Protić	food and agriculture	assistant minister of finance
Risto Jojić	education	minister; professor
Milosav Vasiljević*	national economy	director of the Belgrade Fair
Stevan Ivanić*	social policy/health	chief in ministry of health
Stanislav Josifović	construction	assistant minister of construction

*Nazi agent prior to the German occupation

SOURCES: N.A., microcopy T-120, roll 200, frame 153198; Borković (1979), pp. 33–34; Stefanović (1984), p. 116; Milovanović (1978), vol. 2, p. 27.

Aćimović's Government of Commissars, Restructured July 10, 1941

Commissar	Commissariat	Deputy Commissar(s)
Milan Aćimović	president, interior	Tanasije Dinić Đorđe Perić
Momčilo Janković	justice	Đuro Kotur
Dušan Letica	finance	Milan Horvatski
Ranislav Avramović	transportation	Nikola Đurić
Dušan Pantić	post office	Milorad Dimitrijević
Budimir Cvijanović	food and agriculture	
Velibor Jonić	education	Vladimir-Velmar Janković
Milosav Vasiljević	national economy	Dr. Mihailović
Stevan Ivanić	social policy/health	Božidar Darko Petrović
Stanislav Josifović	construction	

SOURCES: N.A., microcopy T-200, roll 120, frame 134265 (Turner's report to the commander of the southeast); "Rekonstrukcija Saveta Komesara" [The reconstruction of the Council of Commissars], *Novo vreme*, July 11, 1941, p. 1; Borković (1979), p. 67.

Nedić's Government of National Salvation, August 29, 1941

Milan Đ. Nedić	president
Miloš Masalović	chief of the president's cabinet
Milan Aćimović	interior
Čedomir Marjanović	justice
Ljubiša Mikić	finance
Josif Kostić	transportation; post office
Miloš Radosavljević	agriculture and food
Miloš Trivunac	education
Mihailo Olćan	national economy
Jovan Mijušković	social policy and national health
Ognjen Kuzmanović	construction

| Panta M. Draškić | labor |
| Momčilo Janković | minister without portfolio |

SOURCES: N.A., Microcopy T-120, roll 200, frames 153–98; Borković (1979), pp. 105, 146; Stefanović (1984), p. 137.

Nedić's Government of National Salvation, November 7, 1942

Milan Nedić	president
Tanasije Dinić	interior
Bogoljub Kujundžić	justice
Dušan Letica	finance
Đura Dokić	transportation
Josif Kostić	post office
Radosav Veselinović	agriculture and food
Velibor Jonić	education
Milorad Nedeljković	national economy
Stojimir Dobrosavljević	social policy and national health
Ognjen Kuzmanović	construction

SOURCE: Borković (1979), pp. 380–88.

Committee of State Administration for Serbia, October 10, 1944

Ivan Petković	president
Aleksandar Pekezović	interior affairs
Aleksandar Pelivanović	justice
Milan Horvatski	finance
Milan Jojić	transportation
Josif Štok	post office
Buda Cvijanović	agriculture
Dušan Milojković	education
Milutin Bošković	national economy
Aleksandar Đorđević	social policy
Nenad Lancoš	construction

SOURCE: AMHI, Nedić Archive, document 1/21, box 50, the order of General Felber, as cited in Borković (1979a), p. 350.

Ante Pavelić	chief of state
	chief of Ustasha movement
	prime minister
	foreign affairs
Slavko Kvaternik	commander of armed forces
Andrija Artuković	interior
	head of Ustasha Control Office
Mirko Puk	justice
Lovro Sušić	national economy
Ivica Frković	forests and mines
Mile Budak	religion and education
Jozo Dumandžić	corporations
Ivan Petrić	public health
Osman Kulenović	vice president
Milovan Žanić	president of the Legislative Council

SOURCES: Hory and Broszat (1964), pp. 75–92; Hilberg (1985), pp. 708–09; Krizman (1978), p. 27; Jelić-Butić (1977), pp. 104, 199; Novak (1948), p. 547; Colić (1973), pp. 58, 93, 103.

Glavni Ustaški Stan (Main Ustasha Headquarters), March, 1941

Council of the deputy chiefs of state

Andrija Betlehem
Mile Budak
Marko Došen, president
Slavko Kvaternik
Luka Lešić
Stjepan Matijević
Ademaga Mešić

Corps of adjutants

Mijo Bzik
Ivan Javor
Blaž Lorković
Ivan Oršanić
Alija Šuljak, chief

Commissioners

Zdenko Blažeković
Božo Cerovski*
Danijel Crljen
Mira Dugački-Vrličak
Drago Dujmović
Tomislav Grčinić
Vlado Herceg
Mato Jagodić
Vlado Jonić
Šime Cvitanović
Nikola Jurišić
Eugen Kvaternik*
Franjo Laslo
Vjekoslav (Maks) Luburić*
Frane Miletić
Vilko Pečnikar*
Grga Pejnović
Ivan Pregrad
Branko Rukavina*
Aleksandar Seitz
Vlado Singer*
Marijan Šimić
Ante Štitić

*Indicates the police authorities directly responsible to Pavelić for
executing measures against the Jews and the Serbs.

SOURCES: Colić (1973), pp. 95ff; Jelić-Butić (1977), pp. 109, 179.

Notes

ABBREVIATIONS

AMHI   Archives of the Military-Historical Institute,
          Belgrade
N.A.   National Archives, Washington, D.C.

FOREWORD

1. A point documented in S. Meštrović et al. (1993).
2. See Cigar (1995).

CHAPTER 1: THE ROOTS OF SERBIAN FASCISM

1. Petrovich (1976), pp. 230–35; Banac (1984), pp. 82–84; Hehn (1975), pp. 153–71.

2. "Načertanije" first appeared in unabridged published form in: M. Vučković, *Program spoljne politike Ilije Garašanina na koncu 1844 godine* (Foreign Policy Program of Ilija Garašanin at the End of 1844), *Delo* (Work), Belgrade, vol. 38, 1906, pp. 321–36. For the full Serbian text, see Garašanin (1991), pp. 65–77. For English translations, see Garašanin (1993), pp. 68–82; Hehn (1975), pp. 153–71.

3. Hehn (1975), p. 158.

4. Ibid., pp. 168–69.

5. Stojanović (1991), pp. 99–105; for an English translation, see Stojaović (1993), pp. 105–13. This article was first published in Belgrade in August, 1902, and subsequently appeared in Zagreb in *Srbobran* [Protector of Serbs], Zagreb, no. 168–69, 1902. Notably, the contention that Croats had taken Serbian as their literary language is false. The "father" of the

modern Serbian language, Vuk Karadžić, had introduced two Croatian dialects (that of Herzegovina and Dubrovnik) into Serbian in the nineteenth century, at which time Karadžić's Serbian critics protested that "this person is imposing the Croatian language on us." See Karadžić (1965), p. 140.

6. Čović (1993), pp. 28–29.

7. C. Jelavich (1983) analyzed over 150 Serbian elementary and secondary school textbooks in geography, history, and literature, between 1878 (the independence of the Serbian state) and 1914 (the onset of World War I). All lands that would ultimately become Yugoslavia (except Slovenia) were identified as traditionally Serbian lands inhabited by Serbs. Interestingly, Slovenes, Hungarians, Albanians, Bulgarians, and others were routinely identified as such, but the Croats as a people were rarely if ever mentioned to exist.

8. Čubrilović (1991), pp. 113–14; for an English translation, see Čubrilović (1993), pp. 121–23. Čubrilović originally presented "The Expulsion of the Albanians" as a lecture to the Serbian Cultural Club on March 7, 1937, and subsequently as a memorandum to the Yugoslav government. The original document is in AMHI, Arch. of the Royal Yugoslav Army, 2/4, box 69.

9. Čubrilović (1991), pp. 115–16; for an English translation, see Čubrilović (1993), pp. 124–25.

10. For an eyewitness account of Chetnik atrocities committed during the Balkan Wars of 1912–13, see Trotsky (1980), pp. 120–21, 266–68, 275–76. He reported that a Serbian eyewitness to the Balkan War in Macedonia described entire Albanian villages turned into "pillars of fire," Chetnik campaigns of plunder and murder against Turkish and Albanian civilians, and the sight of Albanian corpses with severed heads, piled under the main bridge over the Vardar River in the center of Skopje, the Macedonian capital. "What was clear was that these headless men had not been killed in battle" (pp. 266–68).

11. Stokes (1990), p. 166.

12. Balić (1993), p. 79. Of the 217 mosques that stood in Belgrade during the seventeenth century, only the modest Bajrakli mosque on Gospodar Jevrem Street remains standing today. For the Ottoman heritage in Serbia, see also Kinross (1977).

13. Durham (1914), p. 271. For an account of Serbia's political goals and campaign of genocide (primarily against Muslims) during the Balkan Wars, see Kennan (1993), pp. 38–39.

14. Tucović (1914), pp. 107–108.

15. Durham (1914), pp. 236–39.

16. Ibid., pp. 298–99.

17. Banac (1984), pp. 149–50, 367; Djilas (1958), pp. 203–209.

18. Bilandžić (1985), p. 19; Brown (1992), p. 61; Rothschild (1974), pp. 278–79.

19. Rothschild (1974), pp. 278–79.

20. Browning (1985), p. 41.

21. Banac (1984), p. 151; Bilandžić (1985), p. 19; Rothschild (1974), pp. 278–79.

22. Banac (1984), p. 148, esp. n. 22, which cites Ferdo Čulinović, *Jugoslavija izmedju dva rata*, vol. 1 (Zagreb, 1961), pp. 178–80.

23. The institution of corporal punishment for civil offenses was especially appalling to the Croatian peasantry, since it had been abolished by the Croatian *Sabor* (Parliament) nearly half a century earlier, in 1869. See Banac (1984), p. 148.

24. Ibid.

25. Milan Rojc, "Prilike u Hrvatskoj," *Nova Evropa* 2 (1921), no. 2, p. 57, cited in Banac (1984), p. 148 n. 20.

26. Hoffman and Neal (1962), pp. 59–60; Denitch (1976), pp. 105–107; Bilandžić (1985), p. 19. "Einstein Accuses Yugoslavian Rulers in Savant's Murder. Charges the Slaying of Sufflay, Noted Croatian Leader, Was Inspired by Government. Links King to Terrorism," *The New York Times*, May 6, 1931, p. A1.

27. Tomasevich (1975), p. 9; Maček (1957), pp. 109–12.

28. B. Jelavich (1983), vol. 1, pp. 156–57, 200–202; Hoffman and Neal (1962), pp. 59–60.

29. Pozzi (1935), pp. 21, 23.

30. Jovanović (1928); also cited in Krleža (1990), pp. 619–20.

31. I. Meštrović (1993), p. 193.

32. "Einstein Accuses Yugoslavian Rulers," *The New York Times*, May 6, 1931, p. A1; Almond (1994), p. 200; Banac (1984), p. 269.

33. Pozzi (1935), p. 184.

34. Ibid., pp. 180–81.

35. Ibid., pp. 140, 180, 187–90.

36. Ibid., p. 141.

37. For an outline of the rise of fascism in Royal Yugoslavia, see the following: Stefanović (1984), pp. 11–16; "Srpski nacizam" [Serbian Nazism], in Konstantinović (1981), pp. 366–97; Gligorijević (1965), pp. 35–83; Kuljić (1974), pp. 240ff.

38. According to Ratko Parežanin, an early Zbor ideologist, the acronym *Zbor* (which translates to "rally") stood for the key concepts of their program: Zadružna borbena organizacija rada (the Cooperative Militant Organization of Labor). See Parežanin (1971), p. 33.

39. Parežanin (1971), pp. 43–44. Arch. of Bosnia-Herzegovina, Sarajevo, the State Security of the Royal *Ban* Administration, report of the Police Department in Sarajevo regarding singing the Zbor hymn, "Vojska smene" (Army of Change), June 27, 1938, confidential DZ no. 791, cited in Stefanović (1984), p. 28; AMHI, register 17, box 60, file 7, doc. 10, cited in Gligorijević (1965), p. 58, see also p. 59; Politisches Archiv des Auswärtigen Amtes [the Political Arch. of the Foreign Office], Bonn, the German embassy in Belgrade, vol. 4, report of von Heeren, December 20, 1934.

40. For more on Yugoslav Action's call for totalitarianism and elections within the movement, see Gligorijević (1965), p. 36. See also AMHI, Chetnik arch., doc. 17, file 3, box 269, interrogation of Velibor Jonić, cited in Stefanović (1984), pp. 12–13.

41. Gligorijević (1965), pp. 59–63; Parežanin (1971), p. 47. The Union of Militants was led by Vlatko Fabijančič and Engineer Avgust Kuster.

42. Ljotić (1952), pp. 125–26.

43. Parežanin (1971), pp. 27, 42–44; Gligorijević (1965), p. 63; Stefanović (1984), pp. 15–16.

44. Ljotić (1952), pp. 8–9; Ljotić (1976), p. 112.

45. Ljotić (1952), pp. 9, 12; Ljotić (1961), p. 51; Ljotić (1976), pp. 111–12.

46. Ljotić (1952), pp. 36, 41, 43.

47. Ibid., p. 17.

48. Krakov (1963), pp. 54–55. See also Ljotić (1952), p. 56.

49. Ivanović (1954), p. 14; Stefanović (1984), p. 20.

50. Ljotić (1952), pp. 99, 101.

51. Ibid., pp. 115–16.

52. The first issue of *Otadžbina* was February, 1934; *Buđenje* began on July 22, 1934; *Zbor* began on August 25, 1934. See Gligorijević (1965), p. 67.

53. Gligorijević (1965), p. 67. See also Arch. of Vojvodina, Sremski Karlovci, Koblentz, NS–10–223, German report of the events in Yugoslavia in 1934, cited in Stefanović (1984), p. 24.

54. Parežanin (1971), pp. 51, 54–58, 63; Martinović-Bajica (1956), p. 344; Ljotić (1952), pp. 125–26; Ljotić (1990), p. 427; Popov (1993), p. 10. Also, AMHI, Chetnik arch., doc. 17, file 3, box 269, interrogation of Velibor Jonić, cited in Stefanović (1984), p. 24.

55. Parežanin (1971), p. 63; Ljotić (1952), pp. 125–27. See also Ljotić (1990), p. 12; "Osnovna načela" [Basic Principles], *Zbor*, no. 5, December 12, 1934, pp. 1–6; Ljotić (1952), p. 125; Ljotić (1990), p. 250.

56. See AMHI, 17, doc. 1/3, box 95A, history of the emergence of the

Association of Fighters of Yugoslavia, cited in Stefanović (1984), p. 27. See AMHI, 17, doc. 60, 7, box 22, a record from the session of the Central Committee of the Yugoslav Action, February 17, 1935; *Otadžbina,* no. 53, March 10, 1935, p. 3, cited in Stefanović (1984), p. 26.

57. Politische Archiv des Auswärtigen Amtes [the Political Arch. of the Foreign Office], Bonn, Deutsche Gesandtschaft Belgrad [the German Embassy in Belgrade], vol. 4, the report of von Heeren, December 20, 1934, cited in Stefanović (1984), pp. 27–28.

58. N. A., microcopy T–501, roll 249, frame 60.

59. Odić and Komarica (1977), pp. 40–47.

60. Arch. of Croatia, Zagreb, The Royal *Ban* Administration SB, confidential DZ, no. 53666, the open letter of Dimitrije Ljotić to the royal government; *Otadžbina,* no. 83, October 6, 1935, p. 4; *Službene novine* [the Official Gazette], Belgrade, no. 261, November 11, 1935, p. 2, all cited in Stefanović (1984), p. 36.

61. Gligorijević (1965), p. 80. AMHI, Nedić arch., doc. 49, file 3, box 61; "Sveštenici, opredelite se!" [Priests, Take Sides!], *Otadžbina,* no. 151, February 27, 1937, p. 7, both cited in Stefanović (1984), p. 31.

62. AMHI, Chetnik arch., doc. 1, file 1, box 270, interrogation of Kosta Mušicki, cited in Stefanović (1984), p. 40.

63. Arch. of Yugoslavia 102/7/19, Stanislav Krakov arch., "A Proposal for the Creation of the Section for Propaganda of the Yugoslav National Movement *Zbor,*" cited in Stefanović (1984), p. 38.

64. Rothschild (1974), pp. 249–51.

65. Ibid., p. 250.

66. Ibid., p 257; Odić and Komarica (1977), pp. 30–31; Milovanović (1978), vol. 1, pp. 123–24.

67. Rothschild (1974), p. 257.

68. Ibid., p. 257; Slijepčević (1978), p. 91.

69. Parežanin (1971), p. 202; Ljotić (1961), pp. 201–202; Slijepčević (1978), pp. 91–92.

70. For an explanation of Hermann Göring's role in undermining Ljotić, see Odić and Komarica (1977), pp. 40–43; Slijepčević (1978), pp. 79–85.

71. Slijepčević (1978), p. 65.

72. See Ljotić (1961), p. 22; Parežanin (1971), pp. 219, 142–53; Slijepčević (1978), p. 65; Stefanović (1984), pp. 54–55.

73. AMHI, 17, doc. 20, file 4, box 21, cited in Stefanović (1984), p. 54.

74. Parežanin (1971), p. 204; Popov (1993), p. 5; "Hapšenje Ljotića i 31. člana 'Zbora'" [The Arrest of Ljotić and 31 Members of 'Zbor'], *Vreme* 28, no. 6025, October 28, 1938, p. 1. See Arch. of the Institute for

History of Workers' Movement of Croatia, Zagreb, collection 18-L–27/
1174, "A Message Behind the Prison Bars" (Zbor leaflet); Arch. of the Institute for History of Workers' Movement of Croatia, Zagreb, collection
18-L–27/1180, "Građani!" [Citizens!] (Zbor leaflet signed by "Yugoslav
Patriots"). See AMHI, register 17, doc. 20/4, 22, Ljotić's letters to Anton
Korošec, September 23 and October 12, 1938; Arch. of Yugoslavia, 102/
7/19, Stanislav Krakov file, petition of Lazar Tomić, all cited in Stefanović
(1984), p. 53. See also Ljotić (1961), pp. 197–99.

75. Ljotić's letter of October 12, 1938, to Yugoslavia's minister of the
interior, Anton Korošec, quoted in Ljotić (1961), p. 203.

76. Odić and Komarica (1977), p. 42; Slijepčević (1978), p. 91; Ljotić
(1961), p. 20.

77. Ljotić (1961), pp. 18–19, 22.

78. Rothschild (1974), p. 257; Stefanović (1984), p. 47; Slijepčević
(1978), p. 92.

79. About 20 percent of Yugoslavia's Serbs lived in former Habsburg
lands (Croatia and Vojvodina). See Rothschild (1974), p. 209.

80. Maček (1954), p. 185.

81. Rothschild (1974), p. 259.

82. Ivanović (1954), p. 41. See also AMHI, Chetnik arch., doc. 1, file
1, box 270, interrogation of Kosta Mušicki, cited in Stefanović (1984), p.
57. For the common genealogy of Nedić and Ljotić, see Ljotić (1973), pp.
10, 30, 199, 200; Martinović-Bajica (1956), pp. 19–20.

83. Ivanović (1954), p. 41; Trišić (1960), p. 16; Ljotić (1961), p. 6; Parežanin (1971), pp. 203, 205.

84. Ivanović (1954), pp. 34–35. For the full original text, see p. 35.

85. Arch. of Yugoslavia, Dimitrije Ljotić collection, a 1939 letter from
Nikola Stojanović in the name of the Serbian Cultural Club to Dimitrije
Ljotić, no. 8,674; a 1940 letter from Slobodan Jovanović to Ljotić, no.
8,678; a 1940 letter from Ljotić to Milan Nedić, no. 8,682, all cited in
Stefanović (1984), p. 59. For more on Ljotić's attacks on Cvetković, see
Parežanin (1971), pp. 192–94; Ljotić (1961), pp. 135–54.

86. Stefanović (1984), p. 61.

87. Odić and Komarica (1977), pp. 38–40.

88. Stefanović (1984), p. 66.

89. Ivanović (1954), p. 42. See Arch. of the Central Committee of the
League of Communists of Yugoslavia, the Progressive Student Movement,
no. 405, "Istina o događajima na Beogradskom univerzitetu" [the Truth
about the Events at the Belgrade University]—a leaflet by the Action Committee of Student Associations, cited in Stefanović (1984), p. 81. Ljotićite

writers corroborate that the students of the Department of Technology were *potučeni do nogu* (thoroughly beaten) by the members of the Zbor youth. See *Srpski dobrovoljci* (1966), p. 16.

90. Arch. of the Central Committee of the League of Communists of Yugoslavia, Belgrade, the Progressive Student Movement, no. 405, report by the Action Committee of Student Associations; Arch. of the Central Committee of the League of Communists of Yugoslavia, the Progressive Student Movement, no. 454, the United Student Youth's proclamation entitled "Studentima Beogradskog univerziteta, omladini, radnom narodu, svoj poštenoj javnosti" [To the Students of the Belgrade University, the Youth, the Working People, and the Whole Honest Community]; Arch. of Serbia, Belgrade University, no. 11292/40, all cited in Stefanović (1984), pp. 82–83.

91. Stefanović (1984), p. 82.

92. Ljotić (1961), pp. 227–28; Parežanin (1971), p. 200. See also Arch. of Bosnia-Herzegovina, Sarajevo, the State Security of the Royal *Ban* Administration, confidential doc. DZ 5759/40; Arch. of Bosnia-Herzegovina, Sarajevo, the State Security of the Royal *Ban* Administration, confidential doc. DZ 5258, telegraphic message from the Ministry of the interior, November 6, 1940, all cited in Stefanović (1984), p. 85.

93. Marjanović (1979), pp. 16–17. See also Arch. of Bosnia-Herzegovina, Sarajevo, State Security of the Royal *Ban* Administration, confidential DZ 5,494, the decision of the Section for State Protection of the Ministry of the Interior, confidential no. 48,742, November 16, 1940; Arch. of the Central Committee of the League of Communists of Yugoslavia, collection of the Gestapo, K-IV/296, excerpt from the report "Auslands-Kurzmeldungen," November 9, 1940, concerning the ban on the Zbor movement, all cited in Stefanović (1984), p. 84.

94. Ljotić (1961), p. 219. See also pp. 213–18.

95. Arch. of Yugoslavia, Belgrade, Dimitrije Ljotić collection, no. 8,682, cited in Stefanović (1984), p. 88; Arch. of Bosnia-Herzegovina, Sarajevo, State Security of the Royal *Ban* Administration, confidential doc. no. 8,933/40 and confidential doc. no. 9,875/40, cited in Stefanović (1984), p. 87; Stefanović (1984), p. 94; Parežanin (1971), pp. 227–32.

96. AMHI, Nedić arch., doc. 20, file 7, box 1, interrogation of Aleksandar Cincar-Marković, cited in Stefanović (1984), p. 86.

97. Arch. of Slovenia, Ljubljana, public prosecutor arch., 3/6—41, cited in Stefanović (1984), p. 97; AMHI, microcopy from Bonn, no. 4, frames 187–216, cited in Stefanović (1984), p. 101; Parežanin (1971), pp. 269, 283, 291.

98. Hoettl (1954), pp. 129–30.

99. Ibid., p. 131.

100. There is some discrepancy concerning which clause(s) Hitler refused to make public. See Balfour and Mackay (1980), p. 239; Maček (1957), p. 210.

101. This date is given as March 4 by Balfour and Mackay (1980), p. 227. The date is March 6, according to Parežanin (1971), p. 283.

102. Extracts from "The Yugoslav Crisis of March 1941," September 27, 1941, report of British S.O.E. operative Glanville, obtained from Foreign and Commonwealth Office, London, pp. 3–4.

103. The Crown Council meeting of March 20, 1941, was attended by Pavle's eight coregents, six of whom were Serbs: Radenko Stanković and Ivo Perović; Dragiša Cvetković, prime minister; Aleksandar Cincar-Marković, foreign minister; Gen. Petar Pešić, minister of war; Milan Antić, minister of the Royal Court; Vice-Premier Vladko Maček (the Croat); and Minister Fran Kulovec (the Slovene). See Balfour and Mackay (1980), pp. 227–29; Maček (1954), pp. 209–10. In his memoirs, Maček gives March 19 as the date of the Crown Council meeting.

104. Extracts from "The Yugoslav Crisis of March 1941," September 27, 1941, pp. 4–5.

105. The three dissenters in the royal cabinet, Branko Čubrilović, Srđan Budisavljević, and Milan Konstantinović (all funded by British intelligence), resigned. Pavle persuaded Konstantinović to retract his resignation. See Maček (1957), p. 213; Balfour and Mackay (1980), pp. 227–29, 254.

106. Balfour and Mackay (1980), p. 291; I. Meštrović (1993), p. 264.

107. Balfour and Mackay (1980), p. 243.

108. Extracts from "The Yugoslav Crisis of March 1941," September 27, 1941, p. 18.

109. For the text of Nincić's statement to von Heeren, see Tomasevich (1975), p. 51. See also Balfour and Mackay (1980), p. 259; Maček (1954), p. 220.

110. Balfour and Mackay (1980), p. 258.

111. Fotich (1948), p. 76; Balfour and Mackay (1980), p. 258; Milovanović (1978), vol. 1, pp. 47, 51–52, 55, 58.

112. Hoettl (1954), pp. 135–36.

113. T. G. Mapplebeck's business partner was wealthy Belgrade businessman Žika Krstić. See Balfour and Mackay (1980), p. 255; Milovanović (1978), vol. 1, pp. 52–53.

114. Milovanović (1978), vol. 1, pp. 65–66, 167; Balfour and Mackay (1980), p. 253.

115. Milovanović (1978), vol. 1, pp. 11–77, esp. 51–42; extracts from "The Yugoslav Crisis of March 1941," September 27, 1941, p. 9; Hoettl (1954), pp. 129–30; Balfour and Mackay (1980), pp. 244–45.

116. Under this plan, the new Simović-led government would consist of Gen. Bogoljub Ilić, Mirko Kosić (a close friend of Simović), Dragomir Ikonić, and Radoje Knežević (who had been dismissed from his position as French tutor of young King Petar II). See Milovanović (1978), vol. 1, p. 67.

117. Balfour and Mackay (1980), pp. 253–55.

118. Hoettl (1954), pp. 139, 144; extracts from "The Yugoslav Crisis of March 1941," September 27, 1941, p. 12; Hoettl (1954), pp. 145–47.

119. Parežanin (1971), pp. 276, 283, 303–304; Milovanović (1978), vol. 1, pp. 13, 146, vol. 2, pp. 25, 363; Balfour and Mackay (1980), p. 244.

CHAPTER 2: THE SERBIAN STATE, 1941–1944

1. Hoettl (1954), p. 145.

2. Hitler's decision to invade Yugoslavia in response to the British-supported Belgrade coup was an unexpected development in the Balkans. The findings of a joint German-Serbian commission appointed to invest-igate the March 27 coup, however, gave Hitler an excuse to break the Molotov-Ribbentrop Pact and attack the Soviet Union, a supposed ally. The commission was led by Col. Tanasije Dinić and included Đorđe Perić and Mihailo Mika Đorđević, an assistant to Dragi Jovanović. During inter-rogation, a code-clerk named Anđelković, who allegedly worked for the Soviets, stated that the Soviet chargé d'affaires in Belgrade was prepared to sign an agreement of mutual assistance with the coup government. When Dr. Busse, the consul-general in the Reich Ministry of Foreign Affairs, heard this, he reportedly said, "Thank you. I have got what I wanted." Busse promptly returned to Berlin with a report of his findings, and the investigation was suspended. Several days later, Germany attacked the So-viet Union. In his speech on the eve of the attack, Hitler stated that the Soviet Union had violated its nonaggression pact with Germany by pushing Yugoslavia to war against Germany. Thus, Hitler used the findings of Din-ić's commission as a pretext to justify the long-planned attack on the Soviet Union. See N.A., microcopy T–120, roll 200, frame 153205; Marjanović (1976), p. 65; Arch. of the Secretariat of Internal Affairs of Serbia, Tanasije Dinić file, minutes of interrogation of Tanasije Dinić of February 21, 1946, cited in Borković (1979), p. 52; AMHI, Chetnik arch., doc. 27, file 2, box 269, interrogation of Tanasije Dinić, cited in Stefanović (1984), p. 118.

3. Tomasevich (1975), pp. 71, 75.

4. AMHI, Nedić arch., doc. 6, file 7, box 1, interrogation of Milan

Nedić; Chetnik arch., doc. 27, file 2, box 269, interrogation of Tanasije Dinić; Chetnik arch., doc. 1, file 1, box 270, interrogation of Kosta Mušicki, all cited in Stefanović (1984), p. 105. See also Borković (1979), p. 14.

5. Karapandžić (1958), pp. 17–18; Tomasevich (1975), pp. 74–75; AMHI, microfilm from Freiburg, Germany, no. 11, frames 426–34, cited in Stefanović (1984), p. 106. During the April, 1941, war, the Italians captured about thirty thousand Yugoslav Army soldiers.

6. AMHI, Nedić arch., doc. 11, file 7, box 50A, cited in Stefanović (1984), p. 149.

7. Kostić (1949), p. 18. Microfilm from Bonn no. 2, frame 596, cited in Stefanović, p. 113.

8. See Fotich (1948), pp. 98–99; Tomasevich (1975), pp. 71, 75–79; Irvine (1993), p. 91.

9. AMHI, Nedić arch., doc. 20, file 7, box 1, interrogation of Aleksandar Cincar-Marković; microfilm from Bonn, no. 2, frame 672, both cited in Stefanović (1984), p. 114.

10. AMHI, Chetnik arch., doc. 43, file 1, box 270, interrogation of Đuro Dokić, cited in Stefanović (1984), p. 113.

11. AMHI, Nedić arch., doc. 20, file 7, box 1, interrogation of Aleksandar Cincar-Marković; microfilm from Bonn no. 2, frame 672, both cited in Stefanović (1984), p. 114.

12. N. A., microcopy T–501, roll 245, frame 271; Kostić (1949), pp. 18–19.

13. Microfilm from Bonn, no. 2, frame 595, cited in Stefanović (1984), p. 114; Ivanović (1954), pp. 45–46.

14. Arch. of the Ministry of the Interior of Serbia, uncatalogued, Karl Kraus's record of April 20, 1941, cited in Stefanović (1984), p. 115 and Borković (1979), pp. 28–29.

15. N.A., microcopy T–501, roll 245, frame 271.

16. Karapandžić (1958), p. 24; Parežanin (1971), p. 321; N. A., microcopy T–120, roll 200, frame 153198; Borković (1979), p. 28. Also, microfilm from Bonn, no. 2, frame 604, cited in Stefanović (1984), p. 115.

17. Kostić (1949), p. 21; Parežanin (1971), p. 319. Also, AMHI, Nedić arch., doc. 19, file 7, box 1, interrogation of Dragi Jovanović; Chetnik arch., doc. 27, file 2, box 269, interrogation of Tanasije Dinić; Chetnik arch., doc. 17, file 3, box 269, interrogation of Velibor Jonić, all cited in Stefanović (1984), p. 116.

18. Karapandžić (1958), pp. 22–25; Tomasevich (1975), p. 108; Borković (1979), p. 162.

19. Singleton (1976), p. 93; Browning (1985), pp. 40, 42.

20. Browning (1985), pp. 40, 42.

21. In April, 1941, membership in the Communist Party of Yugoslavia was around eight thousand, half of which was in Croatia. See Jelić (1981), vol. 1, p. 401; Marjanović (1963), p. 97.

22. Stefanović (1984), p. 130.

23. "Apel srpskom narodu" [Appeal to the Serbian Nation], *Novo vreme,* Belgrade, August 13, 1941, pp. 1, 3; "Nastavak liste potpisnika Apela srpskom narodu" [Continuation of the List of Signatories to the Appeal to the Serbian Nation], *Novo vreme,* Belgrade, August 14, 1941, p. 3; "Odjek apela srpskom narodu" [The Public Reception of the Appeal to the Serbian Nation], *Novo vreme,* Belgrade, August 16, 1941, p. 5. The entire Appeal with a list of its signatories is reprinted in Krakov (1963), pp. 105–13. Six Belgrade intellectuals are recorded as having refused to sign this document: writer Isidora Sekulić; professors Bogdan Popović, Nikola Vulić, and Miloš Đurić; painter Sreten Stojanović; and diplomat and writer Ivo Andrić. See Mukerji (1990), pp. 41, 172.

24. "Advokatska komora pridružuje se osudi komunističke i terorističke akcije" [The Bar Association Joins the Condemnation of Communist and Terrorist Activity], *Novo vreme,* Belgrade, August 14, 1941, p. 1.

25. The Serbian Agrarian Party was excluded, because it was supported and supplied by the British government and intelligence agencies. See Milovanović (1978), vol. 2, p. 27; Borković (1979), pp. 95–97; Kostić (1949), pp. 44–46; Karapandžić (1958), p. 84.

26. Balfour and Mackay (1980), p. 209; Tomasevich (1975), p. 109.

27. Tomasevich (1975), p. 108.

28. Ibid.

29. N.A., microcopy T–315, roll 2237, frames 842–45, Harald Turner's report, December, 1941. See also AMHI, doc. 16, file 7–4, box 1; Arch. of the Ministry of the Interior of Serbia, Belgrade, interrogation of Milan Nedić, January 9, 1946, both cited in Borković (1979), p. 151. For a discussion of the collaboration of Kosta Pećanac, see Tomasevich (1975), pp. 126–29.

30. AMHI, Nedić arch., doc. 27, file 1, box 40, cited in Borković (1979), p. 109.

31. N.A., microcopy T–315, roll 2237, frames 842–45, report of the commander of Serbia to the commander of the South East, September 6, 1941; T–501, roll 246, frames 267–69; Krakov (1963), pp. 157–62; Krakov (1968), pp. 47–48; Borković (1979), p. 126. Also, AMHI, Nedić arch., doc. 1, file 1, box 24A, cited in Stefanović (1984), pp. 139–40.

32. Browning (1985), p. 45.

33. Milazzo (1975), pp. 21–27.

34. Browning (1985), p. 45.

35. Ibid., pp. 45–46, 54; Borković (1979), pp. 158–59, 161; Hilberg (1985), p. 683.

36. Mihailo Olćan, "Nastupa novo vreme, dolazi novi duh, a taj duh je, našom srećom i duh našeg naroda" [A New Time is Beginning, a New Spirit is Coming, and This Spirit, through Our Good Fortune, Is the Spirit of Our Nation as Well], *Obnova*, Belgrade, November 21, 1941, p. 5.

37. Borković (1979), p. 162.

38. According to German sources, on December 1, 1941, Nedić had 17,992 armed persons under his command: 3,628 gendarmes, 4,084 Ljotićites and Chetniks loyal to the government, 3,500 Chetniks of Kosta Pećanac (including 1,000 armed older persons at their homes), 1,432 policemen (in Belgrade and other Serbian cities), 348 agents, and 5,000 members of border units. See N.A., microcopy T–501, roll 256, frames 1172–73, report by Harald Turner to the commander of the South East, December 1, 1941. See also N.A., microcopy T–501, roll 256, frame 1160, the order of the military commander for Serbia. For the crossover of former Chetniks of Mihailović to Pećanac Chetniks, see Tomasevich (1975), p. 127.

39. AMHI, Nedić arch., doc. 19, file 7, box 1, interrogation of Dragi Jovanović; Chetnik arch., doc. 27, file 2, box 269, interrogation of Tanasije Dinić; Chetnik arch., doc. 17, file 3, box 269, interrogation of Velibor Jonić; Chetnik arch., doc. 43, file 1, box 270, interrogation of Đura Dokić; Chetnik arch., doc. 1, file 1, box 270, interrogation of Kosta Mušicki, all cited in Stefanović (1984), p. 113.

40. AMHI, Nedić arch., doc. 19, file 7, box 1, interrogation of Dragi Jovanović, cited in Stefanović (1984), p. 114, and in Borković (1979), p. 29.

41. Under Dragi Jovanović's command, the Guard of the Administration of the City of Belgrade, the Special Police, and the civil police consisted of 52 officers, 1,550 guards, 180 civil servants, and 300 police agents. See AMHI, Nedić arch., doc. 19, file 7, box 1, interrogation of Dragi Jovanović, cited in Stefanović (1984), pp. 118–19.

42. Stefanović (1984), pp. 118–19. See also Nenad Stefanović, "Čovek koji je suviše znao i batinao" [A Man Who Knew Too Much and Who Beat Too Much], *Duga*, Belgrade, February 18–March 3, 1995, p. 80.

43. *Zbornik dokumenata* (1978), vol. 12, book 1, doc. 79, pp. 205–207, half-month report of the German field commander, July 14, 1941, concerning the situation in the vicinity of Belgrade; Marjanović (1964), p. 36.

44. Romano (1980), p. 60; Borković (1979), p. 329.

45. Borković (1979a), pp. 318–20. After World War II, Božidar (Boško) Bećarević was interrogated by the Yugoslav police for fifteen years until his execution in 1960. Bećarević's police dossier, unlike that of Dragi Jovanović, has remained secret. See Stefanović, "Čovek koji je suviše znao i batinao," p. 80.

46. Romano (1980), p. 60.

47. Stefanović (1984), p. 66; Odić and Komarica (1977), pp. 40–47; Martic (1980), pp. 219–39.

48. Stefanović (1984), pp. 69–70. Also, *Politika*, no. 10087, June 24, 1936; *Otadžbina*, no. 160, May 13, 1937, p. 3; *Politika*, no. 10,334, March 1, 1937, all cited in Stefanović (1984), p. 8.

49. N.A, microcopy T–501, roll 246, frames 267–69; Kostić (1949), pp. 48–49; Ivanović (1954), pp. 47–48; Karapandžić (1958), pp. 90–91; Krakov (1963), pp. 160, 174; Parežanin (1971), p. 456.

50. Karapandžić (1958), p. 91; Krakov (1963), p. 160; Kostić (1949), p. 50. See also AMHI, Chetnik arch., 1/1, box 270, interrogation of Kosta Mušicki; Nedić arch., 2/4, box 153, both cited in Stefanović (1984), p. 147.

51. Karapandžić (1958), pp. 92–93; Kostić (1949), p. 50; Parežanin (1971), pp. 461–62; *Srpski dobrovoljci* (1966), p. 35. See also Nedić arch. 13/7, box 50A; 2/4, box 153, cited in Borković (1979), p. 170.

52. AMHI, German arch., doc. 1/2, box 27–2, cited in Stefanović (1984), p. 154.

53. Borković (1979), p. 14.

54. AMHI, Chetnik arch. 1/1, box 270, interrogation of Kosta Mušicki, cited in Stefanović (1984), p. 113.

55. Jukić (1974), pp. 106–107; Borković (1979), p. 148.

56. Krakov (1963), pp. 246–47. Two German battalions were stationed in the vicinity of Kragujevac, the 3rd Battalion of the 749th Regiment and the 1st Battalion of the 724th Regiment.

57. Borković (1979), p. 148; Ivanović (1954), pp. 49–57.

58. Historical Arch. of Čačak, no. 132, cited in Stefanović (1984), p. 170.

59. AMHI, Nedić arch., doc. 2, file 4, box 153; doc. 22, file 1, box 154; doc. 2, file 4, box 153; Arch. of Kraljevo, all cited in Stefanović (1984), pp. 170–71. Such German-Serbian courts-martial were formed in Kraljevo, Gornji Milanovac, Guča, Šabac, Valjevo, Ivanjica, Arilje, Požega, Užice, and other towns.

60. Arch. of Serbia, Belgrade, no. 25206, report of the Ministry of Education to the Presidium of the Ministerial Council, December 10, 1941; Arch. of Serbia, Belgrade, the October, 1941, salary list, both cited in Borković (1979), pp. 171–72, 291.

61. Borković (1979a), p. 192.

62. Borković (1979), pp. 286–303, especially 286–88; see Arch. of the Ministry of the Interior of Serbia, Belgrade, interrogation of Milan Nedić, February 1, 1946, cited in Borković (1979), p. 289.

63. Martinović-Bajica (1956), pp. 355–57; AMHI, Nedić arch., doc. 75, file 4–1, box 2, report of the Ministry of the Interior to Nedić's government, May 28, 1942, cited in Borković (1979), p. 292; Kostić (1949), p. 72. On April 1, 1944, the Serbian State Guard and Serbian Border Guard had 13,100 and 5,605 members, respectively.

64. Martinović-Bajica (1956), pp. 355–57; Arch. of the Ministry of the Interior of Serbia, Belgrade, interrogation of Milan Nedić, p. 289.

65. N. A., microcopy T–501, roll 253, frames 283–87.

66. AMHI, doc. 26, file 1–4, box 27; doc. 26, file 1–6, box 27, cited in Borković (1979), pp. 337–38.

67. Fotich (1948), p. 148; Stefanović, "Čovek koji je suviše znao i batinao," p. 81 (this article is part of a serialization of the minutes of the postwar interrogation of Dragi Jovanović).

68. N. A., microcopy T–501, roll 256, frames 509, 867; Kostić (1949), p. 136; Shelah (1990), pp. 288–89; Milazzo (1975), p. 125; Maclean (1949), p. 412; Tomasevich (1975), pp. 166–69, 230.

69. N. A., microcopy T–120, roll 200, frame 153419; Browning (1985), pp. 42–43.

70. N. A., microcopy T–314, roll 1457, frames 1110–12.

71. For the correspondence between Mihailović and the Germans, preparations for the mid-November, 1941, meeting and the meeting itself, see N. A., microcopy T–314, roll 1457, frames 1110–12, 1314–21, 1338.

72. Sources differ on whether Mihailović's meeting with the Germans was held on November 11, 1941, or several days later (see Borković [1979], p. 219). For a detailed account of Mihailović's meeting with *Abwehr* in the village of Divci (near Valjevo) around November 11, 1941, see Karapandžić (1958), pp. 128–57. This source cites written accounts by the participants at this meeting, including Chetnik colonel Branislav J. Pantić and the *Abwehr* captain Josef Matl. See also Karapandžić (1958), pp. 133–34.

73. Karapandžić (1958), p. 143.

74. Ibid.

75. Ibid., p. 144; see also pp. 128–57.

76. Kostić (1949), pp. 32–36; Milazzo (1975), p. 16.

77. Borković (1979a), p. 211.

78. Arch. of the Ministry of the Interior of Serbia, interrogation of Milan Nedić, January 9, 1946; AMHI, Nedić arch., doc. 1–16, file 7–1, inter-

rogation of Milan Nedić in the office of prison no. 2 in Belgrade; as reproduced in Cvijić and Vasović (1991), pp. 223–31, see esp. p. 227; also cited in Borković (1979a), p. 212.

79. AMHI, Nedić arch., microcopy b/2, 150–53, order 4, confidential UB no. 194, cited in Borković (1979a), p. 213.

80. Jukić (1974), pp. 104–105, 108; Borković (1979), p. 219.

81. Cvijić and Vasović (1991), p. 227.

82. N. A., microcopy T–501, roll 246, frames 643–44. AMHI, Nedić arch., doc. 2, file 4, box 153, cited in Stefanović (1984), p. 159.

83. According to German sources, Partisan losses were 1,415 dead, 80 wounded, and 718 imprisoned, while German losses were 11 dead and 35 wounded. Although data are not available for the losses sustained by Serb collaborationists during this campaign, a later report from the Serbian State Guard claimed losses of 1,600–1,700 dead and 1,400–1,500 wounded as of the beginning of 1942 (see Krakov [1963], pp. 298–99). See also AMHI, Nedić arch., report of the Serbian State Guard, February, 1942, cited in Borković (1979), p. 224.

84. AMHI, German arch., London microfilms, 1/297092–097, "Serbia at the end of 1941," cited in Borković (1979), p. 228.

85. Ibid.

86. Tomasevich (1975), pp. 166–69; Moljević (1991), pp. 141–47.

87. Moljević (1991), p. 141; for an English translation, see Moljević (1993), pp. 151–52.

88. Moljević (1991), pp. 142–43; for an English translation, see Moljević (1993), pp. 152–54.

89. *Zbornik dokumenata* (1981), vol. 14, book 1, doc. 35, pp. 101–103.

90. In his shrill but prescient book, French author Pozzi (1935), p. 77, warned of impending war in Europe, citing the parallel between Greater Serbian and Greater German ambitions.

91. Tomasevich (1975), p. 170.

92. Ibid. There exists a question whether the Chetnik directive of December 20, 1941, was written by Mihailović himself or by subordinates who forged their leader's name. In either case, there is no indication that Mihailović disavowed this directive. Concerning the authorship of this directive, see Malcolm (1994), p. 179.

93. Žerjavić (1991), p. 96; Kočović (1985), p. 124.

94. Milazzo (1975), p. 109.

95. Tomasevich (1975), pp. 258–59; Milazzo (1975), p. 109.

96. Tomasevich (1975), pp. 258–59.

97. N.A., microcopy T–501, roll 256, frames 509, 867; Kostić (1949), p. 136; Parežanin (1971), pp. 485–86, 497. See Stefanović (1984), pp. 280, 309.

98. Tomasevich (1975), p. 177; *Spomenica pravoslavnih sveštenika-žrtava fašističkog terora i palih u NOB* (1960), p. 195.

99. Tomasevich (1975), pp. 158, 177, 352, 428, 442 n. 38, 452; Milazzo (1975), pp. 76–77, 151, 163, 165, 178.

100. Martin (1946), pp. 141–42; Milazzo (1975), pp. 138, 150.

101. Milazzo (1975), p. 163.

102. Tomasevich (1975), p. 329 n. 17; Stefanović (1984), p. 307.

103. Milazzo (1975), pp. 163–65.

104. Kostić (1949), p. 187; Milazzo (1975), pp. 178–79; Stefanović (1984), p. 307.

105. Kostić (1949), p. 190.

106. *Zbornik dokumenata* (1957), vol. 19, book 4, pp. 445–47. See also Popović et al. (1988), pp. 351, 359.

107. Popović et al. (1988), p. 353.

108. Ibid., p. 354.

109. *Zbornik dokumenata* (1957), vol. 19, book 4, pp. 1089–90. See also Popović et al. (1988), pp. 356–57, 360.

110. *Zbornik dokumenata* (1968), vol. 36, p. 760. See also Popović et al. (1988), pp. 357–58, 360.

111. Kostić (1949), p. 247. See also Popović et al. (1988), p. 374.

112. According to sources at the U.S. Department of Justice, Office of Special Investigations (as of November, 1994), Yugoslavia filed an extradition request in 1988, but this case was not acted upon. See also Popović et al. (1988), p. 318; Tomasevich (1975), p. 329 n. 17; Stefanović (1984), p. 307.

113. Ford (1992); Lašić-Vasojević (1976), pp. 252–53; Lees (1990); Dragnich (1992), pp. 100–115; Martin (1946); Jukić (1974).

114. Wheeler (1980), p. 73; Tomasevich (1975), pp. 166–69; Moljević (1991), pp. 141–47; Shelah (1990), pp. 288–89.

115. Wheeler (1980), p. 73; Popović et al. (1988), p. 94; Bilandžić (1985), p. 55.

116. Milazzo (1975), p. 125.

117. For example, see Ford (1992), pp. 133–34, 177–78; Roberts (1973), p. 292; Martin (1946), p. 245.

118. Tomasevich (1975), pp. 378–80.

119. *Dokumenti o izdajstvu Draže Mihailovića* (1945), vol. 1, pp. 677, 680.

120. Romano (1980), pp. 72–78; Shelah (1990b), pp. 1340–42; Kupre-šanin (1967), p. 7.

121. Kuprešanin (1967), pp. 21, 25; Romano (1980), p. 73; Borković (1979), p. 329.

122. Glišić (1977), pp. 694, 696; Borković (1979), p. 329.

123. Romano (1980), p. 73; Kuprešanin (1967), p. 21.

124. Romano (1980), p. 74.

125. Glišić (1977), p. 699.

126. Ibid.; see Kuprešanin (1967), p. 58; Vuković (1991), pp. 79–81. As a rule, the Cyrillic alphabet is used by Serbs; the Latin alphabet is used by Croats and Bosnian Muslims.

127. See Glišić (1977), pp. 700–702; Kuprešanin (1967), pp. 22, 93–94. Trišić (1960), p. 95; "Banjički logor u Beogradu" [Banjica Concentration Camp in Belgrade] in: *Enciklopedija Jugoslavije* (1980), vol. 1, pp. 495–96. The origin of some 68,000 burned corpses and 1,400 unburned corpses exhumed at the Jajinci killing site is unclear. These victims may have been incarcerated at Banjica or Sajmište or elsewhere (see Žerjavić [1992], p. 210). For additional survivor testimony on Banjica, see Pejić (1989).

128. The Russian Protection Corps was incorporated into the Wehrmacht on November 30, 1942. For its various designations, see Vertepov (1963), p. 8.

129. Ibid., p. 37.

130. Zernov (1975), pp. 164–85; Vertepov (1963), pp. 9–15, 37, 405. Nearly one-third of those who joined the Russian Corps were already living in Yugoslavia, nearly half came from Romania, and the rest were Russian émigrés living in Bulgaria, Hungary, Greece, Poland, Latvia, Germany, Italy, and France.

131. Vertepov (1963), pp. 404–405.

132. N.A., microcopy T–78, roll 413, frames 6381005–6, directive of November 16, 1941.

133. Vertepov (1963), pp. 24–25; Tomasevich (1975), pp. 347, 414, 425.

134. For cooperation with the Chetniks, see Vertepov (1963), pp. 20, 48, 53, 62, 78, 241, 244. For cooperation with Ljotić's Volunteers, see Vertepov (1963), pp. 146, 173, 241. For cooperation with the Ustashas, see Vertepov (1963), pp. 117, 140, 275–76. For the role of the Russian Corps in the Wehrmacht, see Neulen (1985), pp. 231–32.

135. N.A., microcopy T–501, roll 253, frame 78.

136. For attacks between the Chetniks and the Russian Corps, see Vertepov (1963), pp. 89, 153, 160.

137. Ibid., p. 239.

138. Ibid., p. 19.

139. Borković (1979a), p. 198. For general sources on the Serbian Gestapo, see Kostić (1949), pp. 61–62; Krakov (1968), pp. 352–56; Odić and Komarica (1977), pp. 163–72; Borković (1979a), pp. 198–200.

140. Belgrade German Gestapo report on Strahinja Janjić, July 28, 1942, cited in Odić and Komarica (1977), pp. 163–64.

141. Kostić (1949), p. 61.

142. Report by SS sublieutenant Fritz Strecke, Department of the German Security Police of Serbia, cited in Odić and Komarica (1977), p. 166.

143. Odić and Komarica (1977), p. 164; Kostić (1949), p. 61; Krakov (1968), pp. 353–54; Borković (1979a), p. 198.

144. Odić and Komarica (1977), p. 165.

145. Ibid., pp. 167–68; Kostić (1949), pp. 61–62.

146. Arch. of the Ministry of the Interior of Serbia, Nedić file, cited in Borković (1979a), p. 198.

147. Odić and Komarica (1977), p. 167.

148. Kostić (1949), p. 62.

149. Arch. of the Ministry of the Interior of Serbia, Nedić file, Nedić's memorandum to Bader, February 22, 1943, cited in Borković (1979a), pp. 198–99.

150. Borković (1979a), p. 200; Odić and Komarica (1977), p. 167.

151. Borković (1979a), p. 200; Odić and Komarica (1977), p. 172.

152. Quoted in Odić and Komarica (1977), p. 172.

153. Ibid., pp. 171–72.

154. Tomasevich (1975), pp. 350, 420–21.

155. AMHI, doc. 4, files 1–13, box 19, cited in Borković (1979), pp. 48–49.

156. Arch. of the Ministry of the Interior of Serbia, Belgrade, Nedić file, interrogation of Milan Nedić, February 2, 1946, cited in Borković (1979a), pp. 232–33.

157. AMHI, German arch., doc. 19/1-a, box 70-A, the statement by Neubacher during the investigation in Belgrade, cited in Borković (1979a), p. 161; AMHI, Nedić arch., doc. 1/2-1-1, box 1, speech of December 13, 1942, cited in Borković (1979a), p. 34; Nedić (1943), pp. 105, 108; Cvijić and Vasović (1991), pp. 63, 65.

158. N.A., microcopy T–501, roll 256, frames 907–23, memorandum of Milan Nedić to General Bader, January 1, 1943.

159. N.A., microcopy T–501, roll 256, frames 924–37, January 22, 1943; microcopy T–501, roll 256, frames 960–65, January 29, 1943.

160. N.A., microcopy T–120, roll 61, frames 49474–85; Parežanin (1971), pp. 341–42; Kostić (1949), pp. 411–12. See also AMHI, Nedić

arch., doc. 19, file 7, box 1, minutes of interrogation of Dragi Jovanović, cited in Borković (1979a), p. 171; Chetnik arch., doc. 38, file 1, box 269, interrogation of Milan Nedić, cited in Stefanović (1984), p. 233. For a detailed description of the Hitler-Nedić meeting, see Borković (1979a), pp. 160–77, esp. p. 168; Stefanović (1984), pp. 232–34.

161. Present at the September 18, 1941, meeting between Nedić and von Ribbentrop and acting as translator was Robert Krohnholz, the German consul-general to Serbia, who recorded the minutes. Also present for part of this meeting were Felix Benzler, Hermann Neubacher, and Edmund Veesenmeyer. See N.A., microcopy T–120, roll 61, frames 49475–85 (minutes of the von Ribbentrop-Nedić meeting of September 18, 1943). See also AMHI, Nedić arch., no. 19, file 7, box 1, interrogation of Dragi Jovanović, cited in Stefanović (1984), p. 233; Borković (1979a), p. 171, 233. See also Arch. of the Ministry of the Interior of Serbia, Belgrade, Nedić file, interrogation of Milan Nedić, February 2, 1946, cited in Borković (1979a), pp. 232–33, and p. 170.

162. For a well-reasoned discussion of Neubacher's support for a Greater Serbian Federation, see Marjanović (1977), pp. 486–501. See also AMHI, German arch., doc. 19, file 1-a, box 70-A, statement by Neubacher during the investigation in Belgrade, cited in Borković (1979a), p. 172. For a Chetnik perspective, see Trišić (1960), p. 52.

163. Deutsche Nachrichten Büro, "Vođa Rajha primio je pretsednika vlade generala Milana Nedića" [Führer of the German Reich Received the President of the Government General Milan Nedić], *Obnova*, Belgrade, September 20, 1943, p. 1. No minutes are known to exist for the Hitler-Nedić meeting, but the content of their discussion can be inferred from the subsequent communiqués of their respective governments and from the postwar testimony of Nedić and Neubacher. See Arch. of the Ministry of the Interior of Serbia, Belgrade, interrogation of Milan Nedić, February 2, 1946; AMHI, German arch., doc. 19/1-a, box 70-A, the statement by Neubacher during the investigation in Belgrade, cited in Borković (1979a), pp. 172–73; see also p. 176. During a conference in August, 1944, Hitler commented how Nedić had bowed before him in an oriental way at their meeting of September 18, 1943. When Hitler contrasted Nedić's manners to those of Milan Stojadinović, Neubacher replied: "Nedić is a Serb of a conservative type, if you like, a Serbian democrat whose politeness is based on completely different traditions than that of Stojadinović, a Westerner. The latter studied in Munich, had a practice as an official in Bavaria, perfectly learned how to drink beer and, therefore, he can move in Germany like a German!" See Neubacher (1956), p. 135.

164. Lochner (1948), p. 466.

165. N.A., microcopy T–501, roll 256, frame 867.

166. Arch. Serbian Ministry of the Interior, Nedić file, uncatalogued, interrogation of Milan Nedić, February 2, 1946, cited in Borković (1979a), p. 233.

167. N.A., microcopy T–120, roll 780, frames 371763–64, Neubacher's report to von Ribbentrop, July 6, 1944.

168. Warlimont (1962), p. 499; for an English translation, see Warlimont (1964), p. 469. For a discussion of Hitler's opposition to Greater Serbia, see Marjanović (1977), pp. 499–501.

169. Arch. Yugoslavia, no. 110, file 85/765, the personal file of Milosav Vasiljević, cited in Stefanović (1984), p. 231.

170. Odić and Komarica (1977), p. 172.

171. N.A., microcopy T–501, roll 249, frame 259.

172. Parežanin (1971), p. 485; Kostić (1949), p. 136; Karapandžić (1971), p. 101. See also AMHI, Chetnik arch., doc. 13/1–64, box 257; Chetnik arch., doc. 12/1, box 276; Chetnik arch., doc. 43/1, box 270, interrogation of Đuro Dokić; Arch. Yugoslavia, 110/100/2310, Mihailo Olćan file, all cited in Stefanović (1984), p. 280.

173. See Stefanović, "Čovek koji je suviše znao i batinao," p. 81. See also Arch. of the Ministry of the Interior of Serbia, uncatalogued, interrogation of Milan Nedić, February 3, 1946; AMHI, no. 19, file 7, box 1, interrogation of Dragi Jovanović, both cited in Borković (1979a), p. 332.

174. Kostić (1949), p. 164; Martinović-Bajica (1956), p. 367. For a discussion of prominent Serbian officials who left Belgrade under German protection in early September, 1944, see Arch. of the Ministry of the Interior of Serbia, interrogation of Tanasije Dinić, February 27, 1946, cited in Borković (1979a), pp. 344–45.

175. Stefanović, "Čovek koji je suviše znao i batinao," p. 83.

176. On August 17, 1944, the German military commander of the South East and the Nedić government discussed preparations for the withdrawal of the Germans and their Serbian collaborators. See N.A., microcopy T–312, roll 780, frames 371746, 371754.

177. Arch. of the Ministry of the Interior of Serbia, Nedić file, interrogation of Milan Nedić, January 5, 1946, cited in Borković (1979a), p. 346.

178. AMHI, Nedić arch., doc. 1/1, file 2, box 169, cited in Borković (1979a), p. 343.

179. AMHI, Nedić arch., doc. 3/6–45/6, box 59, cited in Borković (1979a), p. 346.

180. AMHI, Nedić arch., doc. 2/2, file 2, box 164, cited in Borković (1979a), p. 347.

181. Karapandžić (1958), pp. 383–84; Kostić (1949), pp. 174, 180, 182;

Stefanović (1984), pp. 294–303, 307, 322–23; Borković (1979), p. 380; Tomasevich (1975), pp. 461–62. See also AMHI, Nedić arch., doc. 2/2, file 2, box 164, cited in Borković (1979a), p. 347.

182. Parežanin (1971), pp. 496–500.

183. N.A., microcopy T–501, roll 258, frames 736–37, report of the commander of the South East, October 21, 1944; microcopy T–120, roll 2955, frame 470213. See AMHI, Nedić arch., doc. 19, file 7, box 1; Arch. of the Ministry of the Interior of Serbia, Nedić file, statement of Milan Nedić, January 5, 1946, both cited in Borković (1979a), pp. 348 and 351; see also p. 349.

184. N.A., microcopy T–120, roll 780, frames 371712–13. Also, Arch. of the Ministry of the Interior of Serbia, Nedić file, statement of Milan Nedić, January 5, 1946, cited in Borković (1979a), p. 356.

185. AMHI, Nedić arch., doc. 1, file 21, box 50, the order of General Felber, cited in Borković (1979a), p. 350.

186. Ljotić (1976), p. 152.

187. Kostić (1949), p. 187; Parežanin (1971), p. 503; Karapandžić (1971), p. 180. The Nedić government was relocated to Kitzbühel on October 16, 1944. See Stefanović, "Čovek koji je suviše znao i batinao," p. 84.

188. Dožić (1986), pp. 84–105.

189. Karapandžić (1958), pp. 425–29.

190. Arch. of the Ministry of the Interior of Serbia, Nedić file, statements of January 5 and February 2, 1946; AMHI, Nedić arch., doc. 19, file 7, box 1, statement of Dragi Jovanović; Arch. of the Ministry of the Interior of Serbia, Tanasije Dinić file, interrogation of February 28, 1946, all cited in Borković (1979a), p. 367.

191. Dožić (1986), p. 91.

192. Tomasevich (1975), p. 442.

193. The number of Serbian Volunteer Corps is given as about 4,000 in N.A., microcopy T–120, roll 780, frame 371714, but a more precise number of 4,624 soldiers plus 217 officers is found in N.A., microcopy T–120, roll 780, frames 371712–13. The number of Serbian State Guards is 2,000 according to Borković (1979a), pp. 359–60, and 1,600 according to Kostić (1949), p. 203. See also Stefanović (1984), pp. 322–23; Milazzo (1975), pp. 178–79; Tomasevich (1975), p. 442 n. 38.

194. AMHI, Nedić arch., doc. 19, file 5, box 61, cited in Stefanović (1984), p. 323; Hermann Neubacher (1956), p. 192.

195. Kostić (1949), pp. 254, 256. Also, AMHI, Nedić arch., doc. 33, file 3, box 61, cited in Stefanović (1984), p. 328.

196. Walters (1988), p. 292; Wheeler (1980), pp. 118–19; Tomasevich (1975), pp. 108–109, 331; Roberts (1973), pp. 76–77; Milazzo (1975), p.

86; Browning (1985), p. 54; Lendvai (1971), p. 65; Hilberg (1985), p. 683; Borković (1979), pp. 245–52; Borković (1979a), pp. 7–14, 283–301; Romano (1980), pp. 60, 209; Stefanović (1984), pp. 154, 159; Zametica (1992), p. 8.

197. Borković (1979), p. 20.

198. Milazzo (1975), p. 86.

199. *Zbornik dokumenata* (1949), vol. 1, book 5, pp. 212–14.

200. In his postwar testimony, Dragi Jovanović stated that there were, in total, twenty acts of Partisan sabotage in Belgrade throughout the German occupation. See Stefanović, "Čovek koji je suviše znao i batinao," p. 80.

201. In June, 1944, the Serbian monarchy, reluctantly and with British pressure, called publicly for support for the Partisans, after which the Partisans began to attract many recruits from among Mihailović's Chetniks. See Tomasevich (1975), pp. 347, 414, 425; Singleton (1976), p. 97; Clissold (1949), p. 214; Borković (1979a), pp. 331, 358; Maclean (1949), pp. 534, 540–41; Hoffman and Neal (1962), p. 77; Vertepov (1963), pp. 24–25, 146. In one documented case, 3,000 Chetniks of the Čegar Chetnik Corps near Niš abandoned their Chetnik commander, Maj. Mirko Ćirković, to become Partisans *en masse* in September, 1944, joining the 14th Partisan Division. See Martinović-Bajica (1956), pp. 212, 446.

202. This amnesty was extended to those Chetniks, Croatian Home Guards, and Slovenian Home Guards who assisted the Partisans and who, theoretically, were not guilty of rape, murder, or arson—actions notoriously characteristic of the Chetniks. "Odluka o opštoj amnestiji lica koja su u četničkim jedinicima Draže Mihailovića učestvovala ili ih pomagala ili su učestvovali u jedinicama hrvatskih ili slovenačkih Domobranaca" [Decree of General Amnesty to the Individuals Who Participated or Supported the Chetnik Formations of Draža Mihailović or Participated in the Units of the Croatian or Slovene Home Guards], *Službeni List Demokratske Federativne Republike Jugoslavije*, February 1, 1945, vol. 1, no. 12, p. 6, cited in Harpke (1984), p. 14. Excluded from this amnesty were Ustashas, Slovene White and Blue Guards, followers of Ljotić, and members of Nedić's administration.

203. Patriarch Gavrilo Dožić, as quoted in Martinović-Bajica (1956), pp. 9–10.

204. Dožić (1986), p. 80.

205. Littlejohn (1985), p. 255. See the Ljotićites' tribute to Hitler on the occasion of his birthday: "Rođendan Vođe Rajha" [The Birthday of the Reich Führer], *Naša borba* (Slovenia), April 21, 1945, p. 2, as reproduced in Ivanović (1954), pp. 36–39. Contrast this with a revisionist Ljotićite

emigration publication in which Ljotić is portrayed as staunchly opposed to Hitler (see *Light of Truth: Selected Philosophical, Moral, and Political Ideas of Dimitrije Ljotić* [1984]).

CHAPTER 3: SERBIAN COMPLICITY
IN THE HOLOCAUST

1. See Browning (1983), pp. 55–90; Shelah (1987), pp. 243–60.

2. Browning (1983), pp. 60–61.

3. Browning designated the constellation of Turner, Benzler, Fuchs, Neuhausen, and the military commander for Serbia as "the five kings of Serbia." See Browning (1983), p. 59.

4. Such cooperation was particularly evident in the diplomatic negotiations behind, financing of, and construction of the Semlin *Judenlager,* or Sajmište, where half of the Jewish population of Serbia perished. See Browning (1983), p. 59.

5. For example, see Hilberg (1985), pp. 679–92.

6. See, for example, Eck (1958), pp. 262–64, 266–67, 269.

7. For the place of non-Muslims in the Ottoman Empire, see Freidenreich (1979), pp. 28–29; Petrovich (1976), p. 9; B. Jelavich (1983), vol. 1, pp. 39–40; Barnai (1990).

8. Petrovich (1976), pp. 9–10.

9. Freidenreich (1979), pp. 28–29; "Consul-General Longworth to the Earl of Clarendon. Belgrade, September 25, 1860," in: Great Britain, Foreign Office (1877), pp. 785–87; Petrovich (1976), p. 9; B. Jelavich (1983), vol. 1, pp. 39–40.

10. Petrovich (1976), pp. 26, 30–31, 48; West (1941), pp. 468, 519–20; "Men of Blood," *The Economist,* London, August 17, 1991, pp. 43–44.

11. Karađorđe's insurgents began by massacring unarmed Muslim civilians, usually not the individuals or officials who had committed injustices. To coerce hesitant Serbs to join the rebellion, insurgents would set fire to their homes or would hang a Turk at their door and denounce the householder to the Ottoman authorities. See Petrovich (1976), pp. 48–49; B. Jelavich (1983), vol. 1, p. 231.

12. B. Jelavich (1983), vol. 1, p. 198.

13. Petrovich (1976), pp. 9–10; Freidenreich (1979), p. 30; "Acting Consul-General Ricketts to Sir H. Bulwer. Belgrade, July 26, 1863," in: Great Britain, Foreign Office (1873), pp. 728–29.

14. "Acting Consul-General Ricketts to Sir H. Bulwer. Belgrade, July 26, 1863," in: Great Britain, Foreign Office (1873), pp. 728–29; Freidenreich (1979), p. 29; B. Jelavich (1983), vol. 1, p. 198.

15. B. Jelavich (1983), vol. 1, p. 202; Stokes (1990), p. 5.

16. For colorful portrayals of Miloš Obrenović, see Petrovich (1976), p. 209; B. Jelavich (1983), vol. 1, pp. 203, 207, 239.

17. Like Karađorđe, Miloš possessed an ungovernable temper. The slightest resistance to his wishes meant imprisonment. Opponents were routinely murdered. Miloš had Serbian Orthodox Archbishop Nikšić assassinated in his palace. See Laffan (1989), p. 35.

18. Freidenreich (1979), pp. 30–31; Franco (1910), pp. 205–206.

19. *Zbornik Zakona i Uredaba u Knjaževstvu Srbije* (1877a), pp. 194–95: Law no. 2244 of November 4, 1861; Franco (1910), pp. 205–206; Freidenreich (1979), pp. 30–31. See the following entries in: Great Britain, Foreign Office (1873): "Consul-General Longworth to Sir H. Bulwer. Belgrade, November 23, 1867," pp. 726–27; "Acting Consul-General Ricketts to Sir H. Bulwer. Belgrade, July 26, 1863," pp. 728–29. Also see "Acting Consul-General Watson to Sir H. Elliott. Belgrade, November 19, 1871," in: Great Britain, Foreign Office (1877), pp. 807–809.

20. "Consul-General Longworth to Earl Russell. Belgrade, August 10, 1865," in: Great Britain, Foreign Office (1873), pp. 734–36; Freidenreich (1979), p. 30.

21. *Zbornik Zakona i Uredaba u Knjaževstvu Srbije* (1877a), pp. 340–41: Law no. 1660 of October 30, 1856.

22. *Zbornik Zakona i Uredaba u Knjaževstvu Srbije* (1877), pp. 194–95. Law no. 2244 of November 4, 1861.

23. Freidenreich (1979), p. 30.

24. Nedomački and Goldstein (1988), p. 123.

25. Loeb (1877), pp. 19–20; Franco (1910), pp. 205–206.

26. See "Consul-General Longworth to Sir H. Bulwer. Belgrade, November 23, 1867," in: Great Britain, Foreign Office (1873), pp. 726–27; "Lord Stanley to Lord Lyons. Foreign Office, March 30, 1867," in: Great Britain, Foreign Office (1877), pp. 679–80; "Acting Consul-General Watson to Sir H. Elliott. Belgrade, November 19, 1871," pp. 807–809. Also see Temperley and Penson (1938), p. 211: "Correspondence Respecting the Condition and Treatment of the Jews in Servia and Roumania, 1875–76 [14 May 1877]" and p. 275: "Correspondence Respecting the Condition and Treatment of the Jews in Servia [12 April 1867]."

27. The issues of *Svetovide* are identified as nos. 134, 135, and 137. See Loeb (1877), pp. 33, 50–57.

28. "Acting Consul-General Blunt to Earl Russell. Belgrade, March 28, 1865," in: Great Britain, Foreign Office (1873), pp. 733–34. See also Matić (1988), p. 206; Franco (1910), pp. 205–206; Loeb (1877), pp. 34, 59–65.

29. "Acting Consul-General Blunt to Earl Russell. Belgrade, March 28, 1865," pp. 733–34.

30. "Lord Stanley to Lord Lyons. Foreign Office, March 30, 1867," pp. 679–80.

31. "The Jews in Servia: Motion for Papers" in: Great Britain, Parliament (1867), pp. 839–42.

32. Ibid., p. 844.

33. The Serbian Constitution of 1869 consisted of 133 articles. Article 132 concluded, "The Law of October 30, 1856, No. 1660, and the Law of November 4, 1861, No. 2244 remain valid." Law No. 1660 forbade Jews to engage in commerce in the Serbian interior; Law No. 2244 forbade Jews the right of domicile in the Serbian interior. For the text of the Serbian Constitution, see Mrđenović (1988), p. 88.

34. Loeb (1877), p. 35.

35. "A Statement, signed by many of the Jewish inhabitants of Belgrade, respecting the deplorable condition of their co-religionists in Servia, and praying for the protection of the British Government. Belgrade, August 5, 1869" in: Great Britain, Foreign Office (1877), pp. 781–82.

36. "Acting Consul-General Watson to Sir H. Elliott. Belgrade, November 19, 1871," pp. 807–809. See also Franco (1910), pp. 205–206.

37. Quoted from "Acting Consul-General Watson to Sir H. Elliott. Belgrade, November 19, 1871," pp. 807–809.

38. Löwenthal (1972), p. 869. See also Franco (1910), pp. 205–206.

39. Stokes (1990), p. 166.

40. Ibid., p. 137.

41. For example, the anti-Semitic tract, *Nedajmo Srbiju Čivutima* (Let's Not Give Serbia to the Kikes), written by "Several Serbian Patriots" in 1882, urged Serbs to follow "the example of German and Hungarian patriots" and "register in the Serbian Anti-Jewish (Anti-Semitic) Society that should be founded *as soon as possible* in Belgrade," p. 14. Italics and parentheses are in the Serbian original. *Vjerozakonsko učenje Talmuda ili ogledalo čivutskog poštenja* (Religious Teaching of the Talmud or the Mirror of Kike Honesty), issued in response to the Treaty of Berlin of 1878, was a translation from a German text, to which the translator, a Serbian Orthodox priest, added his own introduction: "Now when European diplomats force Serbia and Romania to recognize Jews and their religion as equal to other citizens before the law . . . when Jews are infiltrating more and more not only in cities but also villages, it is critically important for every family in all regions where there are Jews to read and learn by heart this book, because this book is a true mirror of the Jews from which it is

evident that to them divine law itself, the Talmud, demands them to cheat, steal, grab, have pawn shops, plunder, hate, destroy, exploit, and kill all people who are not Jews." See Pelagić (ca. 1878), p. 5.

42. Around 1880, Pašić founded the National Radical Party on a platform that attacked the obligations imposed by the Treaty of Berlin, including those connected with the Jews. See Stokes (1990), p. 186.

43. There is a dearth of scholarship on this subject. For example, the biography of Pašić by Dragnich (1974) contains no substantive discussion on his policies toward Serbia's Jews. In a broad study of the Jews of interwar Yugoslavia, Freidenreich (1979), p. 172, stated without further comment: "Most sympathetic to Jewish causes were the Radicals, the largest Serbian party. Nikola Pašić, party chief and frequent prime minister until his death in 1926, projected an image of himself as a great friend of the Jews."

44. Stokes (1990), p. 340 n. 26.

45. Löwenthal (1972), pp. 868–85; Franco (1910), pp. 205–206.

46. Franco (1910), pp. 205–206. See also Freidenreich (1979), pp. 32–34.

47. The leader of the 1903 plot to assassinate King Aleksandar Obrenović was Col. Dragutin Dimitrijević (known as "Apis"), who also played a prominent role in the 1914 assassination of Archduke Franz Ferdinand. See Crankshaw (1963) pp. 378–79; Banac (1984), p. 110; Denitch (1994), p. 174.

48. At the root of the Serbian officers' assassination of Obrenović was the king's failure to champion Greater Serbia. Obrenović had cultivated friendly relations with Austria-Hungary, and his acceptance of Austro-Hungarian claims to Bosnia-Herzegovina and the Sandžak, incorporated into the empire in 1878, frustrated Greater Serbian aspirations. With the ascent of Petar I Karađorđević to the throne, the army officers obtained, in large part, their foreign policy wishes: Petar I took a pro-Russian stance and Serbian relations with Austria-Hungary worsened, contributing to the chain of events that culminated in World War I. See Crankshaw (1963), pp. 371–89.

49. See Petrovich (1976), pp. 535–37; Banac (1984), pp. 142–43; Djilas (1991), p. 30. Petar suppressed the Black Hand by cultivating another faction of conspiratorial and ultranationalist Serbian army officers, the White Hand. See Banac (1984), p. 146.

50. Freidenreich (1979), pp. 180–81.

51. *Knjiga o Jevrejima: Sveska 1: Kod koga treba da kupujemo?* [Book about Jews: Volume 1: At Whose Store Should We Shop?]. Belgrade: Industrijska štamparija, 1904, pp. 5, 7, 31 (pamphlet, author denoted as "A.S.").

52. Milivoj M. Petrović (editor in chief), "Kako nas štiti vlast" [How the Authorities Protect Us], *Glasnik pravoslavne crkve* [Herald of the Orthodox Church], Belgrade, no. 16, 1912, p. 256.

53. For the treatment of the Jews in Croatian lands under Habsburg rule, see Schwarz (1910), pp. 363–65; Nedomački and Goldstein (1988), p. 136. The Croatian province of Dalmatia did not come under Habsburg rule until 1814, following the defeat of Napoleon (see Darby et al. [1966], pp. 30–33, 52–54; Kečkemet [1971], p. 121.

54. The Edict of Tolerance *(Toleranzpatent)* of 1781 largely abolished discrimination against Protestants and permitted Protestants, but not Jews, to convert to Catholicism. The edict itself did not address the rights of Jews concerning domicile, livelihood, or education, but special legislation extended the Jews' rights in these areas. Generally, the Jews were forced to abandon certain traditional customs and assimilate more fully into Germanic culture. See Kann (1974), pp. 186, 191. For the impact of this legislation on the Jews of Croatia, see Nedomački and Goldstein (1988), p. 137.

55. The legal position of Jews in Croatian lands is discussed in Schwarz (1910), pp. 363–65; Matić (1988), p. 206.

56. Schwarz (1910), pp. 363–65; Matić (1988), pp. 206–207; Löwenthal (1972), pp. 868–85; Franco (1910), pp. 205–206; Nedomački and Goldstein (1988), p. 138.

57. Schwarz (1910), pp. 363–65.

58. Freidenreich (1979), p. 180.

59. Ibid., pp. 179, 183.

60. Romano (1980), p. 572; Matić (1988), p. 207; Freidenreich (1979), pp. 183–85.

61. Freidenreich (1979), pp. 173, 184; Maček (1957), pp. 204–205. For representative Zbor publications, see "O Jevrejima" [On Jews], *Naš put,* Petrovgrad, Serbia, no. 4, March 26, 1939, p. 2; "Opomena Jevrejima" [Warning to Jews], *Naš put* [Our Way (publication of the Yugoslav National Movement 'Zbor')], Petrovgrad (modern Zrenjanin, Vojvodina), no. 3, March 19, 1939, p. 3.

62. The accused editor was acquitted on the convoluted logic that, since his attacks were against the Jewish *race* but not the Jewish *religion,* the editor had not violated the constitution, according to which Jews were a *religious* minority, but not a *national* minority. See Freidenreich (1979), pp. 184–86.

63. Gilbert (1984), p. 64; Freidenreich (1979), p. 186; Matić (1988), p. 208.

64. "Inostrani pregled: Patrijarh Varnava za borbu protiv komunizma" [Foreign Report: Patriarch Varnava for the Fight against Communism],

Glasnik srpske pravoslavne patrijaršije [Herald of the Serbian Orthodox Patriarchate], Belgrade, nos. 1 and 2, February, 1937, pp. 33–34. Patriarch Varnava's meeting with German journalists was also reported in the German press on January 4, 1937.

65. "Kroz crkvenu štampu: Domaći listovi i časopisi: Tri aveti" [Through the Religious Press: Domestic Papers and Journals: 'Three Specters'], *Glasnik srpske pravoslavne patrijaršije* [Herald of the Serbian Orthodox Patriarchate], Belgrade, nos. 5 and 6, April 12, 1937, p. 197. This version of "Three Specters" is excerpted from the original, which appeared in *Pregled crkve eparhije žičke* [Church Review of the Eparchy of Žiča], written by Serbian Orthodox priest M. Pašić.

66. Freidenreich (1979), p. 182.

67. Dawidowicz (1966), p. 391. Dr. Isaac Alcalay, chosen as chief rabbi by King Aleksandar in 1929 and appointed to the newly created Senate by the king in 1932, was the second Jew to ever hold a position in the Yugoslav Skupština (Parliament). See Freidenreich (1979), pp. 106, 175.

68. "Uredbe i o uredbama protiv Jevreja," *Jevrejski glas,* Belgrade, vol. 13, no. 31 (October 16, 1940), pp. 1–3. For an English translation, see Freidenreich (1979), pp. 239–42.

69. Freidenreich (1979), p. 173.

70. Ibid., p. 186.

71. Ibid., p. 179.

72. Krakov (1963), p. 223; Parežanin (1971), p. 219.

73. Parežanin (1971), pp. 475–76.

74. For the list of contributors to *Naša borba* during its first year of publication, see "Godina dana 'Naše borbe': Saradnici 'Naše borbe' od 7 Septembra 1941 do 23 Avgusta 1942!" [A Year of "Naša borba": Contributors to "Naša borba" from September 7, 1941, to August 23, 1942], *Naša borba,* August 30, 1942, p. 5.

75. Borković (1979a), p. 174; Parežanin (1971), pp. 34, 63; AMHI, Nedić arch., doc. 1, file 6, box 98, cited in Borković (1979a), p. 273.

76. M. Jevtić, "Svedočanstva: Jevreji u doba Karađorđa i kneza Miloša" [Testimonies: Jews at the Time of Karađorđe and Prince Miloš], *Naša borba,* Belgrade, November 23, 1941, p. 9; M. Jevtić, "Svedočanstva: jevreji u doba kneza Aleksandra, kn. Mihaila pa do najnovijih dana" [Testimonies: Jews at the Time of Prince Aleksandar, Prince Mihailo to the Most Recent Days], *Naša borba,* Belgrade, November 30, 1941, p. 9.

77. A. T., "Borba za čistoću rase. Jevreji nikada više neće biti lekari, apotekari, advokati i sudije" [The Struggle for Racial Purity. Jews Never Again Shall Be Physicians, Pharmacists, Lawyers, and Judges], *Obnova,* Belgrade, November 3, 1941, p. 4.

78. "Jedno neobrađeno naučno polje . . . dokumentovana istorija jevrejskog pitanja u Srbiji" [An Unexplored Field of Science . . . a Documented History of the Jewish Question in Serbia], *Obnova,* Belgrade, December 9, 1941, p. 8.

79. For an index of the British diplomatic correspondence concerning the Jews of Serbia, see Temperley and Penson (1938), p. 211, ("Correspondence Respecting the Condition and Treatment of the Jews in Servia and Roumania, 1875–76 [14 May 1877]"), and p. 275, "Correspondence Respecting the Condition and Treatment of the Jews in Servia [12 April 1867]." The relevant British diplomatic correspondence, including the written appeals to the British from the Serbian Jewish communities, can be found in Loeb (1877), pp. 41–92.

80. Mojić (1941), p. 40. The author was secretary-general of Zbor, the Serbian fascist party.

81. "Naši seljaci i radnici—robovi jevrejski" [Our Peasants and Workers—Jewish Slaves], *Obnova,* Belgrade, October 20, 1941, p. 3. The excerpt was taken from Mojić (1941), pp. 34–35.

82. Par. [Ratko Parežanin], "Kroz knjige i listove: 'Zakoni i dela Jevreja'" [Through Books and Magazines: The Laws and Deeds of the Jews], *Obnova,* Belgrade, September 8, 1941, p. 6.

83. Kostić (1949), p. 50.

84. AMHI, Nedić arch., doc. 2, file 4, box 153, cited in Stefanović (1984), p. 128.

85. Löwenthal (1957), pp. 8–9.

86. Romano (1980), p. 65.

87. M. M., "Jevreji sa pravoslavnim krštenicama. Dvanaesti dobrovoljački odred uhvatio je u Nišu sedam beogradskih Jevreja, koji su živeli pod srpskim imenima" [Jews with Orthodox Baptismal Certificates. The Twelfth Volunteer Detachment Caught Seven Belgrade Jews in Niš Living under Serbian Names], *Obnova,* Belgrade, February 1, 1942, p. 7.

88. Shelah (1990), pp. 288–89.

89. Throat-slitting has a long tradition among Serbian guerrilla fighters in war. See Lees (1990), pp. 143, 147, 249; Durham (1914), pp. 185, 193, 236–38; Tomasevich (1975), p. 260; Maček (1957), pp. 232, 236, 238, 250.

90. Shelah (1990), pp. 288–89; Romano (1980), p. 75; Löwenthal (1957), pp. 42–43.

91. Löwenthal (1957), pp. 42–43.

92. Shelah (1990), pp. 288–89.

93. Tomasevich (1975), p. 194.

94. Cvijić and Vasović (1991), p. 149.

95. Romano (1980), pp. 217–18. Draža Mihailović relocated his Chetnik headquarters to Kalinovik in early 1943 (see Parežanin [1971], p. 214).

96. "Za nekoliko dana biće u Beogradu otvorena jedna istorijska izložba. Rad jevrejstva, masonerije i komunizma u Srbiji i u svetu" [In a Few Days an Historical Exhibition Will Open in Belgrade. The Work of Judaism, Masonry, and Communism in Serbia and the World], *Obnova*, Belgrade, October 17, 1941, p. 3; "Tajne prostorija u Garašaninovoj ulici broj 8. Juče je u Beogradu otvorena velika Antimasonska izložba" [Secrets of the Rooms on Garašanin Street no. 8. Yesterday in Belgrade a Large Anti-Masonic Exhibition Opened], *Obnova*, Belgrade, October 23, 1941, p. 3; "Jedan društveno-politički događaj. Kroz antimasonsku izložbu. Izložba će se otvoriti ove nedelje" [One Socio-Political Event. Through the Anti-Masonic Exhibition. The Exhibition will Open This Week], *Obnova*, Belgrade, [date illegible], 1941, p. 6; "Kroz Antimasonsku izložbu koja je danas otvorena. Interijer jevrejske sobe usred Beograda i misli koje čoveku padaju na pamet povodom toga" [Through the Anti-Masonic Exhibition That Opened Today. The Interior of the Jewish Room in the Middle of Belgrade and Thoughts Which Occur to a Person on That Occasion], *Obnova*, Belgrade, October 22, 1941, p. 5; "Povodom Antimasonske izložbe. Skinut je veo sa mnogih tajni" [On the Occasion of the Anti-Masonic Exhibition. The Veil Has Been Removed to Reveal Many Secrets], *Obnova*, Belgrade, November 8, 1941, p. 5.

97. Odić and Komarica (1977), p. 89; S. D. K., "Svedočanstva: Izložba svetskih negativnosti" [Testimonies: An Exhibition of the World Negativities], *Naša borba*, Belgrade, October 26, 1941, p. 9.

98. Dr. Laza Prokić, "Veliki uspeh antimasonske izložbe" [Great Success of the Anti-Masonic Exhibition], *Obnova*, Belgrade, November 4, 1941, p. 5; "Tajne prostorija u Garašaninovoj ulici broj 8. Juče je u Beogradu otvorena velika Antimasonska izložba" [Secrets of the Rooms on Garašanin Street no. 8. Yesterday in Belgrade a Large Anti-Masonic Exhibition Opened], *Obnova*, Belgrade, October 23, 1941, p. 3. Other prominent collaborators in Perić's Section of State Propaganda included Momčilo Bakić, Milan Banić, Milovan Popović, and Miodrag Đorđević. See Borković (1979a), p. 274.

99. Odić and Komarica (1977), pp. 52–53; Stefanović (1984), p. 65. For information on the Nazi propaganda publication *Signal*, see Mayer (1976, 1978, 1979).

100. Stevan Klujić worked for the BDS *(Befehlshaber der Sicherheitspolizei und des Sicherheitsdienstes)*, i.e., the commander of the Security Police and Security Service. See Odić and Komarica (1977), pp. 52–53; Borković (1979a), p. 166.

101. S. D. K., "Svedočanstva: izložba svetskih negativnosti," p. 9. For an example of Balić's journalistic writings, see Momčilo Balić, "Svedočanstva: Jevreji kao monopolski velikozakupci i velikoprodavci" [Testimonies: Jews as Monopolistic Lessees and Wholesalers], *Naša borba,* October 5, 1941, p. 7.

102. "Ogromna poseta publike Antimasonskoj izložbi" [Enormous Attendance by the Public at the Anti-Masonic Exhibition], *Obnova,* Belgrade, October 27, 1941, p. 4.

103. "Juče je 20.000 posetilac antimasonske izložbe doživeo, zaista, prijatno iznenađenje" [Yesterday the Twenty-thousandth Visitor of the Anti-Masonic Exhibition Had a Very Pleasant Surprise], *Obnova,* Belgrade, November 3, 1941, p. 4. The twenty-thousandth visitor was presented with "a fine woolen blanket and two pounds of lard . . . very handy for the coming winter"; Borković (1979a), p. 276; "Ogromna poseta publike Antimasonskoj izložbi" [Enormous Attendance by the Public at the Anti-Masonic Exhibition], *Obnova,* Belgrade, October 27, 1941, p. 4; "Velika poseta antimasonske izložbe" [Great Interest in the Anti-Masonic Exhibition], *Obnova,* Belgrade, October 28, 1941, p. 4; Dr. Lazar Prokić, "Veliki uspeh antimasonske izložbe" [Great Success of the Anti-Masonic Exhibition], *Obnova,* Belgrade, November 4, 1941, p. 5.

104. "Povodom Antimasonske izložbe. Skinut je veo sa mnogih tajni," p. 5.

105. "Antimasonske poštanske marke" [Anti-Masonic Postage Stamps], *Obnova,* Belgrade, December 23, 1941, p. 8. *Scott 1993 Standard Postage Stamp Catalogue,* vol. 4 (1992), p. 610. Stamps from the Anti-Masonic Exhibition are listed under Scott nos. 2NB15-18 (illus. nos. OSP5-8).

106. Prokić (1941), pp. 25–26.

107. Romano (1980), pp. 60, 64.

108. Shelah (1987), p. 247.

109. Borković (1979), p. 330.

110. AMHI, Nedić arch., Belgrade municipal government to Department of Social Welfare, February 3, 1942, cited in Browning (1983), p. 63. See also Löwenthal (1957), p. 26; Romano (1980), p. 81.

111. Browning (1983), pp. 60–61.

112. Ibid., p. 85; Shelah (1987), p. 253.

113. "Tragedija naših sugrađana Jevreja" [Tragedy of our Jewish Fellow Citizens], *Politika,* Belgrade, November 1, 1944, p. 3.

114. N.A., microcopy T-120, roll 200, frames 153408-09, Felix Benzler's report about his meeting with Nedić on September 2, 1941, September 2, 1941.

115. Museum of the Revolution of Yugoslavia, Belgrade, doc. M-372/16,

cited in Borković (1979), p. 305. The Osnabrück camp was called Oflag VI C. See Cvijić and Vasović (1991), p. 210.

116. AMHI, doc. 12, file 2A-1, box 1, cited in Borković (1979), pp. 305–306.

117. Romano (1980), p. 60.

118. Shelah (1990b), pp. 1340–42; Löwenthal (1957), pp. 8–9; Romano (1980), pp. 75, 209.

119. "Uredba o pripadanju imovine Jevreja u Srbiji" [Decree on the Ownership of Jewish Property in Serbia], *Obnova*, Belgrade, August 30, 1942, p. 5; "Uredba o pripadanju imovine Jevreja Srbiji" [Decree on the Belonging of Jewish Property to Serbia], *Službene novine*, August 28, 1942, p. 1; Hilberg (1985), p. 682; *Zbornik dokumenata* (1978), vol. 12, book 3, pp. 743–814, report by the German Plenipotentiary for the Economy in Serbia, Franz Neuhausen, second half of 1942 to the end of 1943.

120. Milovanović (1978), vol. 2, p. 91; *Glasnik srpske pravoslavne crkve* [Herald of the Serbian Orthodox Church], Belgrade, nos. 2 and 3, March 1, 1942, p. 10.

121. "Srpska pravoslavna crkva protiv razornih elemenata i komunizma: Arhijereji srpske pravoslavne crkve izjavljuju da će se boriti na strani generala Nedića" [Serbian Orthodox Church against Destruction Elements and Communism: Representatives of the Serbian Orthodox Church Declare That They Will Fight on the Side of General Nedić], *Obnova*, Belgrade, October 28, 1941, p. 1.

122. "Rodoljubive reči jednog sveštenika" [Patriotic Words of a Priest], *Obnova*, Belgrade, December 1, 1941, p. 6.

123. A. T., "Borba za čistoću rase. Jevreji nikada više neće biti lekari, apotekari, advokati i sudije," p. 4.

124. For the text of the decree of January 30, 1942, see Metropolit Josif of Skopje, "Naredba vojnog zapovednika za Srbiju o zabrani prelaza Jevreja u drugu veru" [Decree by the Military Commander for Serbia on the Prohibition of Jews Converting to another Religion], *Glasnik srpske pravoslavne crkve* [Herald of the Serbian Orthodox Church], Belgrade, March 1, 1942, p. 12.

125. Mihailo Olćan, "Nastupa novo vreme, dolazi novi duh, a taj duh je, našom srećom i duh našeg naroda" [A New Time Is Beginning, a New Spirit Is Coming, and This Spirit, through Our Good Fortune, Is the Spirit of Our Nation as Well], *Obnova*, Belgrade, November 21, 1941, p. 5.

126. See Dobrijević (1989), p. 92; Velimirovich (1989), pp. xii–xiii. Rebecca West's diary of her travels throughout Yugoslavia, although unabashedly polemical and pro-Serbian (see Buck [1992], pp. 1131–32), nevertheless offers an intriguing description of Nikolaj Velimirović, the

bishop of Žiča: "He struck me now, as when I had seen him for the first time in the previous year, as the most remarkable human being I have ever met, not because he was wise or good, for I have still no idea to what extent he is either, but because he was the supreme magician. . . . He was so apt for magic that had it not existed he could have invented it." See West (1941), p. 720.

127. Paris (1961), p. 49.

128. A total of 2,720 clergymen were detained at Dachau: two-thirds were Polish. Among the 50 clergy from Yugoslavia, 35 were Catholic Slovenes or Croats, and less than 15 were Orthodox Serbs. Of these 50, four died at Dachau. See Berben (1975), pp. 276–77.

129. Serbian Orthodox Patriarch Gavrilo Dožić was held in Dachau with Velimirović. Dožić's memoirs do not record any episodes of torture or mistreatment at Dachau (see Dožić [1986], pp. 80–82). For a general discussion of the imprisonment of clergy at Dachau, see Musioł (1968), pp. 89–90. For further sources on Velimirović's internment at Dachau, see also Stefanović (1984), pp. 307, 328; Borković (1979a), p. 367; Tomislav Vuković, "Mit u pet slika: O suvremenoj srpskoj mitologiji, a u povodu prijenosa posmrtnih ostataka episkopa Nikolaja Velimirovića" [A Myth in Five Images: About Contemporary Serbian Mythology on the Occasion of the Transfer of the Remains of Bishop Nikolaj Velimirović], *Danas*, Zagreb, May 7, 1991, pp. 38–39. This last source, published in Croatia just prior to the onset of war, is accurate.

130. Velimirović (1985), p. 59.

131. Velimirović (1985), pp. 161–62. See also p. 91.

132. AMHI, no. 7/1, box 1, interrogation of Dragi Jovanović, cited in Stefanović (1984), p. 307; Neubacher (1956), pp. 186–87. For an assessment of Ljotić's influence in Vienna and Berlin, see Martic (1980), pp. 219–39.

133. Neubacher (1956), pp. 186–87. See also AMHI, doc. 7, file 1, box 1, interrogation of Dragi Jovanović, cited in Stefanović (1984), p. 307. See also Arch. of the Ministry of the Interior of Serbia, the statement by Milan Nedić concerning the arrest of Dr. Gavrilo Dožić and Bishop Velimirović; AMHI, doc. 19, file 7, box 1, interrogation of Dragi Jovanović, both cited in Borković (1979a), p. 270.

134. See Romano (1980), pp. 201, 208. Before World War II, about 10,500 Jews lived in Belgrade, about 350 in Niš, about 250 in Novi Pazar (Sandžak), about 70 in Kragujevac, about 70 in Smederevo, and an insignificant number in other towns of Serbia proper—totaling about 11,240. Nedić's Serbia included the Banat region of Vojvodina, containing a population of 640,000 (including about 130,000 *Volksdeutsche*). On June 5,

1941, Banat was accorded an autonomous status but was reincorporated into Nedić's Serbia on December 26, 1941. See Borković (1979), p. 15.

135. Löwenthal (1957), pp. 42–43; Romano (1980), p. 75; Hilberg (1985), p. 692; Browning (1983), p. 90.

136. Considerable revisionism exists concerning Dimitrije Ljotić. For example, in his postwritings, Miloš Martić (a signatory to the "Appeal to the Serbian Nation") portrayed the Zbor movement in a more favorable light, even presenting a rationale for the Zbor's anti-Jewish stance, while omitting all mention of the Zbor movement's active complicity in the Holocaust. See Martic (1980), pp. 219–39, esp. 231–32. Rašević observed in 1953 that, in the post–1945 period, the topic of Ljotić's deep-rooted anti-Semitism does not appear in the Ljotićite press at all (see Rašević [1953], p. 12). This observation remains valid at the time of this writing. See, for example, the revisionist *Light of Truth: Selected Philosophical, Moral, and Political Ideas of Dimitrije Ljotić* (1984). For more on Serbian complicity in the Holocaust, see Manoschek (1993).

CHAPTER 4: COLLABORATION AND RESISTANCE IN CROATIA AND BOSNIA-HERZEGOVINA

1. For an insightful analysis of Italian policy toward the Balkans and the reasons for Italian support for Croatian separatism, see Sadkovich (1987), pp. 1–11.

2. Jelić-Butić (1977), p. 67; Tomasevich (1975), p. 70.

3. Maček (1957), pp. 189–90, 220–21, 228–30; Milazzo (1975), p. 5; Jukić (1974), pp. 74–75; Curtis (1992), p. 38.

4. Ostović (1952), pp. 103–104. Of 419 delegates who voted on the first Yugoslav Constitution on June 28, 1921, 223 voted in favor (184 Serbs, 18 Muslims, 11 Slovenes, 10 Croats), 35 against, 161 abstentions (including 83 Croats).

5. Pavlowitch (1971), p. 80; Hory and Broszat (1964), pp. 19–21.

6. In her memoirs, the mother of Dimitrije Ljotić used the same term *ustashas* to describe armed Serbian rebels in Bosnia in 1875. See Ljotić (1973), pp. 67, 80–81, 181.

7. B. Jelavich (1983), vol. 1, p. 201; Pavlowitch (1971), p. 80; Djilas (1991), p. 109.

8. Shelah (1990), p. 1552.

9. Nešo Temelkovski, "Osvetnikot" [The Avenger], *Glas* [Voice], Skopje, no. 12, 1992, pp. 40–41; B. Jelavich (1983), vol. 1, p. 202; Tomasevich (1975), p. 10. The assassin had a number of aliases.

10. Krizman (1978), pp. 564–73. The statement that the early Ustasha movement was composed largely of intellectuals is entirely false but often

repeated. See, for example, Avakumovic (1971), p. 140. See also Tomašić (1942), p. 79.

11. Djilas (1991), pp. 109–13; Djilas (1973), pp. 131–33.

12. Djilas (1991), p. 109. See also Tomasevich (1975), pp. 63, 105 n. 39.

13. Jelić-Butić (1977), pp. 64–65.

14. Milazzo (1975), p. 6; Jukić (1974), pp. 74–75, 92; Tomasevich (1975), p. 105.

15. See Singleton (1976), pp. 87–89; Poliakov and Sabille (1983), p. 134; Bošković et al. (1988), p. 317; Hory and Broszat (1964), map at end; Pavlowitch (1971), p. 116; Maček (1957), pp. 230–33; Milazzo (1975), pp. 6–10. For the precise demarcation line between the German and Italian occupation zones in the Independent State of Croatia, see Jareb (1960), p. 101.

16. Djilas (1991), p. 212 n. 47.

17. Lašić-Vasojević (1976), pp. 252–53; Tomasevich (1975), pp. 105–108; Milazzo (1975), p. 9; Dawidowicz (1966), p. 390; Djilas (1991), pp. 211–12 n. 47.

18. Tomasevich (1975), p. 100.

19. Hausner (1968), pp. 125–26.

20. The German authorities appear to have understood that the GUS was the real seat of authority in the Independent State of Croatia. As late as September, 1941, all known German diplomatic correspondence concerning the racial laws was conducted with the GUS rather than with the Ministry of the Interior. See N.A., microcopy T-120, roll 4748.

21. Colić (1973), pp. 95ff; Jelić-Butić (1977), pp. 99–103, 109, 179.

22. Tomasevich (1975), p. 106; Denitch (1994), p. 34.

23. Jukić (1974), pp. 97–98, 120.

24. Krizman (1980), p. 49.

25. Jelić-Butić (1977), p. 175; Morley (1980), p. 151.

26. Tomasevich (1975), pp. 227–28.

27. Slijepčević (1978), p. 517.

28. Tomasevich (1975), pp. 229–30.

29. Milazzo (1975), p. 80; Great Britain, Naval Intelligence Division (1944), p. 382.

30. N.A., microcopy T-120, roll 4748 (filmed without frame numbers), cable from German ambassador Siegfried Kasche to the foreign office in Berlin, May 29, 1941; letter from Pavelić's chief of staff, Colonel Sabljak, to the German embassy, September 20, 1941. See also Krizman (1978), p. 480; Krizman (1980), p. 136; Pattee (1953), pp. 99–101.

31. Hilberg (1985), pp. 710–11.

32. The first Jews were incarcerated at Pag on June 24, 1941; these camps were closed at the end of August, 1941. For additional references to the concentration of Jews at Pag, see Shelah (1990c), p. 1719; Morley (1980), p. 160; Matić (1988), p. 211; Zemljar (1988), pp. 52, 131, 159, 161. After the camp at Pag was disbanded, the commander of the Fifth Italian Army Corps, General Balocco, ordered corpses exhumed and burned to prevent an epidemic. In Slano, three mass graves were found to contain 791 corpses, including 407 men, 293 women, and 91 children (see Romano [1980], pp. 123–24, 579; see copies of the original Italian documents in Zemljar [1988], pp. 222–34). An Italian physician who examined several graveyards on Pag in early September, 1941, estimated 8,000 to 9,000 total victims at Pag (see Zemljar [1988], p. 239). The figure of 8,000 Jewish victims at Pag is cited in Poliakov and Sabille (1983), p. 132, but this must reflect all victims.

33. Romano (1980), p. 579.

34. For an analysis of the differential German and Italian responses to the plight of the Croatian Jews during World War II, see Steinberg (1990), pp. 220–41. For a bibliography on the Italian rescue of Jews, see Marrus (1987), p. 74 n. 36. See also Freidenreich (1979), pp. 191–92.

35. Löwenthal (1972), p. 879; Stulli (1989), pp. 14–15; Freidenreich (1979), p. 218; Romano (1980), pp. 580–81, 588–89; Goldstein (1988), p. 191.

36. In August, 1941, according to German estimates, there were 4,000 to 5,000 Jewish refugees in Dubrovnik and Mostar. By November, 1941, the 415 Jews of Split were joined by approximately 2,000 refugees from the German occupation zone; the 87 Jews of Dubrovnik were joined by approximately 1,600 refugees from Bosnia and Herzegovina, 117 refugees from Germany, and 147 refugees from Austria, Poland and Czechoslovakia. See Stulli (1989), pp. 14–15; Löwenthal (1972), p. 879.

37. Although Mussolini had approved the enforcement of anti-Jewish legislation in the Italian occupation zone of the Independent State of Croatia, the Italian occupation forces routinely hindered the enforcement, to the consternation of German authorities. See Marrus (1987), pp. 74 n. 36, 216–17; Freidenreich (1979), p. 192; Romano (1980), pp. 580–81, 588–89; Carpi (1990), pp. 729–30; Löwenthal (1972), p. 879; Poliakov and Sabille (1983), pp. 140–41, 148–49, 168–70; Matić (1988), p. 211.

38. Löwenthal (1957), p. 22; Romano (1980), p. 154.

39. Löwenthal (1957), p. 22; Romano (1980), p. 154.

40. The Ustasha concentration camps Slano and Metajna were opened under the authority of Juraj Crljenko, a former Ljotićite, who had pre-

viously attempted without success to create a Zbor party on Pag. Slano was divided into a Jewish camp and a Serbian camp; Croats and Gypsies were confined in the "Serbian" camp. See Zemljar (1988), pp. 46, 61, 69–70, 159, 164.

41. Romano (1980), p. 123.

42. Ibid., pp. 588–89. The Jewish Rab Battalion, one of two all-Jewish Partisan units formed during the war, was composed of 243 former Rab inmates and later merged with other Partisan units.

43. Romano (1980), pp. 580–81, 588–89; Silk (1947), p. 40; Löwenthal (1957), p. 22; Löwenthal (1972), p. 879; Stulli (1989), pp. 14–15; Matić (1988), p. 211. Of the 121 Jews whose names are memorialized on plaques in the synagogue in Split, 54 were deported to Banjica and 56 were deported to Jasenovac (see Kečkemet [1971], pp. 197–202).

44. The source for this figure is the Federation of Jewish Communities of Yugoslavia (see Romano [1980], pp. 580–81, 588–89). According to Dawidowicz (1966), pp. 391–92, in prewar Yugoslavia there were 76,000 Jews, with 30,000 in the Independent State of Croatia and 12,000 in Serbia. Total losses were 60,000.

45. Hilberg (1985), p. 718; Romano (1980), pp. 580–81, 588–89; Shelah (1990c), p. 1719; Freidenreich (1979), p. 307 n. 11.

46. Clissold (1949), pp. 114–15; Hoettl (1954), p. 161; Maček (1957), pp. 230–33; Hoffman and Neal (1962), p. 70; Dawidowicz (1966), p. 390; Pavlowitch (1971), p. 110; Jukić (1974), p. 125; Singleton (1976), pp. 88–89; Milazzo (1975), p. 10; Tomasevich (1975), pp. 108, 265 n. 3; Hehn (1979), p. 70; Romano (1980), p. 91; Banac (1992), p. 154.

47. Hoettl (1954), p. 148.

48. See Banac (1984), p. 35.

49. Hoettl (1954), p. 148.

50. Djilas (1991), pp. 211–12 n. 47; Maček (1957), pp. 239–40.

51. Maček (1957), pp. 230–33; Pavlowitch (1971), p. 110; Singleton (1976), pp. 88–89; Clissold (1949), pp. 114–15; Hoffman and Neal (1962), p. 70; Dawidowicz (1966), p. 390; Romano (1980), p. 91; Jukić (1974), p. 125; Milazzo (1975), p. 10; Tomasevich (1975), pp. 108, 265 n. 3; Hehn (1979), p. 70; Banac (1992), p. 154; Hoettl (1954), p. 161.

52. AMHI, London microfilm collection, report of Rudolf Lüters, the commander of the German Army in the Independent State of Croatia, to Field Marshal Alexander Löhr, cited in: *Bosanski muslimani: Čimbenik mira izmedju Srba i Hrvata: Interview Adila Zulfikarpašića* (1986), p. 65. See also *Zbornik dokumenata* (1978), vol. 12, book 3, p. 172; Milazzo (1975), p. 10: "The émigré Ustaši group had very little domestic support

and was utterly unfit to rule a greater Croatia. Even according to members of the Ustaši organization, the movement had at most about 40,000 'followers,' or barely 6 percent of the population. The largely rural Croatian population was traditionally loyal to the Peasant party; several efforts of the Ustaši leaders to win Maček over to some sort of collaborationist posture failed." Milazzo's calculation of 6 percent Ustasha "followers" appears too high. According to wartime census data, which might have exaggerated the Croatian population for political reasons, the population of the Independent State of Croatia was nearly 7 million, of which 4,817,710 were classified as Croats (and this would include the Muslim population of 900,000). See *Hrvatski list* [Croatian Newspaper], Osijek, May 20, 1941, p. 8, cited in Samardžija (1993), p. 41. Scholarly postwar demographic studies estimate the total population of Croatia and Bosnia-Herzegovina in 1941 to have been 6,605,000 (see Žerjavić [1991], p. 92). By any constellation of these figures, even excluding Serbs and Muslims altogether, 40,000 Ustasha followers would represent 1 percent support among the Croats, a figure close to the German estimates of support.

53. Maček (1957), pp. 239–46.

54. See Djilas (1991), p. 172; Denitch (1994), p. 62.

55. Supek (1992), p. 102.

56. Mijo Bobetko, "Prvi partizani u Hrvatskoj" [The First Partisans in Croatia] in: *Dvadeset prva: List XXI Brigade* [The Twenty-first: The Newspaper of the 21st Brigade], no. 3, 1943, pp. 20–22.

57. The July 7 Prize, awarded by the Yugoslav government to honor Partisan heroes, took its name from the date of the first official Partisan uprising in Serbia led by Tito in 1941.

58. N.A., microcopy T-81, roll 544, frame 712; T-312, roll 450, frame 121; T-312, roll 464, frame 387. Concerning these sources: *Funkhorch* (radio intercept) companies monitored all military and paramilitary frequencies, forwarding their reports to *Abwehr* (German military intelligence). In general, radio intercept provided the most reliable intelligence information available to both sides during World War II.

59. N.A., microcopy T-120, roll 5799, frames H310829–30; Croatian Islamic Centre (1978), pp. 68–69; "Krvavi dokumenti o četničkim zločinima u Hercegovini 1941. godine" [Bloody Documents about Chetnik Crimes in Herzegovina, 1941], *Zatvorenik*, Zagreb, vol. 2, no. 16, 1991, pp. 10–12; Maček (1957), pp. 231–32; Benković (1947), p. 40.

60. Irvine (1993), pp. 115–19.

61. Djilas (1991), p. 98; Maček (1957), pp. 238, 250; Hehn (1979), p. 70; Tomasevich (1975), pp. 106–107, 159.

62. As of 1941, the population of Yugoslavia, 16 million, was distrib-

uted as follows: Serbia (41 percent), Croatia (24 percent), Bosnia-Herzegovina (17 percent), Slovenia (8 percent), Macedonia (7 percent), and Montenegro (3 percent). The figure for Serbia can be subdivided into Serbia proper (26 percent), Vojvodina (11 percent), and Kosovo (4 percent). See Žerjavić (1991), pp. 92–93.

63. From 1941 through 1945, there were a total of 228,474 Partisans in Croatia, of which 140,124 were ethnic Croats and 63,710 were ethnic Serbs. See Jelić (1978), p. 304.

64. Irvine (1993), p. 171.

65. Đuro Zatezalo, *Četvrta konferencija Komunističke partije za okrug Karlovca, 1945* (Karlovac, 1985), pp. 53–55, cited in Irvine (1993), pp. 171–72. Most of the Serbian defectors returned in response to an offer of amnesty. Of more than one dozen prominent defectors brought to trial in mid-July, 1944, five were executed and the rest received long prison sentences.

66. Djilas (1977), p. 314.

67. Supek (1992), p. 101.

68. Ibid., p. 111.

69. Jelić (1978), p. 291. For a detailed study of the 1,609 National Liberation Committees in Croatia during 1942, see Sirotković (1990), p. 17.

70. Trgo, "Hrvatska," p. 370.

71. As of May, 1944, the ten-member presidency of the ZAVNOH included Andrija Hebrang and Ivan Gošnjak (Communist Party); Franjo Gaži, Stjepan Prvčić, and Filip Lakuš (Croatian Peasant Party); Rade Pribićević and Simo Eror (Serbian-led Independent Democratic Party); and Catholic priest Svetozar Ritig, poet Vladimir Nazor, and Ante Mandić (no party affiliation). See the Museum of Revolution of the People of Croatia, photoarchive no. 2602/65-21, cited in Ivanković-Vonta (1988), p. 255.

72. Roberts (1973), pp. 76–77.

73. Tomasevich (1975), p. 331.

74. Milazzo (1975), pp. 109–10; Tomasevich (1975), pp. 226–29; Popović et al. (1988), p. 73.

75. Popović et al. (1988), p. 73.

76. Ibid., pp. 93–95.

77. *Zbornik dokumenata* (1981), vol. 14, book 1, doc. 180, p. 672, report of Ilija Trifunović-Birčanin to Draža Mihailović concerning current issues of the Chetnik organization, October 20, 1942. See also Popović et al. (1988), pp. 174, 179.

78. Hory and Broszat (1964), pp. 133–34. See also Popović et al. (1988), p. 173; Jareb (1960), p. 111.

79. N.A., microcopy T-77, roll 883, frames 5, 631, 890–92; Colić

(1977), pp. 61–79 (esp. p. 68). See also Tomasevich (1975), pp. 107–108.

80. Bilandžić (1985), p. 75.

81. Colić (1977), pp. 61–79, esp. p. 68.

82. Tomasevich (1975), p. 105; Beloff (1985), p. 74. For an analysis of the position of the Bosnian Muslims in the Independent State of Croatia, see Malcolm (1994), pp. 185–91.

83. These Muslim resolutions were printed in 1941, distributed as documents to the Ustasha authorities, and distributed publicly as leaflets in thousands of copies. After the war, three of these resolutions were reprinted in the journal *Bosanski pogledi* [Bosnian Views], vol. 1, no. 1, October-November-December, 1955, pp. 61–68. In 1984, these resolutions were reprinted in book form. See *Bosanski pogledi: Nezavisni list muslimana Bosne i Hercegovine u iseljeništvu, 1960–1967* (1984), pp. 509–16.

84. Abramski-Bligh (1990), pp. 705–706.

85. Ibid., p. 706.

86. Redžić (1987), pp. 87, 119–20, 155, 166–67, 183.

87. Erignac (1980), pp. 9, 28, 45; Bender and Taylor (1972), p. 146; Redžić (1987), p. 56.

88. Serbian post–World War II propaganda characteristically cites the Serbs' victimization by the Ustashas but ignores the role of Ljotić, Nedić, and Chetnik formations in the genocide of Jews, Gypsies, Muslims, and Croats. See Paris (1961), originally distributed by an American-based Chetnik organization in Chicago; Novak (1948), which accuses the Croatian Catholic clergy of fascism (the author was a signatory to the "Appeal to the Serbian Nation"); Stranjaković (1991), issued in conjunction with the Serbian invasion of Croatia; Dedijer (1992), which compared the Jasenovac concentration camp to Auschwitz. Bulajić (1991) propagates discredited figures for Serbian World War II losses and is transparently a propagandist for the Belgrade regime. On February 2, 1993, Milan Bulajić visited Ohio State University in Columbus, where he was interviewed for "The Serbian Hour" on WCPN-FM (Cleveland Public Radio), which was broadcast on February 7, 1993. Bulajić stated that the publication of his English-language work *The Role of the Vatican in the Breakup of the Yugoslav State,* echoing a familiar anti-Catholic theme, was subsidized by the Serbian government.

89. In October, 1941, the Serbian Orthodox Church issued a report alleging that 180,000 Serbs had perished at the hands of the Ustashas between April and August, attributing collective guilt to the entire Croatian nation. See Tomasevich (1975), pp. 265–67; Wheeler (1980), pp. 125–26.

90. Djilas (1991), p. 124.

91. Paris (1961), p. 5. Bishop Velimirović is quoted from a 1954 article published in the Serbian Orthodox ecclesiastical review *Sveštenik* [Priest].

92. Paris (1961), p. 9. "Edmond Paris" is the author of several rabidly anti-Catholic works, extolling Serbs as having suffered the greatest persecution in the history of the world and praising Eastern Orthodoxy. He is presented on the book jacket as a French historian from a Catholic family, but the details of his biographical sketch (for example, birthplace and education) are so vague as to defy verification. He consistently lapses into Serbian orthography, even when quoting from Croatian documents. For example, see pp. 65, 66, 84, 89, and 135, in which the Croatian newspaper *Nedjelja* is cited by its Serbian equivalent, *Nedelja*.

93. Kočović (1985), p. 126.

94. The two most reliable estimates of Gypsy losses throughout Yugoslavia during World War II are 18,000 and 27,000. See Žerjavić (1992), p. 168; Kočović (1985), p. 125.

95. Paris (1961), p. 9; Djilas (1991), pp. 125–26; Jukić (1974), p. 7; Curtis (1992), p. 42; Romano (1980), p. 582; Singleton (1976), p. 86; Freidenreich (1979), p. 191.

96. Peter Jennings' ABC-TV evening news broadcast, December 23, 1991.

97. Mayers and Campbell (1954), pp. 20–23. See also Žerjavić (1993), pp. 9, 11.

98. Vanja Bulić, "Mrtvi su ujedinjeni za sva vremena. Dr. Vladeta Vučković: Dok je Evropa brojala mrtve, mi smo pripremali demografske gubitke" [The Dead Have Been United Forever. Dr. Vladeta Vučković: While Europe Counted Her Dead, We Were Preparing Demographic Losses], *Duga*, no. 412, Belgrade, December 9–22, 1989, pp. 45–48; Vladeta Vučković, "Sahrana jednog mita" [Burial of a Myth], *Naša reč* [Our Word], Middlesex, England, no. 368, October, 1985. One interview in two parts was published in the Croatian press. See Mirko Galić, "Intervju: Vladeta Vučković (1) Mit o žrtvama" [Interview: Vladeta Vučković (1): The Myth about Victims], *Danas*, Zagreb, July 10, 1990, pp. 63–65; Mirko Galić, "Intervju: Vladeta Vučković (2) Krivac za krivu brojku" [Interview: Vladeta Vučković (2): The person Responsible for the Wrong Number], *Danas*, Zagreb, July 17, 1990, p. 63. In personal communications with the author, Dr. Vučković confirmed the authenticity of these interviews.

99. Letter from Dr. Hans Jochen Pretsch of the Auswärtiges Amt [Foreign Office], Bonn, Germany, July 8, 1992. In June, 1963, the Yugoslav government delivered an undated memorandum that claimed 950,000 Yugoslavs killed in World War II.

100. Mirko Galić, "Intervju: Vladeta Vučković (1) Mit o žrtvama," pp. 63–65. Vučković stated: "I could have remained silent and let everybody wonder where the figure of 1.7 million came from. . . . Nobody will like me after this; some find me guilty for having miscalculated the number of victims right after the war, and some because I am disputing it now."

101. Pasic (1989), p. 65.

102. Ibid., pp. 65–84. See also Žerjavić (1991), pp. 101–102; Željko Krušelj and Đuro Zagorac, "Sporna knjiga mrtvih" [The Contested Book of the Dead], *Danas*, no. 405, Zagreb, November 21, 1989, pp. 24–25.

103. Mayers and Campbell (1954), pp. 20–23. In addition to wartime mortality, an additional 700,000 to 800,000 living in Yugoslavia at the outbreak of the war were lost through migration or expulsion. Thus, after the war, 445,000 *Volksdeutsche* were expelled, primarily from Vojvodina. When the Istrian peninsula was transferred to Yugoslavia after the war, some 150,000 (most of the Italians and many Croats) there emigrated to Italy. Out of a total of 700,000 Yugoslavs who had been prisoners or workers in German war industries, 100,000 remained abroad. At the close of the war, more than 100,000 fled from Yugoslavia, and many of these immigrated to the United States (also see Hoffman and Neal [1962], p. 41). These total emigration figures are also corroborated by Žerjavić and Kočović, who cited 669,000 and 638,000, respectively (see Žerjavić [1991], p. 98).

104. Kočović (1985), pp. 65, 70, 79, 89, 93, 99, 120, 124–25, 172–83.

105. Ibid., p. 101.

106. Žerjavić (1991), p. 96; Žerjavić (1989), pp. xiii–xvi.

107. Žerjavić (1992), pp. 70–72. The figure of 82,000 Serbs given for Serbs killed as Partisans may include some Serb civilians who were massacred.

108. Žerjavić (1992), pp. 72, 77.

109. Ibid., p. 210. This figure for mortality in concentration camps in Serbia is corroborated by the estimate of 50,000 (see Glišić [1977], p. 715).

110. British journalist Nora Beloff described an encounter with a Serbian Orthodox priest, the editor of a widely read Serbian weekly publication, who rejected the idea of reconciliation with Croats, claiming that "the Croats" had killed more than 800,000 Serbs at the Jasenovac concentration camp. Commenting on this, Beloff wrote: "A nought should probably be subtracted from the propaganda figure. But few Serbs would ever say so: for many of them, the higher your figure the greater your patriotism." See Beloff (1985), p. 202.

CHAPTER 5: SERBIAN HISTORICAL REVISIONISM AND THE HOLOCAUST

1. "Tragedija naših sugrađana Jevreja" [Tragedy of our Jewish Fellow Citizens], *Politika,* Belgrade, November 1, 1944, p. 3.

2. Dawidowicz (1966), p. 391, and Freidenreich (1979) reiterate the notion that Jews were traditionally persecuted by Croats and hospitably received by Serbs. For example, Freidenreich (1979), p. 179, states: "In general, the official attitude of the Yugoslav government toward the Jewish minority until the very end of the interwar period was sympathetic. This, to a large extent, was due to the tradition of tolerance of the Serbian Orthodox Church." An examination of church documents leads one to an opposite conclusion, yet not one single Serbian Orthodox Church document is cited within this otherwise comprehensive book!

3. Lendvai (1969), pp. 149–50, 154–56, 158; David Binder, "Rankovic's Fall from Power: Casebook on Party Maneuvers," *The New York Times,* July 8, 1966, p. 1; David Binder, "Deposed Leader Accused of 'Struggle for Power' in State Security Service," *The New York Times,* July 2, 1966, p. 1; Commission on Security and Cooperation in Europe [Helsinki Commission] (1991), p. 131.

4. This propaganda line is well encapsulated in the opinion piece by Teddy Preuss, "Serbia an Ally Spurned," *The Jerusalem Post,* June 9, 1994, p. 6.

5. Harry Ofner [letter to the editor], *Midstream,* January, 1994, p. 47.

6. Erignac (1980), pp. 9, 28, 45; Bender and Taylor (1972), p. 146.

7. "Rođendan Vođe Rajha" [The Birthday of the Reich Führer], *Naša borba* (Slovenia), April 21, 1945, p. 2, as reproduced in Ivanović (1954), pp. 36–39.

8. Fotich (1948), p. 134. Compare with the critique by Marjanović (1976), pp. 58–59.

9. Keitel's order of September 16, 1941, stated: "(a) Every act directed against the German occupation military forces shall be regarded as of communist origin, regardless of circumstances of particular cases; (b) As a retaliation for the life of one German soldier it shall be taken—as a general rule—that it [the death of one German soldier] equals a death sentence for 50–100 communists. The way of execution must strengthen the horrifying effect." See *Zbornik dokumenta* (1949), vol. 1, book 1, doc. 159, pp. 431–32, order of the head of the German High Command, September 16, 1941.

10. Romano (1980), p. 67.

11. Browning (1985), pp. 50–51. See also AMHI, doc. 16/7–3, box 1, cited in Borković (1979), p. 148.

12. Löwenthal (1957), pp. 32–33.

13. The "memorandum" of the Serbian Academy of Science and Arts (known by its Serbian acronym as SANU) was issued on September 29, 1986, and distributed to the Serbian emigration in 1987 (see Serbian Academy of Science and Art [1987]). See "'Memorandum' SANU" (1991), pp. 256–300; for an English translation, see "The SANU 'Memorandum'" (1993), pp. 289–337. Also, a typewritten English translation is available from the Library of Congress under "Suppressed Memorandum of Members of Serbian Academy of Science and Art (SANU), September, 1986," published by the Serbian Literary Association.

14. Vuk Drašković, "Piscima Izraela" [To the Writers of Israel] (December 17, 1985, Belgrade), *Naša reč*, Middlesex, England, no. 373, November, 1986, pp. 8–9; also reprinted in Kostić (1988), pp. 250–54.

15. The first official plenary session of the Serbian-Jewish Friendship Society (March, 1989) emphasized that "the Serbian people cannot be connected in any way with concentration camps and pogroms to which the Jewish people were exposed through history." See Dragan Tanasić, "Prva zvanična skupština Društva srpsko-jevrejskog prijateljstva: Čas himničkog iskupljenja" [The First Official Plenary Session of the Serbian-Jewish Friendship Society: An Hour of Hymnical Redemption], *Intervju* [Interview], March 17, 1989, pp. 46–47. A 1992 article by Friendship Society principals stated that the extermination of the Jews in Serbia was carried out "by Germans exclusively." See Ljubomir Tadić and Andrija Gams, "Istina o odnosu Srba i Hrvata prema Jevrejima" [The truth about the Relationship of the Serbs and Croats toward the Jews], *Politika*, March 6, 1992, p. 16.

16. Gordana Janićijević," "Njene rane život ne može da izleči. Klara Mandić: 'Stalno se pitam zašto je Dafina to uradila'" [Life Cannot Heal Her Wounds. Klara Mandić: "I Constantly Ask Myself, Why Did Dafina Do It"], *Duga*, Belgrade, June 11–24, 1994, pp. 90–93.

17. Jeffrey Gedmin, "Comrade Slobo," *The American Spectator,* April, 1993, pp. 28–33; Roger Cohen, "Serb Says Files Link Milosevic to War Crimes," *The New York Times,* April 13, 1995, p. A1. For an in-depth analysis of genocide as a premeditated and coordinated policy of the Belgrade regime, see Cigar (1995), pp. 47–61.

18. Ljiljana Habjanović-Đurović, "Dobar posao sa firmom koja ne postoji" [Good Business with a Company That Does Not Exist], *Duga*, April 30–May 13, 1994, p. 30.

19. Kostić (1988), p. 257.

20. Ibid., p. 148.

21. *Literary Gleanings* was issued under the pseudonym of R. Oraški. See Kostić (1988), p. 257.

22. Kostić (1988), p. 12. See Ivanović (1954), p. 67.

23. Kostić (1988), pp. 8–9, 14, 29, 31–32.

24. Ibid., p. 42.

25. Ibid., p. 47.

26. Ibid., p. 51.

27. For a detailed description, from both German and Chetnik perspectives, of Draža Mihailović's meeting with the Germans during mid-November, 1941, see Karapandžić (1958), pp. 128–57.

28. Kostić (1988), pp. 53–54.

29. Ibid., p. 105.

30. Lendvai (1969), pp. 149–50, 154–56, 158; David Binder, "Rankovic's Fall from Power: Casebook on Party Maneuvers," *The New York Times,* July 8, 1966, p. 1; David Binder, "Deposed Leader Accused of 'Struggle for Power' in State Security Service," *The New York Times,* July 2, 1966, p. 1; Commission on Security and Cooperation in Europe [Helsinki Commission] (1991), p. 131.

31. Löwenthal (1972), pp. 868–85.

32. Milan Milivojević, "Terrorist State," *Borba,* Belgrade, February 6, 1986, p. 2.

33. Božidar Dikić, "Causes of International Terrorism," *The Review of International Affairs* [published by Jugoslovenska Stvarnost], Belgrade, vol. 37, September 5, 1986.

34. Jennifer Parmlee, "Gadhafi Sees Election Aiding U.S.-Libya Ties. 'So-Called Terrorism' Defended in Interview," *The Washington Post,* September 6, 1988, p. A23; Mario Modiano, "Belgrade is Hijack Base," *The Sunday Times,* London, December 1, 1985, p. 1; Guido Olimpio, "Belgrado, Atene e Bagdad ecco la via del terrore" [Belgrade, Athens and Baghdad—Here Is the Road of Terror], *Il Tempo* [Time], December 4, 1985, p. 19.

35. John Sweeney, "Saddam Supplies Serb War Machine . . . Iraqi Mig-23s Seen over the Battlefields," *The Observer,* London, May 31, 1992, p. 1.

36. Olivera Erdeljan, "Jevreji ponovo raspinju Hrista" [The Jews Are Crucifying Christ Again], *Pravoslavlje* [Orthodoxy (official publication of the Serbian Orthodox Church)], Belgrade, January 15, 1992.

37. Lerman and Spier (1993), p. 108.

38. Andrei Ostal'skii, "Priznanie Rossiei Slovenii i Khorvatii vyzvalo buriu v Belgrade. Taniug obiavliaet èto reshenie rezul'tatom . . . 'evreiskogo zagovora'" [Russian Recognition of Slovenia and Croatia Has Provoked a Storm in Belgrade. Tanjug Declares This Decision Is the Result of . . . 'a Jewish Conspiracy'], *Izvestia,* Moscow, February 6, 1992, p. 5.

39. In 1991, about 7,000 Jews lived in Yugoslavia, apportioned as follows: Croatia (2,000), Bosnia-Herzegovina (2,000), and Belgrade, Serbia

(2,000), and the Vojvodina province of Serbia (1,000). By comparison, the Jewish population of Slovenia was 77.

40. "Stop the Death Camps" [paid advertisement], cosigned by the American Jewish Committee, American Jewish Congress, and B'Nai B'rith, *The New York Times*, August 5, 1992, p. 5.

41. Ruth E. Gruber, "Serbia's Jews Walking Gingerly amidst Chaos," *Jewish Exponent*, New York, August 5, 1994, p. 13.

42. "All Things Considered" segment on National Public Radio, originating in Washington, D.C., May 19, 1993.

43. For examples of reporting in the Israeli press sympathetic to the victims, see "After she was raped, the mother requested to breast-feed her baby. The rapist cut off the baby's head and handed it to her," *Yediot Aharanot*, August 8, 1992; "Ten Men Were Laid in a Row—Their Noses and Testicles Cut Off," *Ma'ariv*, August 10, 1992; both cited in Kofman (1996), in press. See also "Never Again! Anywhere!" [editorial], *Jerusalem Post International Edition*, August 15, 1992, p. 8: "Now we have again squalid words like 'death camps,' 'murdered children,' 'sealed trains' and 'ethnic purity' smearing our daily newspapers. All of it is coming out of Bosnia, and most of it is being laid on the mat of the belligerent Serbians who are turning this border war into a neo-Nazi nightmare. . . . New York's *Newsday* has carried eyewitness accounts of mass executions and starvation of prisoners at concentration camps."

44. For analyses of official and media responses in Israel to the war in Croatia and Bosnia-Herzegovina, including the role of the pro-Serbian lobby, see Primoratz (1995), pp. 193–204; Kofman (1996), in press.

45. *Ma'ariv*, August 9, 1992, cited in Kofman (1996), in press.

46. A series of seemingly identical articles, implying the Bosnian origin of many or most West Bank Palestinians, appeared within a few months. See M. R. Lehmann, "Bosnia—Motherland of the 'Palestinians,' " *Algemeiner Journal*, November 13, 1992; Paul Giniewski, "The Palestinian-Bosnian Connection," *Midstream* 38, no. 9, December, 1992, pp. 2–3.

47. Ye'or (1985), pp. 105, 305.

48. Kofman (1996), in press.

49. Ibid.

50. Paul Lungen, "Yugoslav Jews Cast an Ambitious Eye to Future," *The Canadian Jewish News*, January 18, 1990, p. 12.

51. Igor Primorac [Primoratz], "Astonishing Argument" (op-ed), *The Jerusalem Post*, January 23, 1994, p. 6.

52. Teddy Preuss, "Serbia an Ally Spurned," *The Jerusalem Post*, June 9, 1994, p. 6.

53. See note 30.

54. Figures on Jewish emigration from Yugoslavia to Israel are summarized in Freidenreich (1979), p. 193.

55. See Žerjavić (1992), pp. 71–72, 77–78; Romano (1980), pp. 123–24, 579.

56. The Serbian appropriation of the Holocaust is problematic, since the Holocaust was a unique genocide, the attempted complete annihilation of Jews (and Gypsies) throughout Europe. Indeed, there have been many genocides; there was one Holocaust.

57. Klara Ma[n]dić, "Fascism Reawakens in Croatia, Charges Jewish Leader," *The Jewish Advocate*, Boston, January 24–30, 1992.

58. Immediately before the fall of Petrinja, where Ankica Konjuh died, Croatian military forces there consisted of six untrained young men with machine guns, while Serbian forces had overwhelming military superiority (see Peter Popham and Laurie Sparkham, "Endgame in the Balkans," *The Independent Magazine*, London, September 21, 1991, pp. 20–26). According to police records in Sisak, Croatia, Marijana Jurinjak stated that her neighbor Ankica Konjuh remained in Petrinja after its fall to Serbian forces on September 20, 1991. Also, according to the testimony of civilians from Petrinja who were imprisoned in Serbian-controlled Glina and later released, over 240 people were massacred and buried in mass graves, after the fall of Petrinja (report of the police station in Sisak, no. 511-10-01/01-Sp.–40/92, April 29, 1992).

59. Minutes of the second session of the working committee of the Federation of the Jewish Communities of Yugoslavia, held in Belgrade on December 23, 1991.

60. Personal communication from Nenad Porges, president of the Jewish Community of Zagreb, Croatia, February 20, 1992; personal communications with the Federation of the Jewish Communities of Yugoslavia, Belgrade.

61. Letter from the Serbian-Jewish Friendship Society (Molerova 11, 11000 Belgrade, Serbia), August 4, 1993, which begins, "We, the Jewish members of the Belgrade chapter of the Jewish Serbian Friendship Society . . . " and concludes with eight signatures.

62. Ruth E. Gruber, "Jews in Middle of Yugoslavian Rivalries," Washington *Jewish Week*, January 4, 1990.

63. Radovan Pavlović, "Akteri 'Opere' na sudu" [The Actors of the "Opera" on Trial], *Politika* Belgrade, November 13, 1992, p. 10. See also Batsheva Tsur, "Anatomy of a Balkan Frame-up," *The Jerusalem Post*, February 3, 1993, p. 7. "Opera" was part of a larger pattern of terrorism. For example, one Serbian organization, the "Labradors," was responsible for some 450 explosions in Zagreb during the last half of 1991. See Vladimir

Jovanović, "Labradori i Šinteri" [Labradors and Dogcatchers], *NIN*, Belgrade, May 20, 1994, p. 24.

64. Affidavit by Mirjam Ferera, member of the presidency of the Jewish Community of Dubrovnik, Croatia, December 18, 1991. See Franić et al. (1992), unpublished. Both documents are in the author's possession.

65. Rep. Helen Bentley circulated a "Dear Colleague" letter, February 18, 1992: "I would like to invite you or a member of your staff to attend a briefing with Dr. Klara Mandić, a prominent Jewish leader from Belgrade, Yugoslavia, regarding manifestations of anti-Semitism in the current civil war that is ravaging that country. Dr. Mandić was born in 1944. She is a graduate of the Faculty of Dental Surgery in Belgrade, and is a Jewish leader, founder and General Secretary of the Serbian-Jewish Friendship Society which promulgates good relations between the Serbian and Jewish peoples who have lived together in Yugoslavia for centuries. Dr. Mandić organized a Serbian week in Israel last year during which twenty-three Serbian cities became sister cities to twenty-three in Israel. She also organized a solidarity visit to Israel by the mayors of fifteen Serbian cities during the Persian Gulf War. Dr. Mandić also is a founder and president of the Israeli-Serbian Business and Information Centre in Belgrade." Letter is in the possession of the author.

66. "Serbs and Jews Remember April 10, 1941," *Newsletter* of the Jewish-Serbian Friendship Society of America, Granada Hills, California, June, 1991. This newsletter recounts as fact the oft-repeated but fictional account by the Italian novelist Curzio Malaparte that he had seen a "forty-pound basket of human eyes" on Pavelić's desk when he had visited him. Even respected scholars such as Nora Levin have cited this spurious source (see Levin [1973], p. 516). Original documentary footage of Malaparte's meeting with Ante Pavelić exists and is in the possession of Obrad Kosovac of Croatian Television, Zagreb. As described in Malaparte's novel *Kaputt,* Italian ambassador Casertano was present with Malaparte and Pavelić, but there was no wicker basket of human eyes on Pavelić's desk. A documentary film entitled *"Oči" Curzija Malapartea* [The "Eyes" of Curzio Malaparte], based upon the original footage, was made by Kosovac in 1993. See also McAdams (1992), pp. 35–39.

67. Verica Lazović and Momčilo Perović, "Ja nisam vođa, ja sam vojskovođa" [I Am Not a Political Leader, I Am a Military Leader] (interview with Vojislav Šešelj), *Intervju*, Belgrade, June 7, 1991, p. 18.

68. Marc Champion, "Duke of the Chetniks Opts for 'Amputation,'" *The Independent,* London, July 30, 1991, p. 9.

69. Dusko Doder, "The 'Chetnik Duke' Stakes His Claim to Greater Serbia," *The European,* London, January 7–10, 1993, p. 8; John Kifner,

"An Outlaw in the Balkans Is Basking in the Spotlight," *The New York Times*, November 23, 1993, p. A1.

70. Popović et al. (1988), p. 12; Tomasevich (1975), pp. 158, 177, 352, 428, 442 n. 38, 452. For Đujić's admiration for Ljotić, see Kostić (1949), pp. 188–90.

71. See Champion, "Duke of the Chetniks Opts for 'Amputation,'" p. 9; Milan Radović, "Vojvoda Šešelj, ujedinitelj vaskolikog Srpstva" [Chetnik Commander Šešelj, the Unifier of All Serbs], *Naša reč* [Our Word], Middlesex, England, no. 411, January, 1990, p. 22: "Recently all the émigré newspapers with the exception of the [satirical] *Ošišani Jež* [Cropped Hedgehog] brought really great news—Dr. Vojislav Šešelj from Zemun was promoted to the rank of *vojvoda* [Chetnik commander] and as such became an honorary member of the Movement of Ravna Gora Serbian Chetniks among the emigrants. The promotion was signed personally by the supreme *vojvoda* Momčilo Đujić on June 28, 1989 . . . [Šešelj] at once assumes the role of a *vojvoda* and a *vladika* [high-ranking religious ruler] unifier."

72. Roland Hofwiler, "Tudjman und seine 'Irrwege' in Richtung 'Auschwitzlüge," *Die Presse*, Vienna, January 28, 1992, p. 4. Also cited in Grmek (1993), p. 307.

73. Duško Vuković, "Delo Luke Sarkotića" [Luka Sarkotić's Work], *NIN*, Belgrade, September 2, 1994, p. 19.

74. As reported by Živan Haravan, secretary of the Union of Civilian Victims of War, who complained of a growing anti-Semitic atmosphere in Serbia, in Ljubiša Stvarić, "Koga čeka kazna" [Who Does Punishment Await?], *NIN*, Belgrade, February 24, 1995, p. 29.

75. Miloš Vasić, Filip Švarm, "Sve srpske pretnje" [All Serbian Threats], *Vreme* [Time], Belgrade, May 24, 1993, p. 16.

76. "The War of the Villages," *The Economist*, London, August 3, 1991, p. 38.

77. Gordana Janićijević, "Njene rane život ne može da izleči. Klara Mandić: 'Stalno se pitam zašto je Dafina to uradila,'" pp. 90–93.

78. Lerman and Spier (1993), p. 107.

79. For Velimirović's postwar views on Milan Nedić, Dimitrije Ljotić, and Draža Mihailović, see Velimirović (1986), pp. 775, 781.

80. Excerpted from "Beseda o budućoj srećnoj otadžbini" [Speech about a Future Happy Fatherland] (see Velimirović [1976], pp. 151–52).

81. Ivan Torov, "Izdaja ili podeljene uloge?" [Treason or Division of Labor?], *Borba*, Belgrade, February 23, 1994, p. 11.

82. Velimirović (1985), pp. 33–34.

83. See Blitz (1996).

84. As a rare instance of Serbian-American public dissent, the following editorial letter merits quotation:

> The mind-set of many Serbian-Americans is unfathomable—even to this Serbian-American. In their minds, everyone else is to blame, especially the Croats and Bosnians. The murder and mayhem unleashed by the Serbs upon their former countrymen is the others' fault. Serbia's culpability is ignored.
>
> Be very clear about this: the overwhelming blame for what is happening in the land of the South Slavs lies with Serbia and its thugs in Bosnia-Herzegovina. The Croats are not blameless and the Bosnians bear some guilt, but it is Serbia alone that stands to be condemned.
>
> Serbian-Americans may bear no blame for what is happening in the Balkans, but their silence may be construed as moral support for Serbia. In the face of such evil, there is no place for the rationalization of slaughter. But that is precisely what many Serbian-Americans are doing—rationalizing the brutality of Serbia by invoking history, by reciting the centuries of the Serbs' servile status under the Turks, of the Croat alliance with Hitler and his henchmen.
>
> But to this Serbian-American, it won't wash.
>
> There is something fundamentally wrong with a people so mired in the bitterness and hatred of the past they can find no peace in the present. But that is Serbia and the Serbs. It is an illness of the mind and soul that infects many Serbian-Americans, that shadows their second and third generations in this nation.
>
> It takes an act of will to escape it, this acceptance of evil among one's own people. A sense of moral loathing is needed, but among Serbian-Americans, virtually nothing is said, no protest is raised, the infamy of the Balkans is met with silence—the silence of shame. . . . From the great Slav enclaves of Cleveland and Chicago, across the Great Divide to San Pedro in California, Serbian-Americans bearing moral witness cannot be found. A normally boisterous people has nothing to say. Theirs is a deafening silence." (from George Mitrovich, "Why the Serbian-American Silence?" [op-ed], *Los Angeles Times,* August 25, 1993, p. B15)

AFTERWORD

1. See Tomasic (1948), pp. 216–17; S. Meštrović et al. (1993), p. 19.

2. Almond (1991); Almond (1994), pp. 340–60; Cohen (1994); Richard Johnson, "Serbia and Russia: U.S. Appeasement and the Resurrection of Fascism," National War College, Washington, D.C., May 4, 1994 (un-

pub. MS); Roy Gutman, "Crossing the Border: Russia Helps Yugoslavia Send Weapons," *Newsday,* March 30, 1995, p. A18. For a chronology of the events leading to the dissolution of Yugoslavia and the international responses, see Alan F. Fogelquist, *Handbook of Facts on: The Break-up of Yugoslavia, International Policy, and the War in Bosnia-Herzegovina,* Institute of South-Central European and Balkan Affairs, Los Angeles, California, 1993. See also Cohen (1994).

3. Brzezinski (1993), pp. 11–15.

Bibliography

BOOKS AND ARTICLES

A., S. 1904. *Knjiga o Jevrejima: Sveska 1: Kod koga treba da kupujemo?* [Book about Jews: Volume 1: At Whose Store Should We Shop?]. Belgrade: Industrijska štamparija.

Abramski-Bligh, Irit. 1990. "Hajj Amin Al-Husseini." Pp. 703–707 in *Encyclopedia of the Holocaust.* Vol. 2. Edited by Israel Gutman. New York: Macmillan.

Almond, Mark. 1991. *Blundering in the Balkans: The European Community and the Yugoslav Crisis.* London: School of European Studies.

———. 1994. *Europe's Backyard War: The War in the Balkans.* London: Heinemann.

Anić, Nikola; Sekula Joksimović; and Mirko Gutić. 1982. *Narodnooslobodilačka vojska Jugoslavije* [The National Liberation Army of Yugoslavia]. Belgrade: Vojnoistorijski institut.

Avakumović, Ivan. 1971. "Yugoslavia's Fascist Movements." Pp. 135–43 in *Native Fascism in the Successor States, 1918–1945.* Edited by Peter F. Sugar. Santa Barbara, Calif.: ABC-Clio.

Balfour, Neil, and Sally Mackay. 1980. *Paul of Yugoslavia: Britain's Maligned Friend.* London: Hamish Hamilton.

Balić, Smail. 1993. "Culture under Fire." Pp. 75–83 in *Why Bosnia? Writings on the Balkan War.* Edited by Rabia Ali and Lawrence Lifschultz. Stony Creek, Conn.: Pamphleteer's Press.

Banac, Ivo. 1992. "The Fearful Asymmetry of War: The Causes and Consequences of Yugoslavia's Demise." *Proceedings of the American Academy of Arts and Sciences* 121 (Spring): 141–74.

————. 1984. *The National Question in Yugoslavia: Origins, History, Politics.* Ithaca, N.Y.: Cornell University Press.

Barnai, Jacob. 1990. "On the History of the Jews in the Ottoman Empire." Pp. 18–35 in *Sephardi Jews in The Ottoman Empire.* Edited by Esther Juhasz. Jerusalem: Jerusalem Publishing House.

Beloff, Nora. 1985. *Tito's Flawed Legacy. Yugoslavia and the West since 1939.* Boulder, Colo.: Westview.

Bender, Roger James, and Hugh Page Taylor. 1972. *Uniforms, Organization and History of the Waffen SS.* Vol. 3. Mountainview, Calif.: R. J. Bender Publishing.

Benković, Theodore. 1947. *The Tragedy of a Nation.* Chicago.

Berben, Paul. 1975. *Dachau 1933–1945: The Official History.* London: Norfolk Press.

Bilandžić, Dušan. 1985. *Historija Socijalističke Federativne Republike Jugoslavije: glavni procesi, 1918–1985* [History of the Socialist Federal Republic of Yugoslavia: Main Trends, 1918–1985]. 3rd edition. Zagreb: Školska knjiga.

Blitz, Brad. 1996. "Serbia's War Lobby: Diaspora Groups and Western Elites." In Thomas Cushman and Stjepan Meštrović (editors). *This Time We Knew: Western Responses to Genocide in Bosnia.* New York: New York University Press (in press).

Borković, Milan. 1979. *Kontrarevolucija u Srbiji: Kvislinška uprava 1941–1944. Knjiga I (1941–1942)* [Counterrevolution in Serbia: The Quisling Administration 1941–1944. Book I (1941–1942)]. Belgrade: Sloboda.

————. 1979a. *Kontrarevolucija u Srbiji: Kvislinška uprava 1941–1944. Knjiga II (1943–1944)* [Counterrevolution in Serbia: The Quisling Administration 1941–1944. Book II (1943–1944)]. Belgrade: Sloboda.

Bosanski muslimani: Čimbenik mira izmedju Srba i Hrvata: Interview Adil Zulfikarpašić [A Factor of Peace between Serbs and Croats: Interview with Adila Zulfikarpašića]. 1986. Zürich: Bosanski Institut.

Bosanski pogledi: Nezavisni list Muslimana Bosne i Hercegovine u iseljeništvu, 1960–1967 [Bosnian Views: The Independent Newspaper of the Muslims of Bosnia-Herzegovina in Emigration, 1960–1967]. 1984. London and Zürich: Stamaco.

Bošković, Hedviga; H. Burić; Vedrana Gotovac et al. 1988. "Katalog." Pp. 216–335 in *Židovi na tlu Jugoslavije* [The Jews in Yugoslavia]. Edited by Ante Sorić. Zagreb: Muzejski prostor.

Brown, J. F. 1992. *Nationalism, Democracy and Security in the Balkans.* Rand Research Study. Brookfield, Vt: Dartmouth.

Browning, Christopher R. 1983. "The Final Solution in Serbia: The Semlin *Judenlager* — A Case Study." Pp. 55–90 in *Yad Vashem Studies.* Vol.

15. Edited by Livia Rothkirchen. Jerusalem: Yad Vashem Martyrs' and Heroes' Remembrance Authority.

———. 1985. *Fateful Months: Essays on the Emergence of the Final Solution.* New York: Holmes and Meier.

Brzezinski, Zbigniew. 1993. *Out of Control: Global Turmoil on the Eve of the 21st Century.* New York: Macmillan.

Buck, Claire, ed. 1992. *The Bloomsbury Guide to Women's Literature.* New York: Prentice Hall.

Bulajić, Milan. 1991. *Genocide of the Serbs, Jews and Gipsies in the Ustashi Independent State of Croatia.* Belgrade.

Carpi, Daniel. 1990. "Italy: Aid to Jews by Italians." Pp. 729–30 in *Encyclopedia of the Holocaust.* Vol. 2. Edited by Israel Gutman. New York: Macmillan.

Cigar, Norman. 1995. *Genocide in Bosnia: The Policy of "Ethnic Cleansing."* College Station: Texas A&M University Press.

Clissold, Stephen. 1949. *Whirlwind: An Account of Marshal Tito's Rise to Power.* New York: Philosophical Library.

Cohen, Philip J. 1994. "Ending the War and Securing Peace in Former Yugoslavia." *Pace International Law Review* 6 (Winter): 19–40.

Colić, Mladen. 1973. *Takozvana nezavisna država Hrvatska* [The So-Called Independent State of Croatia]. Belgrade: Delta-pres.

———. 1977. "Kolaboracionističke oružane formacije u Jugoslaviji 1941–1945" [Armed Collaborationist Formations in Yugoslavia, 1941–1945]. In *Oslobodilačka borba naroda Jugoslavije kao opštenarodni rat i socijalistička revolucija* [The Liberation Struggle of the Peoples of Yugoslavia as a War of All the Peoples and a Socialist Revolution]. Belgrade: Zajednica institucija za izučavanje novije istorije naroda i narodnosti Jugoslavije [Community Institution for Research of Recent History of the Nations and Peoples of Yugoslavia].

———. 1988. *Pregled operacija na jugoslovenskom ratištu, 1941–1945* [Review of the War Operations in Yugoslavia, 1941–1945]. Belgrade: Vojnoistorijski institut.

Commission on Security and Cooperation in Europe. 1991. *Minority Rights: Problems, Parameters and Patterns in the CSCE Concept,* Washington, D.C.

Council of the Order of Vitéz. 1977. *Illustrated Chronicle of the Royal Hungarian Armed Forces (1919–1945).* Munich: Heinloth.

Croatian Islamic Centre. 1978. *Massacre of Croatians in Bosnia-Hercegovina and Sandžak.* Toronto.

Čović, Bože. 1993. *Roots of Greater Serbian Aggression.* Zagreb: Centar za strane jezike.

Crankshaw, Edward. 1963. *The Fall of the House of Habsburg*. New York: Penguin.

Curtis, Glenn E., ed. 1992. *Yugoslavia: A Country Study*. Washington, D.C.: Federal Research Division, Library of Congress; U.S. Government Printing Office.

Čubrilović, Vasa. 1991. "Iseljavanje Arnauta" [The Expulsion of the Albanians]. Pp. 106–24 in *Izvori velikosrpske agresije* [Roots of Greater Serbian Aggression]. Edited by Bože Čović. Zagreb: August Cesarec & Školska knjiga.

Cvijić, Anđelka and Milenko Vasović. 1991. *Milan D. Nedić: Život, govori, saslušanja* [Milan D. Nedić: Life, Speeches, Interrogations]. Belgrade: A Cvijić and M. Vasović.

———. 1993. "Deportation of Albanians." Pp. 121–23 in *Roots of Greater Serbian Aggression*. Edited by Bože Čović. Zagreb: Centar za strane jezike.

Darby, H. C.; R. W. Seton-Watson; Phyllis Auty and others. 1966. *A Short History of Yugoslavia from Early Times to 1966*. London: Cambridge University Press.

Dawidowicz, Lucy S. 1966. *The War against the Jews, 1933–1945*. New York: Holt, Rinehart and Winston.

Dedijer, Vladimir. 1992. *The Yugoslav Auschwitz and the Vatican: The Croatian Massacre of the Serbs during World War II*. Buffalo, N.Y.: Prometheus Books.

Denitch, Bogdan Denis. 1976. *The Legitimation of a Revolution: The Yugoslav Case*. New Haven, Conn.: Yale University Press.

Denitch, Bogdan. 1994. *Ethnic Nationalism. The Tragic Death of Yugoslavia*. Minneapolis: University of Minnesota Press.

Djilas, Aleksa. 1991. *The Contested Country: Yugoslav Unity and Communist Revolution, 1919–1953*. Cambridge: Harvard University Press.

Djilas, Milovan. 1958. *Land without Justice*. New York: Harcourt Brace Jovanovich.

———. 1973. *Memoir of a Revolutionary*. New York: Harcourt Brace Jovanovich.

———. 1977. *Wartime*. New York: Harcourt Brace Jovanovich.

Dobrijević, Mirko. 1989. "Bishop Nicholai Velimirovich's 1921 Visit to America," *Serbian Studies* 5 (2): 92.

Dokumenti o izdajstvu Draže Mihailovića [Documents on the Treason of Draža Mihailović]. 1945. Belgrade: State Commission for the Documentation of Crimes by the Occupier and His Collaborators.

Dožić, (Patriarch) Gavrilo. 1986. *Memoari Patrijarha Srpskog Gavrila*

[Memoirs of Serbian Patriarch Gavrilo]. Part 2. Edited by M. M. Dža-ković. Paris.

Dragnich, Alex N. 1974. *Serbia, Nikola Pašić, and Yugoslavia*. New Bruns-wick, N.J.: Rutgers University Press.

———. 1992. *Serbs and Croats*. New York: Harcourt Brace Jovanovich.

Durham, M. Edith. 1914. *The Struggle for Scutari*. London: Edward Arnold.

Eck, Nathan. 1958. "The March of Death from Serbia to Hungary (Sep-tember 1944) and the Slaughter of Cservenka." *Yad Washem Studies on the European Jewish Catastrophe and Resistance* 2: 255–94.

Erignac, Louis. 1980. *La Révolte des Croates* [The Revolt of the Croats]. Villefranche-de-Rouergue, France: Imprimerie Guibert.

Fogelquist, Alan F. 1993. *Handbook of Facts on: The Break-up of Yugosla-via, International Policy, and the War in Bosnia-Herzegovina*. Los Angeles, Calif.: Institute of South Central European and Balkan Affairs.

Ford, Kirk. 1992. *OSS and the Yugoslav Resistance, 1943–1945*. College Station: Texas A&M University Press.

Fotich, Constantin. 1948. *The War We Lost: Yugoslavia's Tragedy and the Failure of the West*. New York: The Viking Press.

Franco, M. 1910. "Servia." In Isidore Singer (editor). *The Jewish Encyclo-pedia*. New York: Funk and Wagnalls, vol. 11, pp. 205–206.

Freidenreich, Harriet Pass. 1979. *The Jews of Yugoslavia: A Quest for Community*. Philadelphia: Jewish Publication Society of America.

Garašanin, Ilija. 1991. "Načertanije (Program spoljašne i nacionalne poli-tike Srbije na koncu 1844 godine)" [The Outline (The Program for Serbian Foreign and National Policy at the End of 1844)]. Pp. 65–67 in *Izvori velikosrpske agresije*. Edited by Bože Čović. Zagreb: August Cesarec & Školska knjiga.

———. 1993. "Nachertanie (Programme for Serbian Foreign and Na-tional Policy at the End of 1844)." Pp. 68–82 in *Roots of Serbian Ag-gression*. Edited by Bože Čović. Zagreb: Centar za strane jezike.

German Anti-Guerrilla Operations in the Balkans (1941–1944). 1954. Pamphlet 30–243. Washington, D.C.: Department of the Army.

Gilbert, Martin. 1984. *Atlas of Jewish History*. (3rd edition). New York: Dorset Press.

Gligorijević, Branislav. 1965. "Politički pokreti i grupe s nacionalsocijalis-tičkom ideologijom i njihova fuzija u Ljotićevom Zboru." *Istorijski glasnik* [Historical Messenger]. 4: 35–83.

Glišić, Venceslav. 1977. "Concentration Camps in Serbia (1941–1944)." Pp. 691–715 in *The Third Reich and Yugoslavia, 1933–1945*. Edited by Pero Morača. Belgrade: Institute for Contemporary History and Narodna kjniga.

Goldstein, Slavko. 1988. "'Konačno rješenje' jevrejskog pitanja u jugoslavenskim zemljama" ["The Final Solution" of the Jewish Question in the Yugoslav Lands]. Pp. 181–91 in *Židovi na tlu Jugoslavije* [The Jews in Yugoslavia]. Edited by Ante Sorić. Zagreb: Muzejski prostor.

Great Britain, Foreign Office. 1873. *British and Foreign State Papers: 1867–1868.* Vol. 58. London: William Ridgway.

———. 1877. *British and Foreign State Papers: 1871–1872.* Vol. 62. London: William Ridgway.

Great Britain, Naval Intelligence Division. October, 1944. *Jugoslavia: History, Peoples and Administration.* Vol. 2. Geographical Handbook Series, B. R. 493A (Restricted).

Great Britain, Parliament. 1867. *Hansard's Parliamentary Debates.* Vol. 186. London: T. C. Hansard.

Grmek, Mirko; Marc Gjidara; and Neven Šimac. 1993. *Le nettoyage ethnique: documents historiques sur une idéologie serbe* [Ethnic Cleansing. Historical Documents on a Serbian Ideology]. Paris: Fayard.

Hausner, Gideon. 1968. *Justice in Jerusalem.* New York: Schocken Books.

Hehn, Paul N. 1975. "The Origins of Modern Pan-Serbism—The 1844 Načertanije of Ilija Garašanin: An Analysis and Translation." *East European Quarterly* 9 (2): 153–71.

———. 1979. *The German Struggle against Yugoslav Guerrillas in World War II: German Counter-Insurgency in Yugoslavia, 1941–1943.* Boulder, Colo.: East European Quarterly. Distributed by Columbia University Press.

Hilberg, Raul. 1985. *The Destruction of the European Jews.* Vol. 2. New York: Holmes and Meier.

Hoffman, George W., and Fred Warner Neal. 1962. *Yugoslavia and the New Communism.* New York: Twentieth Century Fund.

Hory, Ladislaus and Martin Broszat. 1964. *Der kroatische Ustascha Staat (1941–1945)* [The Croatian Ustasha State (1941–1945)]. Stuttgart: Deutsche Verlags-Anstalt.

Hoettl, Wilhelm. 1954. *The Secret Front: The Story of Nazi Espionage.* New York: Praeger.

Irvine, Jill A. 1993. *The Croat Question: Partisan Politics in the Formation of the Yugoslav Socialist State.* Boulder, Colo.: Westview Press.

Ivanković-Vonta, Zvonko. 1988. *Hebrang.* Zagreb: Bibliotheca Scientia Yugoslavica.

Ivanović, Predrag D. 1954. *Ko su ljotićevci?* [Who Are the Ljotićites?]. Chicago: Serbian Literary Association.

Jareb, Jere. 1960. *Pola stoljeća hrvatske politike. Povodom Mačekove autobiografije* [One-Half Century of Croatian Politics. On the Occasion of Maček's Autobiography]. Buenos Aires: Knjižnica Hrvatske revije.

Jelavich, Barbara. 1983. *History of the Balkans: Twentieth Century.* 2 vols. New York: Cambridge University Press.

Jelavich, Charles. 1983. "Serbian Textbooks: Towards Greater Serbia or Yugoslavia?" *Slavic Review* 42 (4): 601–19.

Jelić, Ivan. 1978. *Hrvatska u ratu i revoluciji, 1941–1945* [Croatia in War and Revolution, 1941–1945]. Zagreb: Školska knjiga.

———. 1981. *Komunistička partija Hrvatske, 1937–1945* [The Communist Party of Croatia, 1937–1945]. Vol. 1. Zagreb: Globus.

Jelić-Butić, Fikreta. 1977. *Ustaše i Nezavisna Država Hrvatska, 1941–1945* [Ustashas and the Independent State of Croatia, 1941–1945]. Zagreb: Liber.

Jovanović, Rajko. 1928. *Glavnjača kao sistem* [The Glavnjača Prison as a System]. Zagreb: Zaštita čovjeka.

Jukić, Ilija. 1974. *The Fall of Yugoslavia.* New York: Harcourt Brace Jovanovich.

Kann, Robert A. 1974. *A History of the Habsburg Empire, 1526–1918.* Los Angeles: University of California Press.

Karadžić, Vuk Stefanović. 1965. *Sabrana dela Vuka Karadžića* [The Collected Works of Vuk Karadžić]. Vol. 1. Belgrade: Prosveta.

Karapandžić, Borivoje M. 1958. *Građanski rat u Srbiji (1941–1945)* [Civil War in Serbia (1941–1945)]. Cleveland, Ohio: printed by Buchdruckerei Dr. Peter Belej, Munich.

———. 1971. *Spomenica Srpskih dobrovoljaca, 1941–1971* [The Memorial Book of the Serbian Volunteers, 1941–1971]. Cleveland, Ohio: The Union of the Yugoslav-American Associations; printed by Iskra, Munich.

Kečkemet, Duško. 1971. *Židovi u povijesti Splita* [Jews in the History of Split]. Split.

Kennan, George F. 1993. *The other Balkan Wars. A 1913 Carnegie Endowment Inquiry in Retrospect with a New Introduction and Reflections on the Present Conflict.* Washington, D.C.: Carnegie Endowment for International Peace.

Kinross, Lord. 1977. *The Ottoman Centuries: The Rise and Fall of the Turkish Empire.* New York: Morrow Quill Paperbacks.

Kočović, Bogoljub. 1985. *Žrtve Drugog svetskog rata u Jugoslaviji* [World War II Victims in Yugoslavia]. London: Veritas.

Kofman, Daniel. 1996. "Israel and the War in Bosnia." In Thomas Cushman and Stjepan Meštrović (editors). *This Time We Knew: Western Responses to Genocide in Bosnia*. New York: New York University Press (in press).

Konstantinović, Radomir. 1981. *Filosofija palanke*. [The Small Town Philosophy]. 3rd edition. Belgrade: Nolit.

Kostić, Boško N. 1949. *Za istoriju naših dana: Odlomci iz zapisa za vreme okupacije* [For the History of Our Days: Fragments from Records Made during the Occupation]. Lille, France: Jean Lausier. Reprint. 1991. Belgrade: Nova Iskra.

Kostić, Lazo M. 1988. *Srbi i Jevreji* [The Serbs and the Jews]. Edited by Radiša M. Nikašinović and Ilija M. Pavlović. Southport, Australia: Serbia Press.

Krakov, Stanislav. 1963. *General Milan Nedić. Knjiga prva: Na oštrici noža* [General Milan Nedić. Book One: On a Knife's Cutting Edge]. Munich: Iskra.

———. 1968. *General Milan Nedić. Knjiga druga: Prepuna čaša čemera* [General Milan Nedić. Book Two: A Glass Full of Bitterness]. Munich: Iskra.

Kreso, Muharem. 1979. *Njemačka okupaciona uprava u Beogradu, 1941–1944* [The German Occupation Administration in Belgrade, 1941–1944]. Belgrade: Kultura.

Krizman, Bogdan. 1978. *Ante Pavelić i Ustaše* [Ante Pavelić and the Ustashas]. Zagreb: Globus.

———. 1980. *Pavelić između Hitlera i Mussolinija* [Ante Pavelić between Hitler and Mussolini]. Zagreb: Globus.

Krleža, Miroslav. 1990. *Deset krvavih godina* [Ten Bloody Years]. Sarajevo: Veselin Masleša.

Kuljić, Todor. 1974. "Srpski fašizam i sociologija" [Serbian Fascism and Sociology]. *Sociologija* no. 2: 240ff.

Kuprešanin, Veljko, ed. 1967. *Banjica*. Belgrade: Istorijski arhiv Beograda, Izdavačko preduzeće Kultura.

Laffan, R. G. D. 1989. *The Serbs: The Guardians of the Gate*. New York: Dorset Press.

Lašić-Vasojević, Milija M. 1976. *Enemies on All Sides: The Fall of Yugoslavia*. Washington, D.C.: North American International.

Lees, Michael. 1990. *The Rape of Serbia: The British Role in Tito's Grab for Power, 1943–1944*. New York: Harcourt Brace Jovanovich.

Lendvai, Paul. 1971. *Anti-Semitism without Jews: Communist Eastern Europe*. Garden City, New York: Doubleday.

———. 1969. *Eagles in Cobwebs: Nationalism and Communism in the Balkans*. New York: Doubleday.

Lerman, Antony and Howard Spier. 1993. *Antisemitism World Report 1993*. London: Institute of Jewish Affairs.

Levin, Nora. 1973. *The Holocaust: The Destruction of European Jewry, 1933–1935*. New York: Schocken.

Light of Truth: Selected Philosophical, Moral, and Political Ideas of Dimitrije Ljotić. 1984. Birmingham, England: Lazarica Press.

Littlejohn, David. 1985. *Foreign Legions of the Third Reich*. Vol. 3. San Jose, Calif.: R. James Bender Publishing.

Loeb, Isidore. 1877. *La Situation des Israélites en Turquie en Serbie et en Roumanie* [The Situation of the Jews in Turkey, Serbia, and Romania.] Paris: Joseph Baer.

Löwenthal, Zdenko, ed. 1957. *The Crimes of the Fascist Occupants and Their Collaborators against Jews in Yugoslavia*. Belgrade: Federation of Jewish Communities of the Federative People's Republic of Yugoslavia.

————. 1972. "Yugoslavia." In Geoffrey Wigoder (editor-in-chief). *Encyclopedia Judaica*. Jerusalem: Macmillan Company, vol. 16.

Ljotić, Dimitrije V. 1952. *Iz moga života* [From My Life]. Munich: Iskra.

————. 1961. *U revoluciji i ratu* [In Revolution and War]. Munich: Iskra.

————. 1976. *Videlo u tami* [Light in Darkness]. Munich: Iskra.

————. 1990. *Odabrana dela* [Selected Works]. Vol. 2. Munich: Iskra.

Ljotić, Ljubica Vl. 1973. *Memoari* [Memoirs]. Munich: Iskra.

Lochner, Louis P., ed. and trans. 1948. *The Goebbels Diaries, 1942–1943*. New York: Doubleday and Company.

Maclean, Fitzroy. 1949. *Eastern Approaches*. New York: Time.

Maček, Vladko. 1957. *In the Struggle for Freedom*. New York: Robert Speller and Sons.

Malcolm, Noel. 1994. *Bosnia — A Short History*. London: Macmillan.

Manoschek, Walter. 1993. *"Serbien ist judenfrei." Militärische Besatzungspolitik und Judenvernichtung in Serbien 1941/42* ["Serbia is Jew-Free." Military Occupation Policy and the Destruction of the Jews in Serbia, 1941/42]. Munich: R. Oldenbourg Verlag.

Marjanović, Jovan. 1963. *Ustanak i narodnooslobodilački pokret u Srbiji 1941* [The Uprising and National Liberation Movement in Serbia, 1941]. Belgrade: Institut društvenih nauka.

————. 1964. *Srbija u narodnooslobodilačkoj borbi: Beograd* [Serbia in the National Liberation Struggle: Belgrade]. Belgrade: Nolit.

————, ed. 1976. *Srbija u ratu i revoluciji, 1941–1945* [Serbia in War and Revolution, 1941–1945]. Belgrade: Srpska književna zadruga.

————. 1977. "The Neubacher Plan and Practical Schemes for the Establishment of a Greater Serbian Federation (1943–1944)." Pp. 486–501 in *The Third Reich and Yugoslavia, 1933–1945*. Edited by Pero Morača. Belgrade: The Institute for Contemporary History and Narodna knjiga.

———. 1979. *Draža Mihailović između Britanaca i Nemaca* [Draža Mihailović between the British and the Germans]. Vol 1. Belgrade: Prosveta, and Narodna knjiga; Zagreb: Globus.

Marrus, Michael R. 1987. *The Holocaust in History.* Hanover, N.H.: University Press of New England for Brandeis University Press.

Martic, Milos. 1980. "Dimitrije Ljotic and the Yugoslav National Movement Zbor, 1935–1945." *East European Quarterly* 14 (2): 219–39.

Martin, David. 1946. *Ally Betrayed — The Uncensored Story of Tito and Mihailovich.* New York: Prentice-Hall.

Martinović-Bajica, Petar. 1956. *Milan Nedić.* Chicago: The First American Serbian Corporation.

Matić, Srđan. 1988. "Kronologija." Pp. 204–12 in *Židovi na tlu Jugoslavije* [The Jews in Yugoslavia]. Edited by Ante Sorić. Zagreb: Muzejski prostor.

Mayer, S. L., ed. 1976. *Signal: Hitler's Wartime Picture Magazine.* Englewood Cliffs, N.J.: Prentice-Hall.

———, ed. 1978. *Signal: Years of Triumph 1941–1942.* Englewood Cliffs, New Jersey: Prentice-Hall.

———, ed. 1979. *Signal: Years of Retreat 1943–1944.* Englewood Cliffs, New Jersey: Prentice-Hall.

Mayers, Paul, and Arthur Campbell. 1954. *The Population of Yugoslavia.* Washington, D.C.: Bureau of Census.

McAdams, C. Michael. 1992. *Croatia: Myth and Reality.* Arcadia, Calif.: Croatian Information Service Monographs.

Meštrović, Ivan. 1993. *Uspomene na političke ljude i događaje* [Memoirs of Politicians and Events]. Zagreb: Nakladni zavod Matice hrvatske.

Meštrović, Stjepan G.; Slaven Letica; and Miroslav Goreta. 1993. *Habits of the Balkan Heart: Social Character and the Fall of Communism.* College Station: Texas A&M University Press.

Milazzo, Matteo J. 1975. *The Chetnik Movement and The Yugoslav Resistance.* Baltimore: Johns Hopkins University Press.

Milovanović, Nikola. 1978. *Pukotine kraljevstva: Rat obaveštajnih službi na tlu Jugoslavije* [Cracks in the Kingdom: The War of the Intelligence Services on the Soil of Yugoslavia]. 2 vols. Belgrade: Sloboda.

Mirnić, Josip. 1968. "Sistem jedinstvenog vojnog rukovodstva mađarskog okupatora u borbi protiv NOP-a u Bačkoj" [System of Unified Military Command of the Hungarian Occupier in the Struggle against the National Liberation Movement in Bačka]. Pp. 7–70 in *Vojnoistorijski glasnik* [Military-Historical Herald]. Vol. 2.

Mitcham, Samuel W. 1985. *Hitler's Legions: The German Army Order of Battle, World War II.* New York: Stein and Day.

Mitrovski, Boro; Venceslav Glišić; Tomo Ristovski. 1971. *The Bulgarian Army in Yugoslavia 1941–1945.* Belgrade: Međunarodna politika.

Mojić, Milorad. 1941. *Srpski narod u kandžama Jevreja* [Serbian People in the Claws of the Jews]. Belgrade: Luč.

Moljević, Stevan. 1991. "Homogena Srbija" [Homogeneous Serbia]. Pp. 141–47 in *Izvori velikosrpske agresije.* Edited by Bože Čović. Zagreb: August Cesarec & Školska knjiga.

———. 1993. "Homogeneous Serbia." Pp. 151–52 in *Roots of Serbian Aggression.* Edited by Bože Čović. Zagreb: Centar za strane jezike.

Morley, John F. 1980. *Vatican Diplomacy and the Jews during the Holocaust, 1939–1943.* New York: Ktav.

Mrđenović, Dušan, ed. 1988. *Ustavi i vlade Kneževine Srbije, Kraljevine Srbije, Kraljevine SHS, i Kraljevine Jugoslavije (1835–1941)* [Constitution and Governments of the Principality of Serbia, the Kingdom of Serbia, the Kingdom of Serbs, Croats, and Slovenes, and the Kingdom of Yugoslavia (1835–1941)]. Belgrade: Nova knjiga.

Mukerji, Vanita Singh. 1990. *Ivo Andrić: A Critical Biography.* Jefferson, N.C.: McFarland.

Musiół, Teodor. 1968. *Dachau: 1933–1945.* Katowice, Poland: Ślask.

Nedić, Milan. 1943. *Govori generala Milana Nedića pretsednika Srpske vlade* [The Speeches of General Milan Nedić, President of the Serbian Government]. Belgrade.

Nedomački, Vidosava and Slavko Goldstein. 1988. "Jevrejske općine u jugoslavenskim zemljama." Pp. 113–42 in *Židovi na tlu Jugoslavije* [The Jews in Yugoslavia]. Edited by Ante Sorić. Zagreb: Muzejski prostor.

"Nekoliko srpskih rodoljuba" [Several Serbian Patriots]. 1882. *Nedajmo Srbiju Čivutima* [Let's Not Give Serbia to the Kikes]. Belgrade: Štamparija zadruge štamparskih radnika.

Neubacher, Hermann. 1956. *Sonder-Auftrag Südost, 1940–1945* [Special Task Southeast, 1940–1945]. Göttingen: Musterschmidt Verlag.

Neulen, Hans Werner. 1985. *An deutscher Seite* [On the German Side]. Munich: Universitas Verlag.

Novak, Viktor. 1948. *Magnum Crimen: Pola vijeka klerikalizma u Hrvatskoj* [The Great Crime: Half a Century of Clericalism in Croatia]. Zagreb: Nakladni zavod Hrvatske.

Odić, Slavko, and Slavko Komarica. 1977. *Noć i magla: Gestapo u Jugoslaviji* [Night and Fog: The Gestapo in Yugoslavia]. Vol. 2. Zagreb: Centar za informacije i publicitet.

Le Operazioni delle Unità Italiane in Jugoslavia (1941–1943) [Operations of the Italian units in Yugoslavia (1941–1943)] 1978. Rome: Ministero della Difesa, Stato Maggiore dell'Esercito, Ufficio Storico.

Order of Battle and Handbook of the Bulgarian Armed Forces. 1943. Washington, D.C.: Military Intelligence Division, U.S. War Department.

Ostović, P. D. 1952. *The Truth about Yugoslavia.* New York: Roy Publishers.

Parežanin, Ratko. 1971. *Drugi svetski rat i Dimitrije V. Ljotić* [World War II and Dimitrije V. Ljotić]. Munich: Iskra.

Paris, Edmond. 1961. *Genocide in Satellite Croatia, 1941–1945: A Record of Racial and Religious Persecutions and Massacres.* Chicago: American Institute for Balkan Affairs.

Pasic, Nicholas. 1989. "In Search of the True Number of World War II Victims in Yugoslavia." *Serbian Studies* 5 (1): 65–84.

Pattee, Richard. 1953. *The Case of Cardinal Aloysius Stepinac.* Milwaukee, Wis.: The Bruce Publishing Company.

Pavlowitch, Stevan K. 1971. *Yugoslavia.* New York: Praeger.

Pejić, Predrag. 1989. *Banjica: Sećanja jednog zatvorenika* [Banjica: Recollections of an Inmate]. Gornji Milanovac, Serbia: Dečje novine.

Pelagić, Vasa. ca. 1878. *Vjerozakonsko učenje Talmuda ili ogledalo čivutskog poštenja, po nemačkom izradio Vasa Pelagić* [Religious Teaching of the Talmud or the Mirror of Kike Honesty, according to the German Text Prepared by Vasa Pelagić]. Belgrade: T. Jovanović.

Petrovich, Michael Boro. 1976. *History of Modern Serbia, 1804–1918.* 2 vols. New York: Harcourt Brace Jovanovich.

Poliakov, Leon and Jacques Sabille. 1983. *Jews under the Italian Occupation.* New York: Howard Fertig.

Popović, Jovo; Marko Lolić; and Branko Latas. 1988. *Pop izdaje* [Orthodox Priest of Betrayal]. Zagreb: Stvarnost.

Pozzi, Henri. 1935. *Black Hand over Europe.* London: Francis Mott Company.

Primoratz, Igor. 1996. "Israel and Genocide in Croatia." In *Genocide after Emotion: The Postemotional Balkan War.* Stjepan G. Meštrović, vol. ed. London: Routledge. Pp. 193–204.

Prokić, Lazar. 1941. *Jevreji u Srbiji* [The Jews in Serbia]. Belgrade.

Rašević, Veljko. 1953. *Ogledi o shvatanjima Dimitrja Ljotića* [An Essay about the Notions of Dimitrije Ljotić]. Paris: Naša reč.

Redžić, Enver. 1987. *Muslimansko autonomaštvo i 13. SS divizija. Autonomija Bosne i Hercegovine i Hitlerov Treći Rajh* [Muslim Separatism and the 13th SS Division: The Autonomy of Bosnia-Herzegovina and Hitler's Third Reich]. Sarajevo: Svjetlost.

Roberts, Walter R. 1973. *Tito, Mihailović, and the Allies, 1941–1945*. New Brunswick, N.J.: Rutgers University Press.

Romano, Jaša. 1980. *Jevreji Jugoslavije, 1941–1945. Žrtve genocida i učesnici NOR* [Jews of Yugoslavia, 1941–1945: Victims of Genocide and Freedom Fighters.] Belgrade: Federation of Jewish Communities in Yugoslavia.

Rothschild, Joseph. 1974. *East Central Europe between the Two World Wars*. Seattle: University of Washington Press.

Sadkovich, James J. 1987. *Italian Support for Croatian Separatism, 1927–1937*. New York: Garland Publishing.

Samardžija, Marko. 1993. *Hrvatski jezik u Nezavisnoj Državi Hrvatskoj* [The Croatian Language in the Independent State of Croatia]. Zagreb: Hrvatska sveučilišna naklada.

Schramm, P. E., ed. 1961–1965. *Kriegstagebuch des Oberkommandos der Wehrmacht (Wehrmachtführungsstab) 1942–1945* [War Journal of the Supreme Headquarters of the German Armed Forces (Operations Staff) 1942–1945]. 4 vols. Frankfurt, Germany: Bernard und Graege Verlag.

Schwarz, Gabriel. 1910. "Croatia." In Isidore Singer, editor. *The Jewish Encyclopedia*. New York: Funk and Wagnalls. Vol. 4, pp. 363–65.

Scott 1993 Standard Postage Stamp Catalogue. 1992. Sidney, Ohio: Scott Publishing Co., vol. 4.

Serbian Academy of Science and Art (SANU). 1987. *Nacrt memoranduma Srpske akademije nauka u Beogradu* [Framework for the Memorandum of the Serbian Academy of Science in Belgrade]. Srpska narodna odbrana [Serbian National Defense], Canada.

Serbian Academy of Science and Art (SANU). 1991. Serbian Academy of "'Memorandum' SANU (grupa akademika Srpske akademije nauka i umetnosti o aktuelnim društvenim pitanjima u našoj zemlji)" ["Memorandum" of the Serbian Academy of Science and Art (a Group of Academicians of the Serbian Academy of Science and Art on the Current Social Issues in Our Country)]. Pp. 256–300 in *Izvori velikosrpske agresije*. Edited by Bože Čović. Zagreb: August Cesarec & Školska knjiga.

Serbian Academy of Science and Art. 1993. "The SANU 'Memorandum' (A Group of Members of the Serbian Academy of Science and Arts on Topical Social Issues of Yugoslavia)." Pp. 289–337, in *Roots of Greater Serbian Aggression*. Edited by Bože Čović. Zagreb: Centar za strane jezike.

Shelah, Menachem. 1987. "Sajmište—An Extermination Camp in Serbia." *Holocaust and Genocide Studies* 2 (2): 243–60.

————. 1990. "Chetniks." Pp. 288–89 in *Encyclopedia of the Holocaust*. Vol. 1. Edited by Israel Gutman. New York: Macmillan.

————. 1990a. "Croatia." Pp. 323–29 in *Encyclopedia of the Holocaust*. Vol. 1. Edited by Israel Gutman. New York: Macmillan.

————. 1990b. "Serbia." Pp. 1340–42 in *Encyclopedia of the Holocaust*. Vol. 4. Edited by Israel Gutman. New York: Macmillan.

————. 1990c. "Ustaša." P. 1552 in *Encyclopedia of the Holocaust*. Vol. 4. Edited by Israel Gutman. New York: Macmillan.

————. 1990d. "Yugoslavia." Pp. 1716–22 in *Encyclopedia of the Holocaust*. Vol. 4. Edited by Israel Gutman. New York: Macmillan.

Silk, Robert. 1947. "The Jews of Split." *Liberal Judaism* (January): 38–41.

Singleton, Fred. 1976. *Twentieth-Century Yugoslavia*. New York: Columbia University Press.

Sirotković, Hodimir. 1990. "Uloga ZAVNOH-a u organizaciji narodne vlasti u Hrvatskoj do završetka njegova trećeg zasijedana" [The Role of the ZAVNOH in the Organization of the People's Authorities in Croatia until the End of Its Third Session]. In *ZAVNOH 1943–1944: Materijali s naučnog skupa održanog u Otočcu 2. i 3. oktobra 1989* [ZAVNOH: Materials from the Scholarly Conference Held in Otočac on October 2 and 3, 1989]. Karlovac: Historijski Arhiv u Karlovcu; Institut za suvremenu povijest u Zagrebu.

Slijepčević, Đoko. 1978. *Jugoslavija: Uoči i za vreme drugog svetskog rata* [Yugoslavia: On the Eve of and during World War II]. Munich: Iskra.

Srpski dobrovoljci: povodom 25-godišnjice njihovog osnivanja [The Serbian Volunteers: On the Occasion of the Twenty-fifth Anniversary of Their Establishment]. 1966. Munich: Iskra.

Spomenica pravoslavnih sveštenika-žrtava fašističkog terora i palih u NOB [The Memorial Book to the Orthodox Priests—Victims of Fascist Terror and Those Who Fell in the People's Liberation War]. 1960. Belgrade: Savez udruženja pravoslavnog sveštenstva FNRJ.

Stefanović, Mladen. 1984. *Zbor Dimitrija Ljotića, 1934–1945* [Zbor of Dimitrije Ljotić, 1934–1945]. Belgrade: Narodna knjiga.

Steinberg, Jonathan. 1990. *All or Nothing: The Axis and the Holocaust, 1941–1943*. London: Routledge.

Stojanović, Nikola. 1991. "Do istrage vaše ili naše" [Until Your or Our Extermination]. Pp. 99–105 in *Izvori velikosrpske agresije*. Edited by Bože Čović. Zagreb: August Cesarec & Školska knjiga.

————. 1993. "Until Your or Our Extermination." Pp. 105–13 in *Roots of Greater Serbian Aggression*. Edited by Bože Čović. Zagreb: Centar za strane jezike.

Stokes, Gale. 1990. *Politics as Development: The Emergence of Political Parties in Nineteenth-Century Serbia*. Durham, N.C.: Duke University Press.

Stranjaković, Dragoslav. 1991. *Najveći zločini sadašnjice: patnje i stradanje srpskog naroda u Nezavisnoj Državi Hrvatskoj od 1941–1945* [The Greatest Crimes of Today: Sufferings and Victimization of the Serbian People in the Independent State of Croatia from 1941 to 1945]. Gornji Milanovac, Serbia: Dečje novine.

Strugar, Vlado. 1969. *Jugoslavija 1941–1945* [Yugoslavia from 1941–1945]. Belgrade: Vojnoizdavački zavod.

Stulli, Bernard. 1989. *Židovi u Dubrovniku* [Jews in Dubrovnik]. Zagreb: Jevrejska Općina Zagreb, Nakladni zavod Matice hrvatske, i Kulturno društvo Dr. Miroslav Šalom Freiberger.

Supek, Ivan. 1992. *Krivovjernik na ljevici* [Heretic on the Left]. Zagreb: Globus.

Temperley, Harold W. V., and Lillian M. Penson. 1938. *A Century of Diplomatic Blue Books: 1814–1914*. Cambridge, England: The University Press.

Tessin, Georg. 1965–1980. *Verbände und Truppen der deutschen Wehrmacht und Waffen-SS im Zweiten Weltkrieg 1939–1945* [Formations and Troops of the German Army and Waffen-SS in the Second World War]. 14 vols. Osnabrück: Biblio Verlag.

Tomasevich, Jozo. 1975. *War and Revolution in Yugoslavia, 1941–945: The Chetniks*. Stanford, Calif.: Stanford University Press.

Tomašić, Dinko. 1942. "Croatia in European Affairs." *Journal of Central European Affairs* (April): 64–82.

Tomasic, Dinko. 1948. *Personality and Culture in Eastern European Politics*. New York: George W. Stewart.

Trišić, Jovan P. 1960. *O Milanu Nediću* [About Milan Nedić]. Author's edition. Windsor, Canada: Avala Printing and Publishing Company.

Trotsky, Leon. 1980. *The Balkan Wars 1912–13*. New York: Monad Press.

Tucović, Dimitrije. 1914. *Srbija i Arbanija: Jedan prilog kritici zavojevačke politike srpske buržoazije* [Serbia and Albania: One Contribution to the Criticism of the Subjugation Policy of the Serbian Bourgeois]. Belgrade: Nova štamparija Save Radenkovića i brata. Reprint. 1974. Belgrade: Radnička štampa.

Velimirović, Nikolaj. 1976. *Sabrana dela. Knjiga IV* [Collected Works, Book 4]. Düsseldorf: Srpska pravoslavna eparhija za Zapadnu Evropu.

———. 1985. *Govori srpskom narodu kroz tamnički prozor* [Speeches to the Serbian People through the Prison Window]. Himmelsthür, Germany: Srpska pravoslavna eparhija za Zapadnu Evropu.

————. 1986. *Sabrana dela. Knjiga XIII* [Collected Works, Book 13]. Himmelsthür, Germany: Srpska pravoslavna eparhija za Zapadnu Evropu.

Velimirovich, Nicholai. 1989. *The Life of Saint Sava.* Crestwood, N.Y.: Saint Vladimir's Seminary Press.

Vertepov, D. P., ed. 1963. *Russkii Korpus na Balkanakh vo vremia II Velikoi voiny, 1941–1945 g.g.: Istoricheskii ocherk i sbornik vospominanii soratnikov* [The Russian Corps in the Balkans during World War II, 1941–1945: An Historical Study and a Collection of Memoirs by Companions-in-Arms]. New York: Nashi Vesti.

Vuković, Tomislav. 1991. *Mozaik izdaje* [Mosaic of Betrayal]. Zagreb: Hrvatsko književno društvo sv. Ćirila i Metoda.

Walters, E. Garrison. 1988. *The Other Europe: Eastern Europe to 1945.* New York: Dorset Press.

Warlimont, Walter. 1962. *Im Hauptquarter der deutschen Wehrmacht, 1939–1945* [In the Headquarters of the German Army, 1939–1945]. Frankfort am Main.

————. 1964. *Inside Hitler's Headquarters, 1939–45.* Translated by R. H. Barry. New York: Praeger.

West, Rebecca. 1941. *Black Lamb and Grey Falcon. A Journey through Yugoslavia.* New York: The Viking Press.

Wheeler, Mark C. 1980. *Britain and the War for Yugoslavia, 1940–1943.* New York: Columbia University Press.

Ye'or, Bat. 1985. *The Dhimmi: Jews and Christians under Islam.* London: Associated University Press.

Zametica, John. 1992. "The Yugoslav Conflict." *Adelphi Papers* no. 270: 1–87. London: International Institute for Strategic Studies.

Zbornik dokumenata i podataka o narodnooslobodilačkom ratu jugoslovenskih naroda [Collection of Documents and Data about the National Liberation War of the Yugoslav Peoples]. 1949. Vol. 1. Belgrade: Vojnoistorijski institut, Borbe u Srbiji 1941 god.

————. 1957. Vol. 19. Belgrade: Vojnoistorijski institut, Borbe u Hrvatskoj 1943.

————. 1968. Vol. 36. Belgrade: Vojnoistorijski institut, Borbe u Hrvatskoj 1944.

————. 1978. Reissue. Vol. 12. Belgrade: Vojnoistorijski institut, Dokumenti Nemačkog Rajha 1943.

————. 1981. Reissue. Vol. 14. Belgrade: Vojnoistorijski institut, Dokumenti četničkog pokreta Draže Mihailovića 1941–1942.

Zbornik Zakona i Uredaba u Knjažestvu Srbiji u dosadanjim Zbornicima neštampanih a izdanih od 2. Februara 1835. do 23. Oktobra 1875. god [A Collection of Laws and Acts in the Principality of Serbia in the Up-to-Date Collections, issued from February 2, 1835, to October 23, 1875]. 1877. Vol. 14. Belgrade: Državna Štamparija.

———. 1877a. Vol. 30. Belgrade: Državna Štamparija.

Zemljar, Ante. 1988. *Haron i sudbine.* [Charon and Destinies]. Belgrade: Beogradski izdavačko-grafički zavod.

Zernov, Nicolas. 1975. "First Council of the Russian Church Abroad in Sremski Karlovtsi (21 November–2 December, 1921): The Notes of One of the participants." *Eastern Churches Review* 7: 164–85.

Žerjavić, Vladimir. 1989. *Gubici stanovništva Jugoslavije u drugom svjetskom ratu* [Population Losses in Yugoslavia During World War II]. Zagreb: Jugoslavensko viktimološko društvo.

———. 1991. "The Losses of Yugoslav Population in the Second World War." In Ivan Crkvenčić and Mladen Klemenčić, editors. *Geographical Papers.* Zagreb: Department of Geography, University of Zagreb. Vol. 8, pp. 83–108.

———. 1992. *Opsesije i megalomanije oko Jasenovca i Bleiburga. Gubici stanovništva Jugoslavije u drugom svjetskom ratu* [Obsession and Megalomania over Jasenovac and Bleiburg. Population Losses in Yugoslavia during World War II]. Zagreb: Globus.

———. 1993. *Yugoslavia — Manipulations with the Number of Second World War Victims.* Zagreb: Croatian Information Centre.

UNPUBLISHED MATERIALS

Franić, Zvonimir; Gordana Vetma; and Dean Tošović. 1992. *Dubrovnik: The Report of the War Damages in the Synagogue and the Tolentino House, October-November-December 1991.* Prepared for the Jewish Community of Dubrovnik, May.

Ferera, Mirjam. 1991. Affidavit describing the bombardment of the synagogue of Dubrovnik, December 18.

Harpke, Michael, J. The Communist Consolidation of Political Power in Yugoslavia, 1944–1945. Master's thesis, University of Wisconsin.

Johnson, Richard. 1994. "Serbia and Russia: U.S. Appeasement and the Resurrection of Fascism." Paper presented at National War College, Washington, D.C., May 4.

Minutes of the second session of the working committee of the Federation of the Jewish Communities of Yugoslavia, Belgrade, December 23, 1991.

Politische Archiv des Auswärtigen Amtes [the Political Archives of the Foreign Office]. Vol. 4. Bonn, Germany. Deutsche Gesandtschaft Belgrad [the German Embassy in Belgrade].

Pretsch, Dr. Hans Jochen. Personal communication, July 8, 1992. Auswär-tiges Amt [Foreign Office], Bonn, Germany. In possession of the author.

Report of the Police Station in Sisak, Croatia. No. 511-10-01/01 Sp.-40/92. April 29, 1992.

Index

of, 130; involvement with Zbor, 15; Rebecca West on, 190n. 126; release from Dachau, 59; sermon of, 130–32

Vučinić, Siniša, 129

Vučković, Vladeta, 108, 199n. 100

Vujković, Svetozar, 48–49

Vulović, Danilo, 17

war casualties: accepted figures, 107–108; and emigration, 200n. 103; erroneous Holocaust statistics, 107; revised figures for, 108–12; source of figures, 108

war in Bosnia: atrocities of, 122–23, 204n. 43; and Greater Serbia, 134; and Israeli pro-Serbian stance, 125; Jewish reaction to, 122; justification for atrocities, 124; and pro-Serbian propaganda, 123

White Eagles *(Beli orlovi)*, 20, 129

"World War II argument," 124, 125

Yugoslav Action movement *(Jugoslovenska akcija)*, 12, 15

Yugoslavia: Axis invasion of, 86; collaborationist government in, 30–31; Communist control in, 119–20; corporal punishment in, 9, 161n. 23; Hitler's invasion of, 28–29; Hitler's policies toward, 85, 86; martial law in, 9; Muslim persecution in, 8; political murders in, 9; relationship with Iraq, 117, 121; Serbian dominance in, 8–9, 119–20; support for terrorism, 120–21; treatment of Jews in, 70–73

Zagreb bombing incident, 127

Zakoni i dela Jevreja, 76

ZAVNOH *(Zemaljsko antifašističko vijeće narodnog oslobođenja Hrvatske),* 96–97

Zbor (Yugoslav National Movement Zbor): anti-Semitism of, 71, 75–76; defections to Stojadinović, 17; disbanding of, 20–21; in elections of 1938, 18; formation of, 14; infiltration by German intelligence, 20; legal status of, 15, 20–21; meaning of term, 161n. 38; membership of, 15; opposition to, by Stojadinović, 17–18; program of, 14–15; support for National Socialism, 15

Žerjavić, Vladimir, 110–12